AT THE MARGINS OF NIHILISM

At the Margins of Nihilism

DECONSTRUCTION AND SOCIAL DEATH

John E. Drabinski

Copyright © 2026 Fordham University Press

All rights reserved. No part of this publication may be reproduced, stored in a retrieval system, or transmitted in any form or by any means—electronic, mechanical, photocopy, recording, or any other—except for brief quotations in printed reviews, without the prior permission of the publisher.

Fordham University Press has no responsibility for the persistence or accuracy of URLs for external or third-party Internet websites referred to in this publication and does not guarantee that any content on such websites is, or will remain, accurate or appropriate.

Fordham University Press also publishes its books in a variety of electronic formats. Some content that appears in print may not be available in electronic books.

Visit us online at www.fordhampress.com.

For EU safety/GPSR concerns: Mare Nostrum Group B.V., Mauritskade 21D, 1091 GC Amsterdam, The Netherlands, gpsr@mare-nostrum.co.uk

Library of Congress Cataloging-in-Publication Data available online at https://catalog.loc.gov.

Printed in the United States of America

28 27 26   5 4 3 2 1

First edition

Contents

PROLOGUE: SEMBÈNE, TENO, AND THE WORK OF THE OUTSIDE   1

Introduction: Whithering the Decolonial   19

1   Social Death as a Kind of Deconstruction   38

2   Racial Formation and the Remainder in Baldwin's Nonfiction   70

3   Nihilism and the Refusal of Refusal in Wright and Fanon   102

4   The Lower Frequencies after Afropessimism   134

Postscript Notes   168

ACKNOWLEDGMENTS   179

NOTES   181

INDEX   189

I wished to reach the point of a certain exteriority in relation to the totality of the age of logocentrism.
—JACQUES DERRIDA

Prologue
Sembène, Teno, and the Work of the Outside

If the Middle Passage was an event that reordered the meaning of thinking, and if the Middle Passage initiated what would come to be called colonialism and global domination by the white West, then there could be no more enduringly urgent question than this: What world did that event produce, and what possibilities and impossibilities comprise that world? An old question, to be sure, but a question always in need of reopening. The truth is, we largely struggle to think outside the infrastructural logic of that world and how it conceived possibility. Even critique is entangled in its terms. That is part of what inheritance means. The past has a way of insinuating itself into the *habitus* of the present and into our imaginations of what is to come.

All to say: Decolonial work is still fresh and urgent work.

But, of the world made by conquest and enslavement, we can say at least this much: The effect and affect of empire introduced a Manichean structure into the heart of our shared world. The metropole and the margin. Colonizer and colonized. White and Black. Global North, Global South. And so on. There are so many iterations of this one and the same infrastructure. Liberation from such an infrastructure begins with the elimination of the metropole. Or at least its neutralization. We cannot dispute that at all. The center produces the abject life of the margins. It is the source point of production and reproduction of the Atlantic world's worst forms of life and death. No other living and dying is possible if that center holds. This kind of insight is productive across multiple fronts, whether we are concerned with theorizing decolonial intellectual worlds or cultural production or political economy or revolutionary action. It is a fecund insight and always worthy of our closest attention and most intimate values.

That leaves a question unasked: What do we make of the margins *as such*? Of the margins not measured by the center? What layered work is done at the margins, including both the work of the metropole and cognates *on* or *against* the margins and the work done *inside* the margins by those who have formed and formulated modalities of being in that (non)space? On the one hand, the margins are created by empire; there is no coherent meaning of "margin" without "center" as its critical, constitutive juxtaposition. This is the source of revolutionary energy that targets the center for elimination and those new visions of what such upheaval makes possible. Radical politics is in many ways just this project. Uproot the center, imagine and plant new roots for a new world. Let me say from the outset that this is righteous and good political work. A liberated imagination liberates entire worlds, overturns oppressive material and cultural conditions, and upends history. New memory and history become possible in that upending.

On the other hand, there is also the question of the margins as such. Are they reducible to what the center has made of them, to what the center has introduced into *our* imagination-memory of them as a mixed collective of oppressor, oppressed, and borderland identities? Empire is domination of more than just land, always. Empire is also domination of how we imagine possibility and how we see, hear, and feel the folds in social and cultural realities. *Realities.* The plural matters. If we think reality as plural, what do the margins signify when understood in their multiple registers? How do those registers signify with chaos as well as coherence? In what way might the Manichean imagination already be upended before revolutionary, radical action and imagination intervenes? Margins might be the site of immense nihilism. In fact, the hegemony of race and empire mandates such immensity. Much of the work that follows is about documenting theorization of that nihilism and the conditions of mandate: social death. Margins might *also* be otherwise. Multiplicity. The fact that life goes on, that there is an obstinacy of *poiesis* and the making of worlds—this is the mandate of time. The future is obstinate. An ethics means little if it does not command us to witness the meaning of that obstinacy, to find ways to listen to it, to adjust theory to the *poiesis* of the margin. Can the margins speak? What aurality is demanded in that speaking?

Two conceptual notes on the question of margins.

In the wake of empire, margins are political, social, and cultural artifacts of domination and extraction. Imperial work, whether work inside the slave trade or colonialism or forms of exclusion in place after independence and emancipation, is possible only if the world is cleaved into at least two spaces and two forms of possibility. *We* live and act here. *They* live and act there. Two spaces that mark difference in embodied presence to the world, in a sense of place inside a political economy, and in relations to the repressive state apparatus, but also difference in epistemology, ontology, and the aesthetic-political imagination. In other words, a broadly and deeply human difference that encompasses the totality of life, death, and whatever relation life/death has in the everyday practices of being. The relation forged between that here-there is a relation of power and comprises the meaning of the entire shared world. Stakes could not be higher. Here or there? These are terms of absolute significance that bear both relation and nonrelation. Nonrelation is the enigma of enigmas. But what is relation itself in this structure? On first glance, the question of the margin is a matter of spatiality, whether that is social-political space or the space of the imagination and imagined possibilities. In some sense, it is indisputably a spatial question. Ghettoization is an old practice that reminds the political center of its other, who is both omnipresent and untouchable, unbeholdable, and in the end subject to extrajudicial terror and murder. Cities wall themselves off in order secure the center's imagination of itself, physically marking an ethical and psychic line between legitimate citizens and their belonging in a category of proper humanity and that strange babble and chaos of the other who lives outside the wall. Margin/center spatiality is a centerpiece of so much human drama, which in global empire, across all of its iterations, only pushed that spatiality deeper into the drama of human cruelty and capacity of mass murder and suffering. Empire in the Atlantic world was and remains unprecedented in scope, time, and intensity. We live in its horizon still. Decolonial work is about discrete thinking against that horizon in the interest of the new. Or recognition of what has lived in the margins as unrecognizable and unutterable to the center, but something else to this humanity lived and thought *otherwise*.

How does "margin" signify the otherwise?

Part of the complexity of the question of signification-otherwise lies in the word margin itself. It is a spatial term. Not only is it a spatial term, but it is also a spatial term that is lived with such material intensity that to think it otherwise is to take the risk of oblivion, the risk that we forget or marginalize, as it were, the material conditions of the margin—thereby doubling the awful. Those conditions are irreducible. But there are also other material conditions, other material forms of life folded into that historical-memorial experience of social death. Those conditions are the concern of a decolonial thought at the margins of nihilism. In order to get at this sense of margin, we have to begin by thinking spatiality in terms of excess. Excess is just that: something that exceeds enclosure, pours out, and signifies beyond the container. Derrida has this in mind when he writes in *Dissemination*:

> A Crisis of *versus*: these marks can no longer be summed up or "decided" according to the two of binary oppositions nor sublated into the three of speculative dialectics (for example, "*différance*," "*gramme*," "*trace*," "*broach/breach*," "*de-limitation*," "*pharmakon*," "*supplement*," "*hymen*," "*mark-march-margin*," and others; the movement of these marks pervades the whole of the space of writing in which they occur, hence they can never be enclosed within any finite taxonomy, not to speak of any lexicon as such).[1]

Derrida's list of terms here is akin to a lexicon of difference as radical difference: difference without recursion to identity. A difference that sits with the impossibility of reconciling difference and identity. A difference as *différance*, which is to say, difference between space and time. The spatiality of excess, this refusal of and resistance to the totalizing work of finite taxonomy, suggests the critical and complex notion that the margins are spatially excessive and therefore belong to another time. Spatiality thought otherwise and thought as an altogether other time, not just the other of or the other in a common time. Diachrony shows up here as a counterinfrastructure whose promise is immense for the project of decolonial thinking.

Time shifts the meaning of space, which shifts the meaning of life and, as we will see, the function and meaning of social death. That is what deconstruction crossed with social death promises. Deconstruction as a modality of thinking, crossed with social death, has a praxical parallel or complement in Gloria Anzaldúa's conceptualization, evocation, and linguistic practice of *la frontera*. Anzaldúa's work on "the new mestiza"—setting aside the complicated cultural politics of the term *mestizaje*[2]—produces concepts and geographies of thinking that link thought to place in important ways. In particular, I have in mind how the between is thought by Anzaldúa as that productive space of *life* which is not a suspension between life and death. Each of these elements is precisely what I also find so interesting about deconstruction: how deconstruction conceives the arrangement between the closure of a system and its opening; how deconstruction argues through gesture and the evocative; how central play with language is to deconstruction; and how play is both a theory and practice of undoing hegemony. Deconstruction makes these broad claims. Where can such claims get footing? This is the question that makes *la frontera* such compelling deconstructive praxis.

Thus, Anzaldúa's importance for the present project lies in its geographical grounding in a theory of the between, of borderlands, of *la frontera*. That theorization refuses abjection by recasting the conceptual and existential meaning of the interstices and between-spaces of life outside systems of social death. What is the fate of being in the margins of nihilism if we think margin as excess? This is Anzaldúa's critical praxis. As well, her theorization importantly refuses abjection without oblivion; the specter of death and the abject form a sort of affective halo around *la frontera* without *la frontera* staying reducible to it. That is, it is not a question of erasing abjection from lived experience or history or social reproduction, but instead a question of how to think the excess of abjection and its resonances. As well, the geography of theory matters. As a theory grounded in the imperial and antiblack, antibrown space of the Americas, Anzaldúa's praxis has an important and unique attenuation to the specificities of *this space here*, the between-spaces of empire in the Americas, which is that space with which the core chapters below are occupied: African American and Afro-Caribbean experience. One of the important features of that experience is that it is located, in terms of its own sense of home, in a place that creates only nonplace inside systems of enslavement, colonialism, and the afterlives of both. Location and dislocation are simultaneous, but the *telos* common to systems of antiblackness bear no hope for relocation.

So, the critical issue is how to make a world *in this place* that is both impossible and unprecedented in its senses of the possible. How can we think the possible at the margins of nihilism without atavism or recurrences of closure? Anzaldúa helps us theorize this problem as thinking and imagination. I have in mind this particular passage in *Borderlands/La Frontera*, from the formative seventh chapter "Towards a New Consciousness" in which she writes:

> But it is not enough to stand on the opposite river bank, shouting questions, challenging patriarchal, white conventions. A counterstance locks one into a duel of oppressor and oppressed; locked in mortal combat, like the cop and the criminal, both are reduced to a common denominator of violence. . . . Perhaps we will decide to disengage from the dominant culture, write it off altogether as a lost cause, and cross the border into a wholly new and separate territory. Or we might go another route. The possibilities are numerous once we decide to act and not react.[3]

There is a lot at work in this passage, and it nicely captures the profound and enigmatic layering of text and idea in *Borderlands/La Frontera*. I am particularly struck by Anzaldúa's shift away from Manichean logic (the counterstance) to a something-else, a "might" and "another route," something that is, in her words, *toward* a new consciousness. This is the movement *from* the space of closure without subaltern possibility as subaltern (social death) *to* the borderlands/*la frontera* of possibility thinking otherwise (refusal, world-making). Such an *otherwise* as possibility remains largely unarticulated. Open ended. Exploratory. Curious. Preoccupied by routes and more routes. And for good reason. Possibility remains un- or underarticulated because it is the emergence of *open* possibilities in the interstices of a system of oppressor/oppressed. New territory. Familiar between spaces. New demands on language. New demands on thinking. New demands on identity words, formations, and relations. *The possibilities are numerous.*

What of the decolonial? Anzaldúa's notion of *la frontera* also interestingly fuses a link between antiblack/antibrown racisms and related forms of colonial domination. This link deepens the meaning of decolonial theory for the African American intellectual tradition. It is a disputed question, to be sure, but I may as well be plain here: I do not think African American history and post-Emancipation African American historical experience is colonial and I do not think the colonial model of domination is particularly illuminating for understanding the practice of antiblack racism in the United States. James Baldwin, like many others in the tradition, was right to raise the question: Ought we think of African Americans—and perhaps also white Americans in the United States—as a distinct *people*? An emerging people, for sure, fumbling around with partially formed foundational concepts of peoplehood, but a distinct people nonetheless. What became the United States was a colony of England until the war for independence, but even before that war it was colonial on a very different model from the one we think of in an age of global decolonial and postcolonial thinking. Indigenous peoples of the United States have lived and continue to live colonialism in its most straightforward form: theft of land, administration from outside the colony (the "reservation"), and cultural and economic manipulation, domination, and exploitation. The Standing Rock protests of 2016 and after served as plenty reminder of this. But African American experiences of antiblack racism elude the colonial model in important ways. This does not diminish those experiences at all. In fact, it sharpens those experiences and lets the visceral unicity of the American practice and praxis of antiblack racism register in the theoretical and cultural imagination with real precision. Precision matters when we want to link history and memory to critical theory and forms of resistance that flow from it.

At the same time, there is a lot to be learned from thinking between forms of antiblackness in the United States and colonialism in other parts of the Black Atlantic world. The Black Atlantic world *is* the Black Atlantic world precisely because the Middle Passage, enslavement, and the long shadow of both in post-

Emancipation life created entire worlds within which we all still live. We see this in the important and vital convergences of thinking after the Middle Passage and slavery across geographies. Indeed, we find mutual exchange in the very beginnings of both intellectual traditions, whether that is the rumor and inspiration of Haiti's successful revolt across plantations in the southern United States or the resonance of jazz and the jazz player as emancipated figure in Aimé Césaire's early poetry. Or, in terms of figures and problematics of concern in the present project, we need only consider the place of Richard Wright in Frantz Fanon's imagination, a place that was surely fraught and complicated, but one that also bore plenty of lessons around violence, sociogeny, and the meaning of Black subjectivity in an antiblack world. What strikes me in the present project as particular interesting and helpful about folding the African American experience into the experience of colonialism is the complex question of the production of margins in racially stratified worlds. The Manichean world, of course, is a cornerstone of Black Atlantic thinking and its relations. What does the postindependence experience of former colonies tell us about post-Emancipation worlds in the United States, how are margins produced in both, what do they produce, and what possibilities might lay hidden from wider view?

Let me reset and make an abrupt geographical shift in order to theorize marginality.

I think about Jean-Marie Teno's 1996 film *Clando* all the time. In fact, in many ways the film has directed my thinking for the past two decades, thinking that has been preoccupied with movement, displacement, time, the postcolonial situation, and formations of identity and meaning in fractured spaces. This has meant, for me, exploring issues of time and alterity, memory and history, vernacular culture, and comparative study in the Atlantic world. How is the Middle Passage an event for the Atlantic world, reordering the terms of thinking, knowing, and being? What does it mean to make worlds in its aftermath? And what is the meaning of decolonization in various sites? For the present project, *Clando* along with two films by Ousmane Sembène quietly shape my thinking toward the place of the outside inside systems of atrocity, exploitation, and neocolonialism. So, a word on both in order to set my interpretative frame and embellish notions of *la frontera* and excess.

Teno's film centers on a moment three-plus decades after independence in Cameroon in its witness to and contemplation of the meaning of the collapse of the postcolonial state into terror and kleptocracy. It follows Sobgui, a former computer programmer who lost his job after being arrested for collaboration with an opposition political movement. Sobgui's entire transgression is just this: He let a friend make photocopies of an opposition flyer for distribution. That's it. And "that's it" is part of the point. Cruelty is not retribution for serious transgression, but instead a feature of deathworlds that want to foreclose any and all possibilities of thinking otherwise. Even permitting a photocopy is already a thinking-otherwise too far. So, in *Clando* we do not get any sense of Sobgui's political commitments, but only his absorption into the punishing world of the repressive state put into terrifying action. He is beaten, fired from his job, and as a result is rendered impotent by the memory of violence and incarceration. But his sense of incarceration is not simply the jail. His entire personhood is carceral. Not long after he is released, Sobgui stands on a busy corner contemplating buying a cigarette from a street vendor when a friend walks up. The friend is happy to see him. Sobgui is expressionless. The friend offers concern and some comfort, reminding Sobgui that he is now free of the cell, no longer jailed, and, although he has lost his middle-class job as a programmer, Sobgui is at least free again. Standing on the corner, Sobgui replies: "I'm in prison. Even here. See the intersection there? That's my new cell."

It is a stunning and cratering moment. Teno lingers on Sobgui's face and posture, letting Paulin Fodouop display his acting excellence—a truly brilliant moment of performance. The pain is total. And it is not the pain of Sobgui alone. It is the pain of the entirety of the postcolonial moment brought to one face and one broken body in a public square. There is hope, there is desire and aspiration and elation, which is then quickly followed by the cruel realities of neocolonialism and the hangover of colonial values and practices in the kleptocratic state. Indeed, nothing is more efficiently passed along as a colonial insight than the notion—a lie, really, but a lie that appears as truth across the formerly colonized world—that kleptocracy is the natural order of things. It is not natural. It is wholly fabricated by elites who could not care less about the promises and aspirations of independence. Yet, here is Sobgui, here is his community-city-nation, here is Africa, here is the Global South after independence. Lost and impotent, delegitimated as body and as citizen, Sobgui drives a *clando*, an unlicensed taxi. He leaves for Germany in search of something meaningful or redemptive and, while in exile, is eventually convinced by his revolution-minded lover and/or his conscience to return. But the return is a dead-end, something we viewers know will be the case (he is one man, and he is not particularly political), but the film stages his return with a shot moving toward a dead-end intersection in the middle of a bustling neighborhood. There is movement. There are the masses. The final shot is a camera fixed on an automobile's dashboard, shaking and rambling as Sobgui is driven on a bumpy street. Toward a dead-end. What is the future? We do not know. The dead-end *does* split right or left, and the car begins to turn. We cannot know where. But what we know is this: Sobgui is literally and figuratively impotent. He cannot position himself for the reproductive act, he cannot imagine how the world carries on beyond him yet with him—impotence as political metaphor, yes, but also as total existential despair. He can't fuck, but he is fucked. He is the kleptocratic postcolonial state and the state is him. There is no distance. Sobgui is no voyeur.

There is no life in the margins in *Clando*. There is only the decimation and violence against the margins by the kleptocratic center, something that is different in some significant ways from other forms of oppression. Or at least that is Sobgui's assessment. He can see no outside. He sees only the repetition of colonialism, repetition that is now from the inside rather than administration from abroad. That shift from the geographic outside—administration from abroad, the strategy and practice of France with its African colonies—to the inner life of the nation (inside the borders, inside the person) enacts a specific kind of evacuation of life's meaning. So, if we are talking about margin/center relations, the stakes could not be higher. How we imagine a living, vital, and militant world-shifting response to metropole-colony consciousness (not just economic and political relationships) is immensely more complicated when the system of atrocity enacts its closure from the inside. Where and who is the enemy? It is in the name of the same become other become terror, rather than the other become terror itself. Manichean logic survives independence and constrains the imagination. The end of this constraint is despair and hopelessness. Nihilism at the margins of nihilism.

Let us stay with francophone African cinema for another moment.

Sembène's 1968 film *Mandabi* is an absolute masterpiece of thinking cinema. This is not surprising to any scholar or even casual viewer of African film. *Mandabi* is innovative for so many reasons, not the least of which is just the fact of its existence and how that fact, when coupled with his 1966 *La noire de . . .* , is the event of the initiation of African cinema into a continental and global tradition. What *La noire de . . .* did for visuality—making Black bodies and faces vibrant on film stock suited to white and only white skin—*Mandabi* does for the politics of small places—making the outskirts of the city, a small corner of an outskirt, really, and the language (Wolof) of a nonglobalized place into a story about colonialism's long, menacing shadow. The cruelty that animates Ibrahima's life is too much, too petty, and too close. It is not just the state, it is the family. If colonialism was a total project, leaving nothing in the colony untouched by corrupt and corrupting violence, then the colonial hangover we call neocolonialism is the same. Bureaucrat, neighbor, family. They all come to beleaguer Ibrahima in the very worst ways as he tries to find balance between his modest good fortune and his Islamic ethic of unconditional hospitality.

But that says nothing about the themes of the film. *Mandabi* is a small story about a small world that, like all of Sembène's cinema, is also a massive, expanding, and expansive story about the meaning of the postcolony. That meaning is mapped on to what had already become, not even a decade after independence in 1968, the vernacular of colonial, anticolonial, and postcolonial relations: the colony and its metropole. Ibrahima's is a story of a kind of decolonial *lumpenproletariat*, outside the system of both hegemony and its negation. In *La noire de . . .* , it is cinematically straightforward. Diouana takes a job in France, leaving her family, boyfriend, and community behind in Senegal. Moving from the colony—however post-the-colony the formal relations between France and Senegal had become in 1966, six years after independence— to the metropole is a movement of estrangement, isolation, and, in the end, fatal violence. We cannot but see Diouana's suicide as the fate of the colonized in the grasps of the colonizer. In *La noire de . . .* , the grasp operates in the imagination, in desire, and in the fantasies that manifest both. France was supposed to be Diouana's escape from the mundane, workerly life in Senegal, but it ends up being only isolation, degradation, and a path of despair that evacuates life of meaning. *Mandabi* is different. In a shift of center/margin relations, Sembène relocates to Senegal and yet finds the specter of France everywhere. This complicates the story we might tell about the two films and the relation between colony and metropole. We might want to say that *Mandabi*'s indulgence of Senegalese sound and image—sound in Wolof, image in vibrant color rather than the black and white of *La noire de . . .* , crafted class difference, and difference in aesthetic charge—leaves France behind. But Sembène's obsessive concern with the immediate *neocolonial* structuring of the postcolonial state renders France once more as a ghostly presence, showing itself in the very dress of the city folks at the city's center and of the poor folks living on the impoverished margins of the city. The suit or the *boubou*? This is Sembène's visual narrative and political incision. The plot unfolds from there. Ibrahima receives a money order (a *mandabi*) from a nephew in France who works as a street sweeper. Like Diouana, he is a laborer, but, unlike her, the nephew understands this work is only for remittances and perhaps, but only perhaps, also another kind of life in the coming years. At most, the metropole is rendered with ambivalence. The center and its closed system mean nothing but violence, and Ibrahima's nephew knows this. He expects nothing except that very little, but very much something of remittances and whatever life might develop from them.

Ibrahima receives the *mandabi* in the mail but is unable to cash it out. He cannot read and does not have proper identification, which means he cannot navigate the city-center banking system. All of this is made even more difficult because illiteracy and lack of state-sanctioned identity documents means he needs assistance and generosity simply to obtain what is already his. He needs proper identification to access his money. In order to get proper identification, he needs money, which he does not have but *could* have if he were able to cash the money order, which he cannot because he does not have the identification he needs, and he can get the identification he needs only with the money he cannot access. It loops and tightens. A knot that will not loosen. A knot that constantly reminds Ibrahima how bound he is by his material and national condition. So, the *mandabi* remains an empty piece of paper, not unlike Sembène's assessment of the terms of Senegal's independence in 1968. Lacking proper state identification and, outside of one character's attempt to assist (a cameo by Sembène himself), Ibrahima goes alone and alienated in search of the means to cash the check. His illiteracy means he needs assistance from someone at every stop along the way: the post office, the bank, the state office for identification. Ibrahima is out of place in the very moment that the state, now independent Senegal, is supposed to have given him a place. The atrocity of neocolonial rule is here, reproducing colonial alienation in the same suit but different language.

Sembène schematizes this in the geography of Ibrahima's movements and the aesthetic, moral, and political values of each place. We never leave Senegal. This is important because Sembène wants us to experience the metropole *inside* the postcolony. In fact, we never leave the city or the impoverished neighborhood alongside it where Ibrahima lives and struggles with his two wives. You cross the street, walk a few dozen yards, and you move from tailored European suits to *boubou*, from the neocolony to the space of something akin to the *lumpenproletariat*. Only a short distance. Same city, same nation, same postcolony. But the border could not be bolder or more violently patrolled. Between the city center and Ibrahima's community, there is a wall dividing what remains from before (his community) and now what lingers after colonialism (what estranges and devastates that community).

Across both films we see the fundamentally *poisonous* character of France. That poison is *pathogenic*, if I may retool a figure borrowed from Frank Wilderson in order to characterize the post/neocolony. The French effect spreads through both direct and indirect contact. Where France enters, things fall apart in the worst ways: they fall backward. For Diouana in *La noire de . . .* , France is the imaginary, the fantasy, the respite from a difficult (if profoundly dignified and anticolonial) life in a struggling neighborhood, a chance for something fancy and flighty to come into a young woman's life. No one could fault Diouana for this desire, and the affect of our rage and (shared) melancholy as she is consigned to nothing but domestic labor and longing for something else is possible only if we understand her desires. But her desires lack political conscience and consciousness, something the Popular School (shots of which feature a Sembène cameo) *could* have taught her were she a student *after* colonialism and had she obtained the full political *conscience* her boyfriend has in the scenes from his apartment—an apartment full of Lumumba posters, a revolutionary posture evoked again in *Mandabi*, in another Sembène cameo, as the director-as-civil-servant sits at a table covered with a portrait of Che Guevara. That revolutionary posture is in and at the margins of neocolonial society, fracturing (or hinting at the fracture of) the closed system of atrocious repetition.

What does it mean to say France is poison and a pathogen? It deepens the anxious postcolonial moment and, in context, to critique, perhaps, the values of Léopold Senghor in the first decade of independence who had imagined a productive relation with the beauties of France. Diouana herself imagines just that. But that imagination is impossible precisely because it fails to infuse historical consciousness with the intractably destructive work of the colonial. She is depoliticized by the neocolonial modification of her desires. A fatal and tragically not dangerous supplement. Diouana does not understand that the future asks something more of us than the past would give, and that postcolonial desire is fraught. Naivete of a certain sort is death. Ibrahima is confounded from a position outside, or we might even say *before*, colonial expectation—why would my brothers and sisters abandon us like this? Another naivete of another sort is alienation. He does not understand that his shared world still works with the same desires as under colonial rule. What are the conditions of desire and its imagination? How is the closed system of colonial domination reified or fractured by desire and imagination? For Sembène it is clear, and this reveals his lingering sense of revolutionary hope we lose in Teno's *Clando*. Sembène sees it all as a question of returning to *the people*. That is, to begin again with what we already failed to value in the ways it *should* be valued: the world-making work of vernacular culture, the beauty and possibility of small places, and life as life otherwise of the margins of hegemony. In *Mandabi*, we see in in the elegy for a culture of communal life, a kind of indigenous communism in Sembène's vision of Islam and the values of the poor. We do not get that from *La noire de* . . . because Diouana never returns. She is lost in the multiple ways that geography blocks the possibility of refusal, resistance, and alternative connection. The concluding sequence to *Mandabi* puts this so directly: A woman and two children appear at Ibrahima's door, hungry but knowing of his generosity. The *right and properly attuned* generosity, a generosity that, in one of those common threads across the Abrahamic religions, welcomes the poor unconditionally. Does it eliminate the pathogen?

Perhaps, in another future. But in *Mandabi*, it is enough to sketch its promise, a promise of which Diouana cannot catch sight in *La noire de . . .* , and to let the unconditional welcome breathe in the margins against neocolonial nihilism. *The welcome inside another time that is outside the time of the colonial.* Those values struggle against the accumulation of capital (and it is a struggle in *Mandabi*, not a given, because Ibrahima is utterly precarious) in the name of another kind of relation. A relation that Sembène captures in the final lines, a final repeated lament in *Mandabi*: "decency has become a sin in this country." Diouana's death by suicide is another postcolony life lost to the vicissitudes of capital. It was her modest desire (small pleasures, a bit of escape and glamour), to be sure, but also the context of her exploitation and nihilism. This all reminds me of a remark in a crucial exchange between Ali La Pointe and El-Hadi Jafar in Gillo Pontecorvo's *Battle of Algiers*, a film released the very same year as *Mandabi* and speaking from the same despair mixed with possibility: At the end of colonialism, our problems just begin and begin again.

I begin with all of this in Teno's *Clando* and two Sembène films in order to outline the terms of the present project and what I hope it opens up for theorizing the intersection of deconstruction and social death. *La noire de . . .* is fundamentally about a social death that, when lived in the barely former colonizer's social, cultural, and political milieu, is the death of a body, a person, and the imagination of a however premature Afropolitan ethos. *Mandabi* shows us a different kind of social death, but a death nonetheless, one that is wholly awful, brutal, and cruel. Ibrahima is *in* the postcolony, yet he is unable to simply cash a money order in a nation wracked with a bureaucratic colonial hangover. He is abject in the eyes of the Western-suited middle class, his poverty a sight and site for derision, embarrassment, and, ultimately, betrayal by a nephew. He wanders socially dead in his *boubou* among the city's exploitative bourgeoisie. His city which is not his.

And yet he also lives on the other side of the margin. Ibrahima's impoverished neighborhood is not abandoned *inside itself,* and from that inside it is neither abject nor a space of nihilism. Instead, at the conclusion of *Mandabi*, Ibrahima is revealed to be famous for his generosity and hospitality; a young mother arrives hungry with her two children, saying simply, "I've heard about your generosity. We've been without food for three days." It is unthinkable outside the neighborhood, yet a given inside it. This is why decency is a sin. What does it mean to think this space as a space of decency, a space of a Muslim ethic of hospitality among the poor, as a theoretical event? That is, what would it mean to take this configuration—moral, geographic, epistemological—as something that shifts how we understand life, death, and meaning outside the interchange of social death and the neocolonial? Sembène's claim is straightforward: The poor do not live as faded or abject copies of the bourgeoisie or neocolonial models of respectability, the proper, and the modern. Ibrahima does not long to wear a European suit—literally and figuratively. He wants to live a life of *decency*. To be sure, comparison is a centerpiece of life under and after colonialism. Shared, national social-political space is often dominated by the ontological and epistemological work of comparison; what it means to be human and how one is knowable *as* a human is often, if not nearly always, structured by relation to a (colonial) measure. But there is also *life* in these interstitial spaces, excesses of the margin, *la frontera* spaces that lie epistemologically hidden from and incomprehensible to the colonial gaze—rendered cinematically by Sembène as narrow, shadowed living spaces and streets—yet live and make worlds under their *own* exchanged gaze. *They have heard of Ibrahima's remarkable generosity, his Islamic virtue*. What does it mean to take this shift in gaze seriously? What is life outside the colonial and the colonizing gaze when that gaze only produces social death? How is the space of refusal different from spaces of resistance of subjugation?

There is something really important and special about Sembène's making anticolonial cinema in the immediate horizon of colonialism, a horizon in which refusal and resistance were both such live, insurgent possibilities. Teno's *Clando* is a very different kind of moment, though, one taken up in the aftermath of this outside-of-the-outside disappearing from view and losing its capacity to sustain life. Sobgui does not return from his alienated life in Germany to a space of sinful decency in Cameroon. Or maybe *Clando* is just a film about oblivion, a case of forgetting deliberately induced by Teno in the interest of revitalizing anticolonial struggle against the neocolonial, kleptocratic state among his outraged viewers. In that way, *Clando* is an important signpost in this consideration precisely because the film *wants* a sense of belonging without margins, wants the abolition of colonial modes of governance and social organization. And it is not a want without real roots and warrant. Indeed, this was the *promise* of independence: The world would be remade by the state with a vision other than the colonial. And yet neocolonialism, already in Sembène's films from 1966 and 1968, then later in Teno's film from 1996, always shows up and keeps the same Manichean economy of life and death in play, producing social death in the repetition of difference in the atrocity machines of comparison, exclusion, and abjection. *Mandabi* offers a reminder at the close of the film: There is also a world outside this machine that is largely, if not wholly, unseeable by that machine. *Clando* cannot quite summon that vision. Sobgui is incarcerated by open space itself. Such is the power and force of the neocolonial kleptocratic state. The space of refusal in *Mandabi* has vanished and there is only resistance. But resistance has brutality and nihilism at its heart. Teno makes sure we see it and cannot look away. This is also part of the world.

In the chapters that follow, this movement or longing for movement to the outside of the machine of comparison and abjection, this turn to a radical outside of system and systematicity, is the methodological and theoretical work done at the intersection of deconstruction and social death. It is also the condition of many visions of revolutionary mobilization and action and of the work of refusal and its inheritances. My concerns are largely theoretical. The existential purchase of that theoretical work lies in recognizing, in every philosophical register, the revolutionary power of obstinate existence and world-making in the interstices. That existence and world-making is enough unto itself. In a theoretical frame, however, it unfurls some of the most important insights of deconstruction's notion of supplementarity and how that sense of the supplement shifts our understanding of the scope of claims to social death. Supplementarity theorizes Ibrahima's right to decency and to another kind of life at the margins of the postcolony. Social death deepens the stakes of supplementarity in its identification of the abject as essential to the functioning of a system and the abject as unremunerated labor. And so the chapters that follow are set out in four phases and sites of analysis—a fully articulated theoretical frame followed by examples from the Black Americas—animated by a conceptually threaded figure, the figure of the slave. The figure of the slave *is* and *is not* as abject, and so, in a speak-back and speak-aside of supplementarity, dismantles claims totalizing abjection. With that, the unremunerated figure dismantles claims by revealing the scope and limits of Europe's colonizing of theory and philosophical practice. Nihilism meets its end in its margins where the figure of the slave is produced *and* speaks without reference to the center that determines the margins as abject. Refusal. Excess. The figure demands double reading, which is inscribed in the system and, in the very moment of its movement to a radical sense of outside, lives outside that system.

A figure of refusal, through and through.

In many ways, this conceptual map is a way of obliquely drawing out critical insights from Zora Neale Hurston's 1934 essay "The Characteristics of Negro Expression." The essay is exactly what the title suggests: a taxonomy with critical commentary that circles around the elements of expressive life among Black folks. Throughout the Black Americas, perhaps, but Hurston's specific attention is to the folkways, habits, embodiment, and foundational cultural practices of African Americans from the most rural South to urban landscapes in the Northeast. For Hurston, it is not a question of the characteristics of *some* Negro expressive traditions, but a question of Negro expression as such, of what kind of features appear across multiple geographies, histories, and memories. The essay is modest and bold at the same time. The modesty lies in the presentation. Unlike so much of her more creative nonfictional pieces, "Characteristics of Negro Expression" really is just a list of features with very few embellishments. But it is also bold in its implications. The taxonomy sets out those conditions under which Black joy in an antiblack world is possible, an affective life in Hurston's work that Lindsey Stewart has documented so well.[4] Hurston wants us to catch sight of joy in moments of abjection, marginalization, and difficult life. But always difficult *life*. What would joy and pleasure mean in this context? In so many ways, that is the deconstructive thread across the present project, its key theoretical intervention, and so a preliminary bit can be said here.

Three features noted by Hurston's essay strike me as particularly important: adornment, angularity, and asymmetry. Each of these features mark a shift of dimensionality in a world committed to controlling and subjugating African Americans inside a one-dimensional world of social death and interracial impossibilities. The essay opens with an evocation of "drama" as an existential characteristic, a broad frame in which the adorning of language (metaphor, simile, double description, verbalization of nouns and making verbs out of nouns), the adorning of space, and the layering of embellishments make drama aural and visual. Angularity of movement and asymmetry of aesthetic expression reiterate the same, namely, that a single dimension or rigid rule is not sufficient for the sustenance of Black life in its expressive worlds. Worlds at the margins of nihilism, yes, but worlds that are not dominated by the rules and systems of nihilism. *The otherwise as adorned, angular, and asymmetric.* What do those worlds *look* and *feel* like, and how does the look and feel say something about alternative, multidimensional modes of being and knowing? Lower frequencies and vernacular refusal. After describing a room in which tables, chairs, and walls are layered with décor, Hurston writes of adornment that

> it indicated the desire for beauty. And decorating a decoration, as in the case of the doily on the gaudy wall pocket, did not seem out of place to the hostess. The feeling back of such an act is that there can never be enough of beauty, let alone too much. Perhaps she is right. We each have our standards of art, and thus we are all interested parties and so unfit to pass judgment upon the art concepts of others.
>
> Whatever the Negro does of his own volition he embellishes. . . . The beauty of the Old Testament does not exceed that of a Negro prayer.[5]

Hurston's evocation of a sort of relativism here—"unfit to pass judgment upon the art concepts of others"—is no mere aesthetic principle. Quite the contrary, it describes an entire structure of refusal that opens up different dimensions of expressing Black life—a life that is folded into the one-dimensionality of nihilism yet not reducible to it. The home is not a container of objects and bodies. Rather, the home is an expression of place, belonging, and, in her vernacular, *the Negro*. What is this Black life that appears in practices of drama, adornment, angularity, and asymmetry? What methods unlock that possibility of appearance?

Angularity and asymmetry further embellish Hurston's characterization of embellishment through an engagement with movement, music, and expressive life. And it is worth saying again: expressive life is a manifestation of something before and behind or underneath expression: life folded into the one-dimensional world of antiblack racism. Dance and music, then, are not Black life itself, but rather leading clues of a lower frequency of being and knowing that makes expression possible. Body, voice, sound as symptom and external sign. This is a symptom and sign of a difference that indicates another structure of difference and differentiation—an intervention inside and also outside the white world and its construction of shared interracial space. Hurston is precise in her discussion of dance, movement, and musicality. "Everything he touches," she writes, "becomes angular," and "anyone watching Negro dancers will be struck by the same phenomenon. Every posture is another angle. Pleasing, yes. But an effect achieved by the very means which an [sic] European strives to avoid."[6]

This last bit, what the white person strives to avoid, is an indication of not just cultural politics, but of dimensionality in being itself. The dimensionality of being generates different ways of knowing folded into the being-knowing structure of nihilism. At the margins of nihilism, a double reading of movement is possible, a reading that puts movement out of place with itself. In Hurston's reckoning, movement as angular becomes expression as asymmetrical *inside* rhythm and its repetition of the same. She writes: "The presence of rhythm and lack of symmetry are paradoxical, but there they are. Both are present to a marked degree. There is always rhythm, but it is the rhythm of segments. Each unit has a rhythm of its own, but when the whole is assembled it is lacking in symmetry. But easily workable to a Negro who is accustomed to the break in going from one part to another, so that he adjusts himself to the new tempo."[7]

This is a remarkable passage that describes, in the work of music and dance, precisely what I have in mind in describing the margins of nihilism as a fold of difference. Hurston is describing dance, rhythm, and relation, but she is also describing the relation of Black life to itself and also the relation of Black life to the interracial world. A doubled discourse, a fold in being and knowing.

A different sense of time. The time of music and movement, and also the time of Black life related to itself. The presence of rhythm and of the asymmetrical is a paradox. But it is not a paradox to be resolved. It is instead a tension in which life is lived and beauty is made.

This brings me back to *Mandabi* and *Clando* as expressions of decolonial anxiety, pause, and movement. I am thinking of how Ibrahima and Sobgui are stuck in the abject space of the margin, largely unable to access whatever joys or pleasures might lie inside the outside. Sobgui is incarcerated by the very space of Cameroon itself. Ibrahima suffers his material conditions. He and his family are hungry and unable to cash the *mandabi* that would change things. Temporarily. Yet hunger as an existential event has multiple temporalities for Ibrahima and his community at the margins. His and their time is angular, asymmetrical, and adorned with ethics and politics. An opening of the system. A pause in hunger is plenty time, a time shared by the neocolonial world of postcolonial Senegal. The body and material life is its own kind of time and need and demand. And condition for revolution. It is also Sobgui's moral and psychological condition. The time and need and demand for some kind of hope and mobilization. The human body needs material and political sustenance. But *Mandabi* has its opening. Ibrahima is also folded into an *other* world that is neither the metropole nor an extension of it. Praise of his generosity and unconditional welcome is a signal of another kind of world inside the outside of that city center which brings only pain, confusion, and humiliation to the margins. This other world is a material culture and politics that shifts tempo, that alters time, that makes worlds *otherwise* than malice. Even in hunger, there is beauty. Even in a closed system of neocolonial domination, there is possibility. Even in conditions of abjection, there is virtue and the possibility of decency. The system of abjection imposes a time. But time is a paradox that opens at the very same moment it closes.

How do we think that opening of a closed system of cruelty?

Introduction
Whithering the Decolonial

> But despite my growing tolerance, for this Chicana *la Guerra de independencia* is a constant.
> —GLORIA ANZALDÚA, *BORDERLANDS/LA FRONTERA*

Two important moments in recent intellectual history give the present project texture and contour. First, the argument made in Gaytri Spivak's famous essay "Can the Subaltern Speak?," which places the work of Jacques Derrida into critical conversation with the subaltern studies group and its broad ideological orientation. That critical conversation lays out the terms in which deconstruction can be a vital resource for anti- and decolonial thinking. Spivak's answer to the essay's title question is complex and nuanced, but also quite straightforward: No, the subaltern cannot speak because the closed systems of *possible* speech and conditions of hearing erase the possibility of speaking and being heard. Colonial domination closes its own system. But there is also the play of absence. The self-immolation of the widow, Spivak's signature example of radical subalternity, sits wordless and without explanation. The widow immolates outside discourses of legitimacy and illegitimacy. An exteriority in the age of logocentrism. The body's fate at the hands of a pyre is akin to, if is not exactly, the fate of the widow's words in a closed colonial, patriarchal system and the closed systems of the native informant and other national-cultural authorities. What is the outside of the system? The widow, and so the subaltern more broadly, is spoken of, described, and explained, but never speaks, as a matter of principle, inside the system of colonial and patriarchal language. Language is no mere tool. That is, for Spivak it is never a question of producing a better or more widely shared instrument for political and cultural communication. Emancipation from colonial subjugation does not consist of an improved shared language. Language and world are inseparable. We make worlds as language and when we make and remake language we make and remake worlds. Martin Heidegger was right when he said that language is the house of Being, except that here we might tweak the phrase a bit, deescalate the question of fundamental ontology, and say that language is the house of *beings*. The consequences of this are real. When a language is colonial, it houses colonial beings. The colonizer and the colonized, a relation of conjunction that consigns the colonized to a certain kind of silence—this is the being of the colonial. And so too with patriarchy and the whole litany of political hegemonies.

At the Margins of Nihilism is a project about how to understand that silence and what it might signify in its refusal of signification. It is about the worlds that silence makes and unmakes. This is a question of erasure and its afterlives.

The other moment that animates this project is Zora Neale Hurston's description of place and embodiment in her essay "Characteristics of Negro Expression." Hurston's essay, while certainly a classic in the African American intellectual tradition, has in many ways been underthematized as a radical intervention in theorizing place and subjectivity as a subaltern, interstitial space. In particular, as noted in detail earlier, I am thinking about Hurston's critical terms such as angularity, asymmetry, adornment, and embellishment, all of which are assembled in order to describe the African American sense of place, practice, and belonging. Belonging, that is, that lies outside the normative demands of the white gaze and its antiblack racist claims. Hurston's aim in the essay is straightforward: to describe and account for features of expressive life among African Americans as neither derivative nor poor imitations of white American and European expressions of the same, but instead as original *forms of existence*. An aesthetic project that is also epistemological and ontological. When Hurston describes angularity and dance as *pleasing* as well as "an effect achieved by the very means which a European seeks to avoid,"[1] she marks a temporal and existential distance from the conditions that produce the African American as a subaltern class, abject category, and marginal other inside a system of social death. This is the key phrase: *seeks to avoid*. The embrace of what the European seeks to avoid describes a sense of life lived for the pleasures and comforts of African Americans *between one another*. Outside the white gaze, outside norms of European subjectivity and intersubjectivity, Hurston moves her discourse into cultural and social space while at the same time understanding that this culture-space, thought otherwise, nevertheless bears a *kind of* relation to the hegemonic white world. The otherwise is the possibility of life exterior to social death. But it bears a relation *to* social death. A paradox akin to the relation between asymmetry and rhythm. Both at the same time, but with the irreconcilable as a regulative concept. Resistance and also refusal.

In a comparative reading, we can see how Hurston narrates a space *toward* which Spivak asks and questions, but does not, or in principle cannot, speak *from*. That is the difference between witnessing a world (Hurston) and critical theory proper (Spivak). Even as both often overlap, draw from a set of concepts bearing important family resemblances, and form a compelling pair of approaches to refusing the economies of social death as a total project, of fundamental ontology, and of any closed system of the world, methodologies of witnessing and critique manifest very different sensibilities. But both sensibilities converge around the question that animate my reflections here: How do we name this *otherwise*? In the readings and theorizations that follow, I consider how gestures and conceptualizations of refusal embellish Hurston's account and Spivak's elliptical indicator in order to help us think about how the work of deconstruction, in its relation to the concept and practices of social death, is a theory of life. This deconstructive sense of life is always a wholly otherwise than what the order of being theorizes as life; the deconstructive sense bears relation to, while also being delinked from, social death, colonialism, and the terrors of the white gaze. And so in the chapters that follow, I stage the tension between closed systems and their exteriors while always coming back to how those exteriors and their relation to closure create interstices in which culture and sociality live and breathe. Living and breathing, it must always be said, is something made *after* political and epistemological critique and never in the mode of naivete. Critical life otherwise. Crafted. Critical theory is not life itself, but its interventions and characterizations do the kind of work of knowledge and cultural production that is necessary to grasp the full significance of what it means to think and live otherwise. To think and live otherwise is more than survival and resistance. It is being (dis)placed in the outside of being. It is refusal. It is improper in the order of colonial being. It is profane to the sanctity of social death. It is sacred of *la frontera* as world-making. It is unordered, wandering, and nomadic like Édouard Glissant's Caribbean subjectivity. It is a sense of freedom after and outside Emancipation. All of these at the margins of nihilism.

To Begin

Intellectual trends are fascinating. Because they are trends, they emerge at what invariably seems to be a diverging crossroads of intense dedication or equally intense ridicule. No one likes a trend, after all, even though likeability is part of what makes a trend trendy. Irritability is an important posture for traditionalists to take. They are, after all, inheritors of previous trends that through historical sedimentation have become cornerstones or dominant subfields. Funny how age works that way. Tradition is made out of a lot of oblivion. This is all especially true when the given matter of intellectual life is oriented toward understanding the fundamental structures of how our social, cultural, and political world(s) work. The stakes seem so high. In fact, they *are* high. When a new trend is an address to the cornerstones of how we live and breathe, moving away from those stones threatens, if not explicitly declared it as an intention, to build an entirely different way of being and knowing. And it is this very sense of high stakes, the notion that other ways of being and knowing are possible or even already actual, that opposes ridicule with genuine dedication. This is the trending of the trend. Every movement has to work to reproduce itself, after all. If we are trying to figure out how the worlds that define us work, whether in the mode of conservation or revolution or refusal, then any sense that we may have found a decisive path into that understanding rivets our critical attention. The meaning of life is at stake. Elaboration of details, formation of critical new vocabulary—new ideas require new words, always—and expansive dialogue, experimentation, and exploration of implications are all part and parcel of fresh new work. Not everyone understands the vocabulary and the debates, of course, precisely because it is new. Thus the intense dedication *and* the vulnerability to ridicule.

For those of us raised in the intellectual culture of the United States in the 1990s, deconstruction, particularly the work of Jacques Derrida, was one of our crossroads. We had to decide: Is deconstruction complete nonsense, or is it the revolutionary intellectual intervention we need in order to upset white Western history's grand hegemonies from the inside? This was not a matter of taste, however much the haters wanted it to be about the aesthetics of writing and accessibility or the ability to pose for a great photograph—all of these were Derrida's virtues and vices. The question of deconstruction was serious business. The entirety of white Western history and its tradition was at stake. The long history of published texts, canonical and foundation-building seminars, symposia, comprehensive exams, all those sites in which traditions are reproduced—this was what was being put in question. In that sense, no matter how petty and cruel it could get, the dispute over deconstruction was earned by the broad, ambitious aims of Derrida's work and the work of his comrade theorists: Dispute the antechamber of the tradition, even if it works against the tradition. Deconstruction aimed at taking away all of the tradition's words and concepts. Indeed, in that way I think we can say that upsetting the white Western tradition *must* appear as nonsense to that tradition's defenders. Perhaps critics working in the then-emerging field of deconstruction were right to take little real interest in making deconstructive work transparent to those who were being put under critical scrutiny. It was a struggle over the future of thinking, after all, and a bit of opacity and incomprehension is probably necessary for genuinely revolutionary thought. (Theodor Adorno had a point when he criticized transparent prose as conserving the worst of open market capitalism.)

Part of the anxiety that Derrida's work incited was also linked to the intimacy of his criticism. He was such an amazing reader of texts. As a parasitic praxis, deconstruction is a mode of dispute that draws upon existing intellectual conflicts and unresolved paradoxes at the heart of philosophy and critical theory. Deconstruction works from embeddedness in a tradition. The place of "clear writing" in moments of critical renovation or revolution and the place of geographies of knowing and being in the economy of truth claims, moral imperatives, and universal or universalizing claims about history and culture—these are all part of the dispute and vision of deconstructive work. Derrida's ability to place us at the unstable center of the canon while also operating as an outsider of and as an exterior force to the white Western tradition is as upsetting as it is confounding, yet also necessary. Matters of life and death are at stake. Not just intellectual life as a world of letters and missives, but also and firstly for deconstruction a vision of what it would mean to live or imagine living outside the hegemonies of everyday authoritarianism. Deconstruction has no interest in authority. Therein lies its most liberatory impulse, but also, for defenders of tradition, its most obnoxious affective appeal. So much still remains to be done *with* these insights. They are insights that ought to embellish other works with the thought of the outside. And deconstruction ought to open itself to embellishment by complementary and family resembling theories.

The question of social death and its ultimate significance played a similar role in turn of the century Black Atlantic theory. Orlando Patterson's paradigm-establishing work *Slavery and Social Death* not only introduced a new critical term, social death, to every field concerned with the study of Black life, but it also offered a grand narrative of the structure and effect of slavery in a global historical context. No matter one's final assessment of Patterson, the ambition of *Slavery and Social Death* is impressive and challenging, generating one of the most important critical terms for the field of Black studies. What does it mean to name the enslaved as socially dead? What does that naming say about the lifeworld structure of life, death, and how the relation between the two produce historically meaningful worlds? Patterson's broad claims invited both dedicated elaboration—the birth, really, of so much of what we now call Afropessimism—and its own kind of ridicule. How dare Patterson make such massive historical claims? Well, for me: thank god Patterson makes such massive historical claims. So much is possible after bold, audacious theorizing. Audacity makes us *think* and we are all the better for that, no matter the destination of our thinking. Work dedicated to producing *the interesting* and *the provocative* is so much more fecund than positivist insistence on being modest, right, and correct. In that way, critical theory that has a dimension of what Maurice Merleau-Ponty in *The Visible and the Invisible* called "wild being" opens up so many more horizons. In doing that ambitious, perhaps at times wild work, Patterson produces another critical theory crossroads: How do we reckon with his difficult insights, take them on, and see how they modify our intellectual sensibilities? Or does that work provide no insight whatsoever? This is a dispute absolutely worth having. To claim social death as not just a *feature* of slavery but also as a *constitutive* or *foundational part* of worlds made in and through the practice of slavery elevates the stakes. How do we remember the past? How do present worlds descending from worlds of slavery retain traces or more of enslavement with social death as a persistent animating force? What is the ultimate purchase of such a broad claim about the structure of slavery, and how do those features live beyond their moment? Ambitious, wild work such as Patterson's illuminates something about the world, tells some sort of truth. What other theoretical interventions can be made in order to further embellish that illumination? How does the notion of social death embellish another theory or other theories? This is what most interests me about *Slavery and Social Death*. Not the question of accuracy or overstep, but what it allows us to see and what we can do with what we see.

How does theory sit between deconstruction and social death? And how does that between illuminate something important about decolonial thinking?

What I am proposing in the pages that follow is a critical comparative study of deconstruction and social death as companion theories of death, theories that place a certain conception of death at the root of the distinction between life and death, or perhaps outside that distinction yet always constitutive of it. Mutual embellishment and creative extension. For me, embellishment is one of the more interesting parts of comparative work, emphasizing creative rereadings and recastings that pull more out of a theory than the original theory might want or expect. This is the power of critical reading and critical assessment of theoretical interventions. Now, when it comes to deconstruction and social death, it must be said that there are very real differences between the two critical theories. The language of each is distinct, internally consistent and rigorously developed, and drawn from a particular set of historical concerns and experiences. This is true of all theoretical innovations, of course, but in this case the two innovations work from entirely different positions in the historical economy of empire. Derrida, by way of Algeria, writes from postwar Europe and to the history of its tradition. Patterson, by way of Jamaica, writes from the United States, but to a massive global-historical framework and vision. What is required to make this sort of creative conjunction and mutual embellishment work?

The critical bridge I build between deconstruction and social death works with what I call, borrowing Andrew Benjamin's turn of phrase, "the figure of the slave" in philosophy and critical theory.[2] This phrase "figure of the slave" can have manifold significations, of course, the most obvious and straightforward being the place of actual enslaved people in social and political theory from the pre-Emancipation era. That figure shows up in numerous places, especially in critical philosophy of race. The ways in which philosophers of race have interrogated the function of the slave and slavery in white Western political and historical thinking has demonstrated how in so many cases broad philosophical questions that *appear* to be disconnected from historical phenomena and political realities—the dream of a pure and uncontaminated discourse—are actually entangled with what is most gruesome about modern human history. But I do not want to work with the figure of the slave in that manner. I am not doing critical philosophy of race. Rather, I am interested in how key moments in Western thought—expressed in the interracial space of the Black Atlantic, entangling being with the history of terror—both rhetorically appeal and demonstrably need an element, inside and also outside systematicity, that remains unremunerated.[3] This is an important tweak of Derrida's notion of the supplement, one made possible by a conceptual transformation produced by contact with Patterson's notion of social death. What labor is done by supplementarity and social death when it comes to the composition of economies of thinking, being, and knowing? How is supplementarity fecund when it is not embellishing those very same economies, but is instead destabilizing them at the very same moment it seals the internal coherence of the system? Deconstruction's paradoxical work. Social death's alienated place in social production and reproduction. In what way is this labor unremunerated? And how does it make the Western tradition appear as a massive, multicentury intellectual plantation? This requires deconstructive reading and sensibility, to be sure, but also a sense of the entanglement of colonialism, an entire orientation of thinkerly life, with the white Western tradition and its production of an other. Social death helps us to see the dramatics of supplementarity and, when blended with the figure of the slave, to see how the supplement draws out the atrocity of the imperial fantasy of white Western culture, epistemology, and social-political lifeworlds. Emmanuel Levinas was not wrong when he said the Western tradition has been largely an expression of the urge for totality and totalitarianism. Social death shows the concrete, traumatic historical experience of that urge and expression. The urge and its practice was formative of entire discrete and interconnected worlds in the Atlantic world, perhaps of the entire globe. Decolonial thinking is the movement out of that world movement charted in part and in possibility by the intersecting work of deconstruction and critical theory rooted in social death.

Every imperial, totalitarian fantasy needs its other. What or who is that other, how does it appear and not appear in the systematicity of those fantasies? What is the life of the figure outside its figuration and the logic of capture or seizure that operates inside that figuration? Enslavement was a total practice. We know something about its history as an economic and political practice. We also know something about the theological and moral justifications for those practices. But if it was a total practice, a practice that captivated the entirety of the Western imagination, then we should not be surprised to see the figure of the slave show up in the foundations of the project of philosophy and critical theory in modes of demonstration, justification, argument, and the taxonomy of ideas, values, and prerogatives. That is to say, *slavery changed thinking itself*. It was an event in the most transformative sense.

It is also the case that the figure of the slave is not entirely captured by what the enslaver imagines. The figure of the slave is the radicalization of death in the economy of thinking, and sometimes dialectic, of life and death, the supplement outside the system that makes the system possible but can never (fully, wholly) appear inside the system of thought. What needs to be asked, then, is how the radicalization of death is also possibly and perhaps necessarily a radicalization of life. To wit: If the supplement marks the interstices between death as an absence that is present (or capable of becoming present) and presence, then that which is both necessary as an antestructure and impossible as a visible component of the system that depends upon its absolute absence has its own economy, however opaque, veiled, and unavailable to imperial vision. A sense of absence that is not subject to variations on the thought of totality. What is and what can be said about a sense of life and death radicalized to such a point that hegemonic Western systems, committed as they are to the figure of the slave as unremunerated conceptual and affective labor, cannot see them? What is that figure's life when it is *not* the unremunerated laborer? What would it mean to ask about this subaltern and its speaking? The enslaved are never solely what the enslaver wants or imagines them to be.

These are broad questions, to be sure, and elliptical at best. Any kind of responsible response must work from examples. Social death, after all, is a concretization of death, not simply an abstract figure that is thought in fits of abstraction. My examples here are textual, rhetorical, and components of argumentation and demonstration. And, as we shall see, exemplarity is itself a complicated moral and political matter, carrying with it all sorts of quiet and unacknowledged imperial values, refusals, and affective life. To give an example or to work from an example is often to say more than one intends to say. The complexity of exemplarity is part of what forms the basis of the critical reflections that follow. So, a first word on exemplarity.

What is an example? This is a particularly compelling matter when we understand that the examples in question concern the margins produced by colonial practice and global empire. Imperial subalterns like "the Indian," "Africa," "the Native," "the African," the infrahuman, the subhuman, the animal, and so on are all products of global conquest and exploitation, living not just as political places and economic relations on a colonial map, but also, if not first, as figures in the imagination to which all sorts of affects cluster. This is what is so important about examples. They are not merely occasional mentions or interchangeable cases for consideration. Examples are not subordinate variations of concepts or figures, but instead co-constitutive of the event of meaning. Examples serve a rhetorical function in the construction of arguments that have to be taken seriously on their own terms, read back into concept and theory as conditions for possibility rather than simply an object under the conditions of cognition—an almost reversal of Immanuel Kant's transcendental aesthetic, enacting a zigzag movement across it, rendering conditions of possibility reversible and vulnerable. For example, when G. W. F. Hegel famously turns to Africa and the African in his *Lectures on Philosophy of History* and we recoil from its grotesque racism, we cannot simply swap out a more palatable, less colonial case in order to save what we like about the theory. The example is more than a substitutable particularity. Every thinker, we must presume, selects words, concepts, and examples with great care and with a view toward important meaning making. Meaning making crosses the logical with the affective; any cleavage of argument and affect is tenuous, if not wholly fabricated. Our rhetorician friends know this. The affective, in turn, invites us to read these crossed moments inside history and the values, prerogatives, and urgencies of the moment. What does the messy inscrutability of the Indian tell us about, say, John Locke's argument about property, about how and why he wants to persuade us? And so too with Hegel's appeal to an African without self-consciousness and the foundations of a philosophy of history. What do the examples expect and demand of us at the level of affect? What beliefs, values, and political subconscious are *activated* in the affective work of the example? Arguments, after all, are designed to convince. When we reread white Western philosophy with this in view, something critical philosophy of race has done well at times, that tradition appears as a global plantation. The follow-up question is how inheritance works for subaltern traditions as well, how the colonial example—the figure of the slave, the unremunerated something or someone—shows up at the edges and also at the center of diagnosis and reckoning. Terrifying, but a crucial theoretical issue with which we must come to terms.

The nuances of exemplarity are contingent upon the example and its function in a particular text or constellation of texts. Of course. But one of the horizons of exemplarity emerges with decolonial significance in that moment in which the example embeds argument in historical, political, and cultural moments of moral asymmetry, hegemony, and atrocity. Those moments have multiple layers of signification, life, and forms of death; no example is one-dimensional or stable. If decolonization has to do with the movement away from center/margin thinking and shifting into a post-Manichean horizon, then this embeddedness of the example in politics and culture also helps us see how interstitial spaces are opened by what the example says, what it does not say, and what remains opaque in order to be read under erasure outside the figure of the slave and the status of the example as a kind of social death. The logic of supplementarity gathers all significations to this place. But, again, this is a matter of reading and rereading the example under erasure, the kind of double reading I offer in the chapters that follow. Let me say a bit more about the general shape and contour of exemplarity, supplementarity, social death, and decolonization in order to read the following chapters with anticipation.

The link between the example and production of abject margins speaks most directly to the colonial text and how it renders its other. If colonialism was a total project and all of the work of literature, history, philosophy, science, and religion was gathered to its elaboration and defense, then we should never be surprised to see the figure in the slave at the center of argument, demonstration, and ideological reproduction. But the more complicated question is: How does exemplarity work in texts *not* generated by the colonial gaze? How does exemplarity work in texts that speak to, against, and from outside that gaze?

In the three figure-based chapters that follow, I explore how social death and deconstruction function in James Baldwin's reflections on the ghetto, in the nihilism of Richard Wright and Frantz Fanon, and in the construction of pessimistic ontology in contemporary Afropessimism. What we see in each of these cases is how senses of voice, speaking, iterability, and aural resonance are articulated and unarticulated when trying to make sense of Black lived experience in an antiblack world. Nihilism is the atmospheric common to all three chapters. For Baldwin, pessimism is the grounding fact of a world in which, for the Black person, "it was intended that you should perish."[4] All the world is a ghetto. For Wright and Fanon, nihilism is an existential sensibility born from a world that makes no place for Black bodies, much less Black people or Black life. All the world is a scene of death. For contemporary Afropessimism, nihilism generates an ontology of the world that contaminates even liberatory desire and expression with antiblackness. All the world is an antiblack pathogen. But these senses of nihilism—each with different rendering, no matter the common atmosphere—resonate very differently when reframed in terms of social death as deconstructive practice and when that reframing moves us to the margins of nihilism. In each of these three chapters I argue that the destabilizing work of deconstructive practice builds instability into the very ontology that is meant to make Black life impossible—ontology as sociogeny generated both by white racism and by theorists reckoning with its long horizon. And, further, I argue that this destabilization opens up a robust, thick-with-meaning sense of the interstitial: an entire world, full of possibilities, actualities, cultural production, and world-making. This interstitial and its fecundity is the birthplace of the Black Atlantic intellectual tradition in the mode of refusal. Sometimes in revolt, but always in refusal. In this sense of refusal, we see the interstices signify with an opacity that opposes itself to claims of abjection and, in that opposition, signify forms of immanent joy at the making life and death outside the life/death binary of antiblack ontologies.

What would it mean to speak to, from, and about this interstitial world-making space outside space? This is what Ralph Ellison calls the lower frequencies at the close of *Invisible Man*. We hear them only with another kind of attunement, a listening and reading that, after Derrida, we can call working under erasure. A fecund sense of reading under erasure that ends in something less opaque than Spivak's example of the self-immolating widow, but something that also remains *in some measure* and *for some people* obscured and hidden. Reading and listening under erasure forges another kind of relation to absence, a relation that refuses the claims of social death and abjection in order to think otherwise.

Whither the decolonial?

An important sense of a decolonial antechamber shows up here in thinking otherwise under erasure. Thinking under erasure is not itself a production of value or life but instead conceives and gives language and sensibility to what is necessary for such production. Under erasure can also be configured in or as the imagination and expression of life in something like what Gloria Anzaldúa calls *borderlands*: spaces of mixture and composite culture located in the between-space of wholly inside the system of social death *and* wholly outside, and therefore alien to, that system. This difference is nuanced and requires attentive reading for silences as well as declarations. Anzaldúa's long meditation in the experimental text *Borderlands/La Frontera* animates so much of what follows in terms of critique precisely because of her careful attention to the complex linguistic and ontological resonance of both *mestizaje* and becoming-*nepantlera*. Both notions reflect a commitment to silence and erasure, which is a commitment not only to thinking the *between* but to thinking it as a fecund space with its own rules and counterrhythms while also, in the mode of what I am here calling the supplement, being implicated in the system that marks the border as a border. The border is still literally and figuratively *land*, a living space, ever precarious and always haunted by forms of social death. What Ellison's notion of lower frequencies offers to this discursive formation and possibility is a sonic figure for thinking life *otherwise*, a link between the spatiality of *la frontera* and the orality of vernacular languages and composite cultural formation. Interstitial life, when framed in this and other companion ways, helps us see how deconstruction can be treated as at once a theory of death—taking responsibility for the structure of social death and the ethical imperatives borne by that form of death—and an opening us, in the exit of the closed system, to a reading and a reckoning with another conception of life. Between life and death, deconstruction is work *toward* the space of *la frontera* and an attunement to the lower frequencies. It is Hurston's angular movement and Spivak's subaltern silence when both are read under erasure.

This is my provocation. Where does it lead us?

To Proceed

How is death built into our very conception of life? And how is death conceived as a variation of life? This is the question of deconstruction. It is also the question of social death in its most nihilistic articulation.

The opening chapter below sets out the theoretical parameters that guide readings in the chapters that follow it. In that way, a lot hangs on the effectiveness of the chapter in generating a helpful or interesting theoretical frame and method of reading. That frame and method operate at the intersection of deconstruction and social death, drawing on what I see as the more radical, boundary-pushing, and even shattering insights that lie at the heart of both notions. Derrida's articulation of deconstruction as a theory of the supplement in *Of Grammatology* tells us a story of how systematicity, with its often-terrifying play of presence and absence, depends upon something that does not itself show up in that play. The supplement is both the condition for the possibility of the system and unpresentable and impossible within it. Social death follows an interesting parallel logic. Patterson's account of social death as a form of atrocious exile argues that the socially dead slave is both inside and outside the system of slavery but is also never merely a contingent part of the political and cultural structure. The structure *needs* the slave in order to function and *needs* social death in order to conceive and practice its forms of life, but the slave—and this is where the double meaning of *death* comes into view—is never fully present to politics and culture. Dependency, dialectical engagement, but also radical withdrawal and oblivion characterize the slave in systems of social death. In that way, both social death and the supplement make systems possible and cannot appear fully or in any significant way in those systems. The figure of the slave is precisely this paradox: an unremunerated radical absence that makes the play of presence and absence, life and death, work. But what lies outside that play? What is the figure of the slave, the supplement, the socially dead outside its function and functioning in relation to what excludes? This is another form of life, a decolonized sense of what interstitial space and its temporality means and how it is structured. A space and time structured not by resistance, but by *refusal*—a nonengagement that forges different senses of relation. The *différance* in *différance*, as it were.

With this theoretical frame in hand, the project transitions to three encounters with nihilism and its work of drawing from and producing the margins. What is the language of the margins? And how might a double reading of the margins disclose something about the possibilities inside and outside being itself?

These next three chapters engage with the legacies the white European gaze, its senses of abjection, and the quiet dependencies of systematic thought on figures of the slave. That gaze is our collective colonial legacy, and it is reproduced across social forms, habits, and institutions. Baldwin's ghetto, Wright's underground, Fanon's truncated dialectic of abjection, and Afropessimism's conception of Black being all reckon with the depth of nihilism produced by Europe's transformation of the Atlantic world, its aftermath in postindependence and post-Emancipation social-political life, and its manifold senses of hold on the theoretical imagination. These chapters take up this entangled set of problematics in the Black Americas in order to track the presence of social death, the supplement, and production of interstices in the margins of nihilism.

The second chapter turns to Baldwin's work with a focus on his negotiation of the dialectic of racial formation. This dialectic produces both white and Black identities in the United States, a productive relation that entwines ideological racial reproduction with our most intimate existential concerns. Who and what am I? Who and what are we together? And what are the limits and possibilities of this "we," however we render it? Reading his nonfiction and also drawing on Raoul Peck's retrieval of an incomplete work on the deaths of Medgar Evers, Martin Luther King Jr., and Malcolm X in his film *I Am Not Your Negro*, I argue that Baldwin repeats key elements of the nihilism we find among his contemporaries Wright and Fanon, but with particular attention to the negative dialectical moment of remainder. What is the remainder for Baldwin? How is the remainder produced as a relation to social death, not as a moment of redemption or resistance and instead as a moment of refusal? This is what Baldwin calls in "Many Thousands Gone," an early essay from 1951, "the relation Negroes bear to one another." With that simple evocation evoking the complexity of Black life lived in an antiblack world, Baldwin folds another sense of life outside the play of life/death in the system of social death. This is a space of refusal, a space made *by* refusal, and also a space of fully meaningful life outside the system of antiblack life, social death, and how the figure of the slave makes nihilistic interracial space possible. Baldwin's iteration of the racial supplement at the margins of nihilism not only destabilizes but also speaks, lives, and navigates a way outside of the capacity of the antiblack world to see and hear. This is Baldwin's version of the lower frequencies, interrupting his nihilism with an antechamber for thinking in a decolonial register.

In the third chapter, I offer a reading of Wright and Fanon that describes their shared conception of a nihilistic ontology of an antiblack world. Wright's fiction, in particular *Native Son* and *The Outsider*, is as much theoretical work as it is literary, describing worlds and making ontological claims that, in the language of "The Man Who Lived Underground," offer only death above ground. The only space for Black existence as such, which is at best a threadbare version of Black freedom, lies isolated, lonely, and underground. Fanon's early work *Black Skin, White Masks* gives a similar account in his description of interracial colonial lifeworlds that offer Black people only despair. With comparison, epidermal racism, and the problem of diction—just to name three elements of racial nihilism—Wright and Fanon give us phenomenologies of the figure of the slave as *lived* in antiblack worlds, worlds in which social death and the violence of antiblack racism *seem* constitutive of the world itself. But in both thinkers there are critical moments in which the voracious system of antiblackness cannot come to its proscribed closure. The system opens ever so slightly, often against the systematic aims of their nihilistic thinking. Vernacular culture plays this role of opening the system, naming either the blues (Wright) or creole language formation (Fanon) as fissures at the edge of closure. My claim in the chapter is that this opening of the system destabilizes nihilism without turning to Fanon's vision of an unprecedented future (his notion of a *new humanism*) and surmounts Wright's nihilism with *la frontera* of life in the Black Americas.

The final full chapter examines contemporary work on Afropessimism, with focus on the work of Frank Wilderson, Jared Sexton, and Calvin Warren, but also the early Achille Mbembe and key insights from Saidiya Hartman. My accounting of those works is framed by a concern with the important intersection of Afropessimism and fundamental ontology. This frame sharpens concern and engagement with Afropessimist thinkers, in particular by allowing us to see how the movement carries a deep commitment to closure and systematicity. As a movement and theoretical sensibility, Afropessimism has important connections to affective life in Wright, Fanon, and Baldwin. This is why staging an encounter with Warren and companion theorists in contact with midcentury Black Atlantic thought is so illuminating. Whatever the points of contact and parallel with midcentury figures, Afropessimism represents a radical and radicalizing innovation. Indeed, and this is something I want to underscore in my exposition of its theorization of being and the nothing, what distinguishes so much of contemporary Afropessimism is its commitment to generating an ontology of antiblackness that saturates and conditions being itself. The being of beings, and whatever cultural and political forms emerge from the world as we know it, are saturated with and conditioned by irreducible racial abjection, persecution, and violence. Thus, the *pessimism* in Afropessimism. The figure of the slave is central to this argument. Part of the Afropessimist account hinges on identifying the afterlives of slavery as a matter of repetition of form. Repetition and reproduction putatively seal up the system of antiblackness and pessimistic forms of dissent and outrage that attend to and speak against Being-as-antiblackness. Where is the opening of the system? The Afropessimist system is neither dialectical nor a system that produces common racial nihilism, precisely because Afropessimism is oriented toward either a pessimistically rendered future or an apocalyptic event in thought—the aftermath of which we cannot know. In that way, Afropessimism is more honest and rigorous than Fanon about that structure of time which *Black Skin, White Masks* opens up. But Baldwin's exit, the remainder of negative dialectics, is instructive here. What and whose lives remain otherwise than Being? This is the foreclosed interstitial space of Afropessimism. But supplemental disruption is built into the very figure of the slave that animates and sustains pessimist thought. I argue that Ellison's evocation of the lower frequencies opens up this sense of disruption and supplementarity through an introduction of dimensionality to being. That dimensionality fissures and opens the Afropessimist system of closure from inside that system with aural and sonic registers. Vernacular life, the life of the lower frequencies, expresses lived refusal of the one-dimensional ontology of antiblackness.

By way of conclusion, I turn in some detail to the question of decolonial thought and its compelling relation to thinking deconstruction and social death together. Decoloniality resonates explicitly and implicitly across the chapters as the *implication* and *extension* of the work of deconstruction and social death, finding in each movement into the interstices of thought a kernel of exit from the Manichean structure of colonial thinking. But what is the broader story of decoloniality in relation to these sites of reflection? How do these sites set out a template for revisiting social, cultural, political, and theoretical formations that reify—whether in buttressing support or in resistance and outrage—colonial configuration of social death and abjection? What exits this system? How is this exit built inside the system and yet opaque to it? How does the opacity of refusal inside the system of life-death-social death upset any and all pretensions to a metropole/colony, center/margin logic? This is precisely where I want the project to conclude and to open to other forms of thinking otherwise: a rigorous accounting of refusal and its alternative temporality, which is neither a prior life nor an afterlife of the figure of the slave. Refusal has its own time. It splits time in the name of life *otherwise*. And that is decolonial time par excellence.

Woven throughout these stories of social death, deconstruction, and the production of interstitial space is the question of decoloniality. And this is where the matter of academic trends reappears.

Though the matter of what to do, how to live, and how to make or remake worlds after the end of direct colonial rule has been a question since the mid-twentieth century's wave of independence struggles and victories, the term or method *decolonial* has become suddenly urgent and, truth be told, vexing to most whose thinking is not deeply embedded in the history of anticolonial discourse. Fanon is in many ways the founding figure for these conversations in the Atlantic world, moving across the Black Americas to the continent of Africa with theoretical and praxical demands for the postcolonial state and for senses of personhood, world, and meaning. The evolution of decolonization as a project bears real debts to Fanon and his arguments in *The Wretched of the Earth*. In that text, Fanon argues that decolonizing work is inherent in political violence, a sense of violence that on first take is directed at political forms of oppression and exploitation but shifts and turns to more complicated questions of the psyche, desire, embodiment, and cultural production and reproduction. Violence, on Fanon's account, is structurally inevitable. The exploitation of the colonized creates what Césaire described in *Notebook of a Return to the Native Land* as a volcano: percolating rage that awaits release.[5] Political mobilization activates this explosive power and directs it toward the kinds of things revolution first targets: evacuate the colonizer, reclaim land, and begin the process of a total reconstruction of state and society. That moment of transition to state and society is where complexity begins and the wide question of decolonization as *decolonial thought* or *decolonial critique* begins. Decolonial thought operates as critique in the classical sense: elaboration of the conditions for the possibility for a(nother) kind of world, one outside systems of life/death regulated by colonial ideals of bifurcation—those who live and the socially dead—and the white European gaze. "The colonial context," Fanon writes, "is characterized by the dichotomy it inflicts on the world. Decolonization unifies this world by a radical decision to remove its heterogeneity, by unifying it on the grounds of nation and sometimes race."[6] The removal of heterogeneity, what Fanon elsewhere calls the Manichean structure of the colonial world, creates space for new forms of knowing, being, and worldmaking rooted in what, since the installation of colonial forms of domination and governance, is an unprecedented sense of human possibility. In *that* sense of the decolonial, we grasp the expansive power of Fanon's call for a new humanism, one that, in Césaire's words, is "a true humanism—a humanism made to the measure of the world."[7]

But like all evolutions, decolonial theory has undergone important modifications, splits, debates, and mutations according to geography, intraracial and intraregional differences, historical period, shifts in memory work, and the exigencies of culture and politics in a given moment. Fanon's and Césaire's visions of decolonization were forged in a specific and intensely urgent moment: the midcentury surge of independence struggle and victory over mixed forms of direct and indirect rule. But things change and new demands surface. One can think of the stressed postcolonial state described in the prefatory remarks above by way of Ousmane Sembène's *La noire de . . .* and *Mandabi*, stresses that become ever more urgent over the next few decades, culminating in Quixote-like protest against the neocolonial in Jean-Marie Teno's *Clando* as the postcolonial matures with stunted decolonial growth. These cinematic testimonies, composed in the aftermath of victories that *began* with Fanonian aspirations, speak to the need to revise, expand, and recommit to decolonization as a chaotic, shifting, attentive, and site-specific political and intellectual project.

This sort of shift in tone and need is no doubt part of any substantial intellectual and political movement. Geography and history shape urgency and need. But it is also a feature of responding to the enormity of the project that was colonialism and indicative of the colonial hangover in neocolonial culture and politics. Colonialism, and this is something I will repeat across the pages that follow, was a *total project*. No aspect of the world of the colonizer or of the colonized lay outside its reach. What it means to think, to be, to act, to judge, to speak—all of these aspects of living and dying are closely bound to colonial, imperial prerogatives. Again, Fanon is the architect of diagnosis and struggle: *Black Skin, White Masks* masterfully outlines the depths of colonial impact on language, desire, imagination, senses of self/other, and stability of the psyche. Conquest, whether settler colonialism or colonialism begun in the Middle Passage, uproots, burns the roots, and replants in what little remains of soil the resources for the deepest and widest senses of alienation. And so anti- and decolonial work has to match that uprooting-to-alienation work with the same kind of energy, with the same kind of intensive commitment to detail and comprehensive revolution. For the colonized, this is readily acknowledged as part of struggles for liberation in the aftermath of independence, however configured. Whether affirmations of Creole language formations in Édouard Glissant's work and the work of others, calls to return to Indigenous languages of Africa in the work of Ngũgĩ wa Thiong'o, or embrace of vernacular modifications of colonial languages in Kamau Brathwaite's nonfiction or James Baldwin's work on Black English, and the work of so many others, the very act of speaking and how speaking produces and reproduces community is a consistent theme in theorizing decolonial intervention. The spatiality of the decolonial is similarly important, helping us see how what Hurston describes as angularity or adornment in her "Characteristics of Negro Expression" is an address to *la frontera* inside the metropole—literally the sounds, movement, bodies, and homes of African Americans living inside empire. How is this a decolonial site of reflection? That is part of the motivation for this project, to begin to answer that question. We can also think of institutions of the state from economic and community arrangements to internal governance to South-South solidarity work to education models to public memorials and their politics—how all of these are part of the agenda of decolonial thinking and praxis. Decolonial questions proliferate at the very moment we consider and reckon with the expansiveness of colonial inheritance.

Theory lies at the heart of this. Humanist traditions lie at the heart of this. The postcolonial moment bequeaths a question, one we see in the plea that closes Fanon's *Black Skin, White Masks*. To be one who questions is to be one thrust into the interrogative. That thrust, that questioning life as another kind of life sends the subject into interrogative space precisely because something about the colonized world has shifted. Or perhaps something(s) and someone(s) exited. Outside that world—not as its one-dimensional margin, but radically outside—is the space of possibility at the margins of colonial nihilism and its worldly inheritances.

All of this applies in reverse to the colonizer, but with important modifications. It is always important to say that Europe lived (with impunity) from the colonial machine of violence, abjection, exploitation, and cruelty for centuries. Out of this life emerged some of the most important features of white

Western self-description and self-elevation: pride of language, the concept of whiteness, the naturalness of racial identity, the meaning of culture, legitimacy and illegitimacy of different hegemonies, and so on. So, decolonial imperatives sit just as much at the feet of the colonizer in the long postcolonial moment as they do at the feet of the colonized. The colonized have been engaged with this work, with mixed results (to be generous) because the neocolonial turn, the colonial hangover and its harm to the social-cultural body, is persistent, insistent, and demanding of all energies and attentions. Decolonization and the practice of decolonial theory and world- and culture-making is fundamentally a *process* dedicated to critical self-examination and critical destructuring, then restructuring institutions. The colonizer, though? We have barely begun to reckon with what it means to have lived from this machine of violence. We have barely begun to reckon with what it would mean to do the work of not only reparation for those harmed, but also the expulsion from the collective self of those deeply sedimented colonial habits of thinking. Calling such aftermaths "privilege" is not nearly enough. Something more incisive, destabilizing, and perhaps *abolitionist* is necessary. This is the decolonial in its most expansive sense, rewriting, perhaps, Heidegger's famous title in order to describe where we are: *the end of philosophy and the task of decolonial thinking*. The postcolonial moment opens this horizon of thought, thrusts us into the interrogative, and in that horizon the decolonial emerges as the moment of keeping us honest, ethical, attentive to the neocolonial, and responsive to the demands of all emerging types of critical intervention.

But it is important to see that the decolonial, as Fanon and perhaps Césaire would have it, is not simply a question of the future. It is not only the question of the unprecedented and its interruption of the world as we know it. Apocalypse is not our only avenue. Decolonial practice at the intersection of deconstruction and social death is also a form of reading for traces, of reading for exits at the closure of systems, and of reading for ways in which the colonial model and world of life and death has already been *refused*. Reading for refusal, seeing refusal as a production and reproduction of another kind of interstices, of *la frontera*, and drawing on the fecundity of these spaces, is decolonial practice in the mode of retrieval. It is reading for the otherwise than antiblack being. It is reading for what was written and lived under erasure. It is reading between deconstruction and social death at the margins of nihilism.

And so we begin.

1
Social Death as a Kind of Deconstruction
The Figure of the Slave under Erasure

> It is the domination of beings that *différance* everywhere comes to solicit, in the sense that *sollicitare*, in old Latin, means to shake as a whole, to make tremble in entirety.
> —JACQUES DERRIDA

> We arrive then at a strange and bewildering enigma: are we to esteem slavery for what it has wrought, or must we challenge our conception of freedom and the value we place upon it?
> —ORLANDO PATTERSON

The matter of decolonial methodology, reading, and intervention is urgent and imperative. What does it mean to read and theorize in a decolonial frame? It means to read and theorize at the margins. And how is a decolonial intervention at once anticolonial and postcolonial? It means to read and theorize at the margins of nihilism. If necropolitics, racial capitalism, and exploitation of the Global South are among empire's many activist children, reproducing the worst of history, then intervention against the scope and reach of empire could not be more urgent and imperative. Let us begin with this assertion.

Our world was transformed by the reach of empire and its violence. That is a trite observation, perhaps, but if we take it seriously we see how it is one that captures empire as an *event* for thinking. Decolonial methodology begins here at the moment, then in the horizon of the event of empire because the event remakes the world in terms of both possibility and necessity. What we *can* think and what we *must* think: This is how empire creates a closed system. Or at least *wants* and *intends* a system that is capable of closure. Shifting to a decolonial intervention, we can ask: How is it possible to and how ought we conceive thinking *after*, even if still *inside* the horizon of, the transformative event of imperial violence? The time of the after, the conceptual spatiality of the inside. This is a key question because empire's transformative even has long done its work inside every aspect of life, working from the interior of subjectivity and subjectivities toward all those external signs of violence and alienation that signal the inexorable and its systematicity. The composition of empire as a closed system ranges from the broadest structures of political economy to the intimate features of the psyche. Senses of possibility and impossibility emerge *from* empire's terror. Empire does not compromise on the question of possibility; closure is the imperative, the legitimation structure, and the motivating energy of conquest, enslavement, occupation, and their various afterlives. That is, empire was world-making in its transformation, an apocalyptic event. We move and breathe and think in the space cleared by imperial apocalypse, a world made out of both what remains and the architecture of thinking that that apocalypse brought to us as the only legible possibility. Centuries have neither repaired that destruction nor built a better world in its ruins. Every sign of progress is a monument to imperial modernity's founding violence: a pile of corpses. This is the Global South's constant reminder, a reiteration of Walter Benjamin's riff on Paul Klee in "Theses on Philosophy of History."

To think in a decolonial register is to reckon with how the colonial is composed, what values guide it, how the closure of systems is conceived and legitimated, and therefore how leaks and fissures might be identifiable at the margins of systematicity. This is a massive general claim. The pages that follow explore each contour of that too-dense sentence. But I can say this to begin: Decolonial critique asks about what remains, how life is possible outside the colonial play of life-death that consigns a population or populations to social death, a life outside that life awarded its sovereignty through acts of killing, and asks what is possible when the Manichean model of the world collapses at the margins, in the interstices, and in *la frontera*.[1] A collapse, yes, but as we will see, this is a collapse that is not—and perhaps cannot be, given the law of legibility—seen as the insurgency it is by the system's center; life at the margins of nihilism marks an insurgency in which the "primary noun Person" might not be at stake, to recall Hortense Spillers's phrase. Visibility and the next apocalypse is not the entire story, perhaps not even the primary story, of thinking and living liberation struggle. Decolonial collapse, thought at the intersection of deconstruction and social death, puts colonial systematicity in modes of dephasement, modes deferral and delay, all in the interest of an-other-life. An entire world emerges in the horizon of decolonial critique.

That world is not *created* in critique but rather revealed outside the economy of Being. *Outside.* Being is always politics. Emmanuel Levinas was right to say that. But life is also always already otherwise. Otherwise, that is, at the margins of colonial nihilism and its afterlife. Critique is therefore not simply a gesture of reflection and parsing of concepts, but also and most important an utterly decadent site of possibility *otherwise.* Cultural and political transformation has its burdens and deserves its pleasures. If the decolonial, sited at the intersection of deconstruction and social death, is about articulating the conditions of illegible life at the margins of nihilism, then it is important to take the decolonial on as a question for critical theory along with its intimate siblings anticolonial and postcolonial. *In the non-name of the margins.* There is a language for this *otherwise*: vernacular, *la frontera*, asymmetry, the unenclosed margin, interstices, and life inside deconstructive practice. All of this language is saturated with paradox. But illegible life itself is a paradox while also affective, culturally explosive, and utterly transformative of the task of thinking.

This already rewrites the decolonial into deconstructive critique, and I would be remiss if I did not note the audacity of this turn. In many ways, the process of decolonization is first about the transformation of concrete, material conditions. Frantz Fanon's various characterizations of the processes of decolonization across *The Wretched of the Earth* provides an astonishingly powerful template. That template lays out the institutional stakes and stakeholders, ranging from native informants to colonized intellectuals to methods of revised and inverted cultural values, modes of governance, and postcolonial statecraft. *The Wretched of the Earth* is not the easiest or most pleasurable read—by design and inherent in the aims and methods. It is plodding, detailed, and after its explosive first chapter it lacks Fanon's signature rhetorical flourishes. We lose Fanon the poet-philosopher and gain Fanon the structural analyst. For good reason. The postcolonial moment and its work of decolonization requires radical praxis and close attention to institutional details. The matter of revising or reinventing political institutions, functions, and relations is serious business and the extent of colonialism—a total project that infects every corner of social and political life—mandates such detailed work. Outlining the terms of radical action is inevitably a laborious task. But revolutionary action is also and simultaneously about politics and culture: how we live together and how we make and remake conditions of that life. Cultural questions do not stand to the side awaiting new life in the aftermath of revolutionary struggle. Rather, the movement of politics and the movement of culture go hand in hand—albeit with political action, for Fanon, as the lead agent, including first acts of purposive violence. The nation is composed of culture and politics both, which means the creation and reinvention of institutions and emerging everyday practices that reproduce the new. Fanon writes at the close of "On National Culture," a chapter in *The Wretched of the Earth*, that

> organized struggle undertaken by a colonized people in order to restore national sovereignty constitutes the greatest cultural manifestation that exists. It is not solely the success of the struggle that consequently validates and energizes culture; culture does not go into hibernation during the conflict. . . . The liberation struggle does not restore to national culture its former values and configurations. This struggle, which aims at a fundamental redistribution of relations between men, cannot leave intact either the form or substance of the people's culture.[2]

This passage largely reflects Fanon's commitment to the new as an unprecedented future, something forged not through nostalgic vision but through the event of revolt. Revolt is radical when it stages and enacts this intensity of uprooting and reconceiving the possibilities of social and political life. The terms of cultural and political relation are unrecognizable in the postrevolutionary, postcolonial state. That is what makes it unprecedented. "After the struggle is over," Fanon writes, "there is not only the demise of colonialism, but also the demise of the colonized."[3] After struggle, that is, the world as we have known becomes unrecognizable. The Manichaeism of colonialism is exactly that deeply embedded in how we know and be. It is embedded in the colony and the metropole, as well as the structure of antiblackness that structures so much of the Atlantic world. This will prove important across the chapters that follow.

But the story of uprooting and restructuring concrete, material conditions is only part of the story. Revolutionary action induces an *event*. After all, whatever the transformation of institutions, there is still the question of expressive culture and the intellect. *The end of colonialism and the task of thinking.* What does it mean to think *after* colonialism? The task of thinking after colonialism is the task of thinking outside, between, after, before, and all varieties of spatially and temporally configuring thought, a task directed against the kinds of Manichean exclusions and hegemonic juxtapositions associated with the psychological and cultural terror of colonial subjugation. Those forms of terror persist in the postcolonial, post-Emancipation state—something that features in the structure of social death in the United States under conditions that are not always consistent with broader practices of colonial rule. I want to set aside the question of the link between antiblackness in the United States and colonialism in the strict sense. Whether or not African Americans have been, perhaps still are, a colonized people is a nuanced and complicated conversation. For my purposes here, it is enough to say that the postcolonial and post-Emancipation state have identical practices and that the matter of decolonial critique, thinking at the margins of nihilism, and the reinterpretation of cultural-political practices, stays relevant across sites. It stays relevant because the production of social death is the production of forms of thought inside a system that wants to say, whose essential meaning, and whose *vouloir-dire* is closure. All that is to say, colonialism *itself* was a task of thinking, and it is expansive, voracious, and persistent. Conquest, enslavement, administration from abroad, and neocolonial practices from inside and outside the postcolony are all *events* in the widest, most comprehensive sense. Fanon's description of the colonized Black subject in *Black Skin, White Masks* is a classic for a reason. What Fanon understands and articulates so well is how the colonizer works from inside the intellect and body, leaving no aspect of thinking, expressing, feeling, or desiring untouched by colonial power. The colonized might be relegated to what he calls the zone of nonbeing, but a subject who occupies that zone and lives its experience is a *constructed* and *thinking* subject. Not a naturally colonized being, of course, but instead and quite plainly a fabricated subjectivity whose entire infrastructure is occupied by the colonial epoch. The time of the psyche is the time of empire. What remains in that subject such that it is able to see the very little, almost nothing that forges paths of resistance? How is possibility for an *otherwise* opened up inside a world that is so brutally closed around the question of domination? That is the decolonial question and one to which Fanon has only the thinnest answer. It is a question for those who follow and think in his wake.

When we turn to the question colonialism's historically and politically fabricated subject, we catch sight of the task of thinking in its full significance. The existential dimension of this is straightforward. For all of Fanon's strong claims about the scope and power of sociogeny in *Black Skin, White Masks*, the fact remains that whatever the transformation and revolutionary reinvention of institutions, the formerly colonized are tasked with the problem of thinking after colonialism. And also thinking what has been thought in the interstitial spaces inside or on the leaky edges of the colonial system—a task for which Fanon is not our thinker. What makes thinking *inside* and *after* colonialism, thinking in and as the postcolony, possible calls to mind what Suzanne Césaire described as the trace conservation of vital energies. The trace conservation of energies draws from an anticolonial life philosophy that renders what is needed to think the colonized out of the colony, into the postcolony. Resistance, transformation, the new. It is, Césaire writes,

a matter of becoming conscious of the formidable mass of different energies that until now have been trapped within us. We must now use them in their plenitude, without deviation or falsification. Too bad for those who consider us dreamers.
    The most disturbing reality is ours.
    We will act.
    This earth, our earth, can only be what we want it to be.[4]

From dream to the reinvention of thinking. But a reinvention that draws on the already-there, the surplus or supplement that sits at the margins of nihilism. Césaire concludes her essay "A Civilization's Discontent" with this provocation, a provocation built on an antecedent series of comments on the decolonial possibilities of surrealism: immersion in landscape, harnessing of energies, the human and land, and all of those "fertile accords." That provocation opens a horizon and then offers a vitalist path away from colonial domination.

The surrealist iteration of vitalist philosophy is interesting on its own terms, but what I find so compelling in this passage is less the legitimacy question for life philosophy—a matter for debate about intellectual inheritance and colonial systems of education—and more how Césaire intimately draws us into the antechamber of thinking. Surrealism on Césaire's rendering is a mode of thoughtful engagement with the world outside and on the margins colonial abjection. Indeed, Césaire's early work makes constant reference to the farmer, the dancer, the plant, the ritual, all of which remind the reader and the critic of colonialism that bodies persist, desire, move, sweat, consume, and enjoy. This is the fecund moment in her theoretical work that exceeds the basics of surrealism; the condition for the possibility of surrealist engagement lies in desire's transformation of itself in the margins of abjection. Desire, for Césaire, is a movement toward and a movement rooted in plenitude, which functions as the remainder of the colonial construction of the zone of nonbeing, a sense of life at the margins of nihilism. Her proclamation *this earth, our earth* is a conceptual and existential expropriation of colonial possession, to be sure; land and nation are critical for postcolonial world-making. But it is more than just expropriation. Possession, whether repossession or possession for the first time, is the subject's claim on its world and how the world, now claimed, makes certain kinds of thinking possible. For Suzanne Césaire, this is through the body, the senses, and the kind of secular Pentecostalism of Caribbean surrealism that speaks a new, emergent language inside the milieu of immersion in Nature and the sensible. And we could add so many postcolonial visions to this early motif from Césaire, whether that is Ngũgĩ wa Thiong'o issuing a call to decolonize the mind through literary practice in African languages, Patrick Chamoiseau's ethics of the Creole name and word, Kamau Brathwaite's infusion of the poetic with patois and its interruptive voice, Fanon's repossession of the capacity of violence and its reformation of subjectivity, and so on. In each iteration, language and the body transform the possibilities of thinking and, in that transformation, make the task of thinking at the end of colonialism both possible and an urgent imperative.

Thinking in the margins of the colonial world. But decolonial thinking is not solely produced by the event. The event forms thinking, gives it shape and contour and, in the colonial context, deep political significance. Thinking also *begins* in a moment of movement, of initiation and passage in which the possibility of the event as event is forged, an antechamber to the system that desires its own closure.

The task of decolonial thinking in this context is about a claim on life, a claim to life that is also a claim on and against death. Life and death are always inextricably intertwined. This is the human condition. But colonialism's force and power lies in its ability to fundamentally alter the meaning of life and death to the point of making colonized life impossible except as a form of social death and other forms of death as impossible except as confirmation of the status of absolute abjection. Abjection, the world structured by a murderous nihilism that only wants its subject to perish, is the horizon in which death *and* life operate for the colonized, the enslaved, and the afterlife of both political modalities in the postcolonial and post-Emancipation epoch. Indeed, there is no epochal distinction. History is a long, cruel time structure of plantation worlds in which living is itself a kind of death. The body's final death is then a kind of affirmation, a final confirmation, of the always already of colonial subjectivity.

What, then, must we do with life and death if we are to begin thinking about the task of thinking? How do we create space for another kind of life and death? How do we find the language for a sense of life and death *already* outside the colonial and at the margins of nihilism in order to initiate the labor of thinking in its full capacity and liberated imagination? This is a question of passage through limits of systematicity. And this is passage through the fraught and terrifying space of abjection made into a closed system, which intensifies the affective life of theorizing inside it. No small part of the chapters that follow is negotiating the effects of that affective amplification and intensification. If, as part of the process of decolonization, thinking as a postcolonial and post-Emancipation project is possible without appealing to apocalypse as first beginning, then it is only possible in its fullest sense if that closed system does not block passage. Closure *wants* to forbid passage. This is the essential meaning and the wanting-to-say of closure. And it is no wild claim to say that proposed passage out of the systematization of nihilism is impossible. Closed systems of abjection calcify after centuries of practice. Repressive and ideological state apparatuses cohere around the project of reproducing social death and its state form. Colonialism was a total project, and it projects an entire world of meaning and its necessary correlate—perhaps *supplement*—of nonmeaning. We become subjects in the horizon of that projection, whether our subject formation is in the moment of colonial domination or in the afterlife of its many reiteration. So we are faced with the question: What opens the system? Or, perhaps better put, how does the system open itself such that passage becomes possible and thinking becomes thinkable? We ask about the antechamber. An antechamber, as we will see, that is sited and caught sight of at the intersection of deconstructive supplementarity and the vicissitudes of social death.

On the Antefecundity of Death and Other Life Stories

What is social death to deconstruction? What is the figure of the slave in that relation, the unremunerated life and supplement to rhetorical, argumentative, material, and theoretical systems? How does that figure of unremunerated supplement work at the intersection of social death and deconstruction? And how do social death and deconstruction as diagnostic methods, crossed in this figure of the slave, enact a critical form of decolonial thinking in the margins of nihilism? This is a critical form of thinking that shakes and makes tremble, to evoke Derrida, and in that shaking and trembling, nuances and splits the meaning of freedom in the discourse of modernity and its quiet postmodern labors.

Let me make some preliminary claims in order to anticipate what is to follow.

These are not questions we are accustomed to asking in the wake of Derrida's work, nor is it the expected avenue to travel through Patterson's conception of social death and slavery. Each thinker and their key idea is ensconced in a tradition with its own kind of scholarship—Derrida in European philosophy, Patterson in the Black studies tradition—that has specific critical tools, modes of criticism, and approaches to problems and disputes. And yet, there is this strange coincidence of theoretical space. To be clear, though, this is not a question of influence, but of comparative work in search of unexpected points of contact. These are points of contact articulated in theoretical space, which, between deconstruction and social death, raise the question of how the production of margin/center creates a death economy inside the play of life and death, while also producing a sense of the interstices that call for different modes of naming, speaking, hearing, knowing, and being. As well, this is a way of engaging the question of decoloniality. When framed in terms of decolonial thinking, the intersection of social death and deconstruction draws out and underscores with pointed clarity a crisis at the heart of white "Western" thinking in the broadest transatlantic sense.[5] Undone by absence, undone by what it installs as a cornerstone of legitimation and characterization, the invocation of the figure of the slave disassembles so many key moments in white Western philosophy after the slave trade. The slave trade changed everything about the structure of the world. Philosophy in that Western tradition is no exception. The slave trade and colonialism were *total projects*, leaving no aspect of the thought, politics, and culture of the colonizer untouched. The unremunerated element in the making and reproduction of systems and their closure should not surprise us for that very reason. Argument, demonstration, description, and diagnosis take place inside the event; the event remakes the world, and so the total project of enslavement, colonialism, and their afterlives in the postcolonial and post-Emancipation moment simply iterates the eventfulness of the event. What is a total project? How is this the case, and what does it mean?

My remarks here respond to the philosophical dimensions of these questions. We can begin with a cluster of general claims. Deconstruction is a theorization of death. Thought in terms of supplementarity, the key deconstructive argument in Derrida's *Of Grammatology* situates what lies exterior to the economy of life, as well as death-as-a-variant-of-life, as the condition for the possibility of meaning, language, and all those constitutive parts of what we conventionally call life and death. Social death, on Patterson's account, is also something quite different than the binary life/death would suggest.[6] Social death lives inside life *and* death as an enigma that makes nonenigmatic atrocities possible: the system of slavery, capitalism, coercive social identity, and all those constituent parts of what we conventionally call life and death. We can already discern at least the possibility of a *resonance* between Derrida's and Patterson's work here, a resonance in which the sound of the concept, so to speak, reverberates in complementary ways precisely because both theoretical interventions operate in the atmosphere of an unnamable death. Not a death that concludes a causal chain, not a death that is merely a variation on a conception of life. Rather, the atmospheric in which social death and deconstruction cross is constituted by the commitment to a radical absence (genocidal violence, abjection, erasure, the negative sublime) that generates both the possibility and impossibility of thinking in the Western tradition since the sixteenth century. With Patterson, we document this atmosphere sociologically. With Derrida, we document this atmosphere theoretically.

The figure of the slave as the unremunerated element in a social and conceptual structure embodies, both textually and inside a phenomenology of reading and meaning-making, a sense of supplementarity that is marked as social death and absence, but a social death and absence that makes a certain economy of life possible. At the intersection of social death and deconstruction, then, there is the *figure* of the slave. Another historical iteration of that certain phrase: *il y a là cendre* . . . [7] What cannot be remunerated because it does not belong to the order of knowing, being, identity, and belonging.

It is no small thing to then propose alongside this the *thought* of decoloniality. So a note on this broader concern. What more can be said about decolonization? Has much at all been said about decolonization? As is the fate of so many conceptual and political innovations in critical theory—or just philosophy and philosophical thinking broadly—what emerged initially as a movement of the people against colonial exploitation and violence (the waves of independence at midcentury and their aftermath) and then as a project of postcolonial culture-making and statecraft, has become a broadly intellectual, theoretical project of the most urgent order. *A project for the task of thinking*. Where does this take us? Decolonial thinking is a project aimed at undermining and disassembling what had come before it, then, in the wake of that disassembly, a task of generating a new ethics for making cultural, political, and intellectual life in a genuinely *post*colonial register. A register, I should add, that is inside and perhaps in the service of a transformed set of institutions, institutional practices, and collective values. The spatiality of this characterization is critical. If the slave trade and colonialism were total projects leaving no aspect of the enslaver/colonial world untouched, then the work of decoloniality is not a siege from the outside, but rather an insurgency inside the system. A kind of deconstruction, then, one anchored in that persistent presence of social death which in the figure of the slave, when named as the root of the generation of concepts, draws out the colonial supplement in white Western philosophy's self-articulation. A decolonial act, one small intervention to unsettle and decenter centuries of sedimented colonial meaning and habit.

That is a lot to demand and a very broad set of claims. Claims are anchored in examples, of course. We can see this work of the unremunerated in elements of canonical white Western texts. In his *Second Treatise of Government*, John Locke argues for propriety over self and body through the extension of subjectivity into nature. The key to this argument is that the labor of the subject *makes* nature into property, which, as an extension of one's own self, falls under the rubric of right. Locke, though, does not simply assert this sense of propriety but instead anchors the claims in a critical juxtaposition: against the Indian.

The Indian's chaos lies in his inability to order and enclose, which renders the nature that surrounds the Indian *not* property and it is therefore ready for seizure. This is a precondition of conquest and settler colonial rule. This is also a moment in which the figure of the slave shows up. Unremunerated, the Indian makes the argument work in *Second Treatise of Government* but does not properly belong in what the argument establishes. Or we can think of Immanuel Kant's example of the South Sea Islander and G. W. F. Hegel's Africa and the African. The South Sea Islander's laziness and inability to develop her talents frames and supplements Kant's argument for the moral profundity of acting from duty alone. Hegel's figure of Africa and description of Africans is not merely racist (though it is certainly that) but also serves as a measure for the development of history without being itself inside the very idea of measure *or* history. For Kant and Hegel, then, these unremunerated figures are both outside the closed system of ethics and history and absolutely critical for the articulation of moral consciousness and the understanding of historical Spirit. In this brief sketch, we catch sight of how foundational features of the white Western tradition claim their roots in secular reason: Property and propriety function as the cornerstone of the right to life and to place, whence obligation, and the meaning of history for the life of civilization(s). But they also turn on the figure of the slave, the supplement, the socially dead in order to think property, morality, and history inside the event of empire.[8]

What is interesting to me, and this comprises the core of the chapters below, is that when recast as a question of nihilism in James Baldwin, Fanon, Richard Wright, and select figures in contemporary Afropessimism, we see how that recast and reframe of the horizon of empire is still in some significant measure *inside* empire's conception of closure. Empire captures nihilism at the very moment it produces it. Now, it should be said that nihilism does shift the cast and framing of the event of empire. These writers display the largely unseeable, other, dark, and wretched side of modernity. That is, they produce phenomenologies of abjection. That critical descriptive accounting documents what it means to have built social death into the very meaning and experience of being. I draw suggestive, critical conclusions, to be sure. There is always more to be said with figures like Locke, Kant, and Hegel who wrote with such global ambition and breadth (and scholarly commentary to match), as well as the diversity of discourses we find in Wright, Fanon, and Baldwin. Any readings of these figures, insofar as they work with concrete examples that aim at raising a series of questions, produce important insights and generate new horizons for critical theoretical reading and assessment. But none of these writers are random or occasional figures. Each is foundational to the past and future of political, moral, and cultural theory in the Black Americas, the Black

Atlantic, and even in the Atlantic world more broadly. Reading nihilism inside the texts of each of these figures is not merely a story about each of these texts and singular figures. Rather, it is a question of an entire sensibility and broad critical frame. To ask in tension with that frame is to propose new paths of thinking at the margins of nihilism—or to affirm those paths sketched, articulated, and elaborated in counternarratives to empire's task of thinking. Thus, I want to generate new horizons that are not figure-specific but instead critical sensibilities set between deconstruction and social death. It is a lot to account for paths against or outside the social, political, and cultural productions of social death. It is speculative and existential at the same time, as well as requiring a sober and often painful reckoning with the inheritance of conceptual systems and prerogatives.

And yet this is precisely what is asked of us if we are to answer to history's moral demand, the demand of the historical ghost haunting those corpses piled at the feet of the angel of history who gaze at us with vulnerability, silence, and a Levinasian sense of the ethical. Does the past obligate? If so, on what terms? In this framing, then, we can see how historical and memorial sedimentation provides a crucial staging for critical theoretical intervention, excavating and assessing figures that structure the rhetorical and demonstrative subconscious. *We argue from a sense of inheritance, however conscious we are of it. Inheritance bears the debt and cost of empire's closed system.* It is here that the figure of the slave is important. The figure of the slave is just that figure: a supplement in an argument about history, ethics, selfhood, and world, and one that obligates in some kind of way. But every figure is also an indicator. The figure of the slave? That figure bears within it and indicates for us the history of atrocity, building that history into some of the most important foundations of thought, thought that was deployed both in defense of empire and as a righteous testimony against it. How can we think about this critical theoretical intervention as a decolonial gesture and effort? What obligations direct those gestures and efforts?

We must raise the question of race and philosophy.

It bears noting that no small bit of ink has been spilled in the twenty-first century so far on the place of race in the European philosophical canon. That scholarship has largely been focused on the emergence of concepts of race, debates about the origins of racial difference, and the place of that difference in imaginations of history, ontology, and morality. One remarkable feature of that research has been how deeply it embeds racial discourse in what had previously been imagined to be a culturally and political neutral set of fields: ethics, epistemology, metaphysics, philosophy of history, and aesthetics. And yet another curiosity, if we are honest, is how few the pages in critical commentary on racial discourse number in comparison to the canonical texts from the same thinker. We nevertheless see in those pages and their link to wider philosophical questions how racism, colonialism, conquest, and the slave trade were part of the total project of philosophy. It was important for Locke, Kant, and Hegel to say something about everything. And there were, perhaps still are, few matters of more pressing and impactful concern than the economy of race and social-historical value.

Work on "philosophy of race" that operates in this frame and register has changed the way we read white Western philosophers and theorists since the modern period. Without a doubt. That change also shifts our understanding of modernity, which had such wide-ranging implications inside the European tradition as it moved through the celebration of secularization, the rise of deliberative reason, and the cynical elaboration of the same for the purposes of eliminationist antisemitism. And so, with that shift, critical philosophy of race has reminded us of the absolutely central, foundational place of racial thinking in the formation of modern consciousness and conscience. But that work has also labored within an economy of reading for presence of race thinking, whether explicit or in the form of traces, in a given figure and texts, which allows us as readers to see the trace of racial thinking in an ethics, in the fragmented presence of epistemology in theories of racial descent, or in political notions of freedom in the links between race, propriety, and natural servitude. *A certain kind of thinking of presence.* Always.

What I want to do here, though, is shift methods of reading in order to fathom a different place and kind of discourse. In particular, I want to think the unremunerated work of the racial other under erasure, to think from absences and discern, in what is not said and is not wanting-to-be-said, a certain kind of *dit* and *dire* of that other as a radical absence that makes the presence of the European tradition possible and then haunt the postcolonial and post-Emancipation afterlives of that tradition. While I work toward, then from three figure and theme cases from the Black Atlantic tradition, my broader aim is to provide a framework for thinking more broadly about the subaltern *inside* the example with the suggestion of its deconstructive force. What is that deconstructive force, and what does it help us see, then think about the white Western tradition? This returns us to the question of Derrida and Patterson.

The key pre-text of this consideration is Derrida's work on the supplement in his early work, most particularly in *Of Grammatology*. It is a simple insight, really: The supplement is named as a structural noncomponent, a part of the structure of a systematic investigation—the origin of language, the meaning of the sign, the very idea of a concept, and so on—that does not appear in that systematic account but nevertheless makes the structure and its internal other possible. This is fundamentally a transcendental consideration, one that places as the condition for the possibility of an origin story, a sign/sense relation, or concept, the supplement that never appears in the play of presence and absence. The supplement dismantles and destabilizes what *wants* to be stable and secure. This is why Derrida will characterize the supplement in *Dissemination* as "inessential yet harmful to the essence, a surplus that ought never to have come to be added to the untouched plenitude of the inside."[9] The supplement as transcendental names a condition that withdraws at the moment its place as a contingency structuring the system is caught sight of and then survives *in* the system as a trace or figure under erasure. It is worth quoting in full where Derrida writes: "The supplement transgresses and at the same time respects the interdict. This is what also permits writing as the supplement of speech; but already also the spoken word as writing in general. Its economy exposes and protects us at the same time according to the play of forces and of the differences of forces. Thus, the supplement is dangerous in that it threatens us with death."[10]

What is this threat of death? And is it a form of death that also opens the possibility of liberation, of emancipation from the hegemony of the same/other at play in the inside of the inside? This is the promise of the supplement. This is a promise made in the form of threat and violence. In this threat, which is both respect for interdiction and an act of transgression, the threat and harm to essence, the violence against the violence of the inside or what Derrida will later call the force of law, we see the precarity of claims to closure. In *Of Grammatology*, this is the question of language and its hegemony. The implicit is compulsive and compulsory, structurally necessary *even as the speaking of that which is structurally necessary would dismantle the structure*. This is deconstruction in a nutshell, at its best and in its most destabilizing. Immanent critique. Parasitic reading.

Parasitic reading works from the text. This is such a crucial part of deconstructive reading, but it is easily lost in the broad and expansive critical vocabulary developed across Derrida's career. It is tempting to lift key terms and critical concepts out of Derrida's massive oeuvre—*différance*, margin, supplement, *pharmakon*, double reading, the cinder, and so on—and see them as interpretative tools that shape his encounter (and ours as readers of his readings) with a given text and movement of ideas. Is Derrida an inductive thinker? Is deconstruction an instrument or overlay brought to a given text? I am thinking here of how much easier it is to read Derrida once one grasps a single concept like *différance*. In a flash, the surrounding vocabulary pulls together and gathers around the magnetic force of a founding term. The founding term, however, is not just a critical method or technique, but a deeper claim about the condition for the possibility of the sign, of writing, of language, of memory, and all of those themes in the Derridean corpus. This is the transcendental claim deconstruction makes on us and on the texts with which it reckons. But the reckoning with the text is also not merely an occasion for demonstrating the force of a concept or example of a transcendental. Quite the contrary, Derrida is *also* insistent that he is a reader, a close reader, and that reading itself reveals the surplus that should not be on the inside but is and in its unwelcome presence harms the stability and integrity of essential structures. This parasitic moment is behind Derrida's early characterizations of his work as double sessions and double readings: The act of encounter with the text is deconstructive work, not just the *application* of a critical concept, an antipositivism that is nevertheless empirical, empirical without the transcendental. And yet, because deconstruction is relentlessly enigmatic, the transcendental always appears because it is the condition for the possibility of reading itself. The condition for the possibility of an inside, but also a surplus. What makes systematicity possible and also an egregious, hegemonic fantasy.

The peculiarity and beautiful complexity of Derrida's work on the supplement is exactly here in the relation between parasitic reading and transcendental claims. And it is a complexity in his work from the very beginning. In *Voice and Phenomenon*, for example, Derrida develops *différance* as a critical concept that, while embedded in readings of Edmund Husserl's work on time, sign, signification, and expressive relation, operates in two ways. First, it is revealed, in the language of *Dissemination*, as the surplus that never should have been inside a closed system of immanence/transcendence. The treatment of Husserl and the rendering of *différance* happen at the same time, generating the enigmatic concept in the act of close reading; quite literally, *différance* is rendered in that reading in the sense of *rendre*, to manifest and also to vomit, to expel from the inside what harms the inside, yet was always interior to the body that it poisons. That sense of immanent critique is what makes deconstruction dangerous and voracious. As a method and approach, all texts are vulnerable. Second, *différance* has its own defined and defining features. Derrida famously explicates it in terms of differentiation, delay, deferral, and related terms. In that definition, we can see how Derrida theorizes *différance* as such, then deploys it in a reading of Husserl in order to establish the delay and deferral at the heart of his account of the sign in the first chapter of *Logical Investigations*. While this reckoning with *différance* has elements of immanent critique, it is also the case that it works as a supervening concept that orders the text under scrutiny. The supplement operates in much the same way, showing up as emergent in a close reading of, say, Rousseau on language, but also as the ordering concept of that reading. Or as a discovery deep in Stéphane

Mallarmé's text that also initiates the double session of Derrida's treatment. Indeed, we can write this across Derrida's work, locating the parasitic moment in the very same method and gesture as the transcendental. The *pharmakon* of the *pharmakon*, perhaps. Without a doubt, simultaneity is the enigma.

This is the conceptual and methodological language that makes it so difficult to talk about deconstruction and life. It is certainly not the case that Derrida's work is a form of nihilism or quietism. The old and boring trope that deconstruction (or postmodernism more generally) claims that everything is meaningless rests on a similar kind of (willful) misunderstanding. Derrida's commitment to impurity is fundamental. There can no more be unconditional meaningfulness than there can be unconditional nonsense. If everything, upon reading for the supplement, is fatally compromised by the necessary yet impossible exclusion of its other, then *différance* and its cognates are names for immovable impurity. Life is entwined with death. Life's conventional tie to presence is what makes it impossible to talk about life as such. Rather, finitude, with all of its messy inner logic, surfaces the supplement of not just death as a modification of life, which would be death as a kind of life, entwined through and through, but death as a radical absence that is incalculable on the model of life. Both life and death defer, and in that deferral postpone closure. Life is delayed by the specter of death. Death is delayed by the specter of life. My life, your life, the life of the sign, and so on. Specters and hauntology here mark both the limit of and the language for a phenomenology of the subject. But what I want to underscore here is how the supplement is incalculable inside any claim to closure, any sort of vitalism, and also any sort of nihilism that would draw finitude into the abyss of death and that abyss alone. The supplement against life. The supplement against death. Here is where words break off and there is only gesture and ellipsis. Recurrence without repetition. Every goodbye ain't gone.

How, then, is deconstruction a kind of theory of social death? And what does that mean for the figure of the slave in philosophy?

Rather than the slave as a topic of concern in particular philosophers, or its place in the history of empire, I want here to think the figure of the slave on the model of Patterson's famous account in *Slavery and Social Death*: the slave as the one who does not circulate in the social, who ~~is~~ (writing the copula as a hypothetical or against itself) as a sense of internal exteriority. A sense of death before or outside of life. Patterson's sociological framing of the problem situates the question of social death in terms of belonging and exclusion, how the exterior is produced by a matrix of social practices that manage bodies toward the end of radical exclusion. It is the sort of approach and characterization that allows him to write a global story of slavery but also bring into view the essential structures of social and political practices in enslaving societies and the afterlife of slavery. A different kind of afterlife, one that is not focused on memory and melancholia but instead on the persistence of social practices that reproduce social death in the wake of emancipation, ostensibly the end of social death. But social death survives emancipation precisely because it is the unnamable that is always named. Belonging as a social problem puts social death in bold. In this register of social death, Patterson writes: "In the intrusive mode the slave was conceived of as someone who did not belong because he was an outsider, while in the extrusive mode the slave became an outsider because he did not (or no longer) belonged."[11] Inside and outside at the same time. How is this possible? The slave is the production of closed system. Life and death are contained within systematicity, just as belonging and nonbelonging and inside and outside are features of closure, not fissures in the system. But deconstruction is also attentive to that emergent life outside the play of life/death, the supplement that makes play possible. Our task, then, in moving social death into conceptual contact with deconstruction, is to understand how Patterson's description and historical account of how the slave functions as the outside is also a *radical* outside—an outside set at the root of the inside/outside distinction. If we do not see this radical shift of register, this work of supplementarity in Patterson's own account, then we will simply understand social death as a different kind of life. Slavery would then be a life of exclusion. Yet this is not Patterson's aspiration, even if at times it would seem to be a limit of his theoretical vocabulary. However, Patterson opens his vocabulary in descriptions of nonbelonging and therein creates a different conceptual space. This radicalizes the distinction between the external exile and the internal exile. In what way is the slave excluded? And how does that exclusion express the vicissitudes of social death?

This shift in framing helps us see the dialectical dependency of the enslaver on the enslaved, and so the ontological significance of the strange, impossible dialectic of producing a lived, socially constructed, and historically sedimented sense of (non)being as social death. Being itself is transformed by the practice of slavery, altering the conditions in which beings become beings, first as a broad structure of social and human reality, then as a robust form of sociogeny. That transformation of being transforms the sense of life and death for all beings in the world of slavery. As well, it shapes the world made by inheritance and what it means to *be* in slavery's afterlife. That is, the exilic experience as a mode of social death is complemented by the meaning of social death for the one who excludes, for the one who determines and initiates relations of nonbelonging. Patterson explains this in reference to the analogy or parallel structure of caste and *systems* of slavery. It is important to note how Patterson uses the language of system and essence in *Slavery and Social Death*, a language that sets up the terms of social death's persistence over time—it has a past, but also a present and future—and also the structure in which the socially dead, as supplement, enact or invite double reading—the space of a productive Derridean intervention. Systematicity is simply the condition under which social death is produced and reproduced. "The liminality of the slave is not just a powerful agent of authority for the master," Patterson writes, "but an important route to the usefulness of the slave for both his master and the community at large. . . . The essence of slavery is that the slave, in his social death, lives on the margin between community and chaos, life and death."[12]

Patterson places the slave in a between-space in this passage, which is crucial for siting the grounds for refusal and resistance. The interstitial is always a conceptual *problem*. Neither life nor death in this case, it is how the margins function as something akin to the anchor of social death but also a pseudo-space of return that sustains life when, in circulation among the enslaving class or caste, there would appear to be only death. How do we speak of the interstices, to the interstices, and from the interstices? This question has an element that dialectically engages with Gayatri Spivak's title question and its companion response: Can the subaltern speak, and what would it mean to even begin to listen? Do we have ears for the margins? This is no small question, yet it is crucial for any history of imperial practice and thought that places social death as a cornerstone, especially if we are also attentive to those peculiar forms of life alive *as* radical exteriority, generated in the lower frequencies of interracial space and time.

What does this mean for reading the figure of the slave in the history of Western thinking and its wake? That can only be clarified, of course, in the exposition of each site and citation, but it is important here to indicate a few key features. First, there is the question of exile. Patterson's articulation of intrusive and extrusive modes describes the constitutive function of the slave as *relation*. The slave is made in relation to the enslaver and exilic conditions are produced out of that relation. It is important to note that the subjectivity (such as it is) of the slave is a fabrication made from the material of the ideological body of the state and society, a sense of creation that makes by force and reproduces through institutions and social habit. Second, relationality for Patterson is articulated with a truncated dialectic. There is no work of negation; this is abjection in its purest and most direct form, producing an oppositional other who, though opposed, cannot summon the capacity to engage the work of the negative. Without that work, there is no dialectical movement. Perhaps this is a methodological or descriptive choice for him, either understanding the production of the slave as a kind of *sens unique* and nothing more or perhaps Patterson simply chooses to focus on the enslaved and not on the mutual sense of dependency between enslaver and enslaved. Third, how we think the relationality constitutive of the slave's exilic condition(s) is crucial. A dialectical invigoration of the site of relation naturally moves us to think this in Hegel's terms, describing the intricacies of the surprising and often dismantling ways in which the Lord lives from the Bondsman's labor. That complex sense of life and dependency is initiated by some form of negation. But framing Patterson's conception of social death this way also limits our scope. If we think dialectically about the site of relation that makes the slave's exilic condition(s), then we *also* have to read that dialectic under the rubric of social death as a surplus inside the essence of the social order. A *deconstructive dialectic*. That surplus shifts the meaning of life and death, twisting relation into odd angles with staggered gaps. How radically do we think about death, about its fragmented and fragmenting relation to the life that lives from social death, and how does this alter relations to all elements of dialectical movement, however stalled or truncated? If we conceive social death as *supplement* to life/death, if we read social death as a kind of deconstruction, then it threatens to stall dialectic before dialectics can even begin to do its work. This is an entirely rich and productive field for inquiry.

In a certain sense, what I am saying here is merely that familiar path worn by Derrida's early work on deconstruction. Locating what fails to appear *even as a failure of appearance* functions as a decisive supplement that disables the system in which dialectical movement (or any relationality that makes meaning and sense) lives, moves, and breathes. This is the surplus that does violence to the essence, the specter haunting any and every system. Naming that supplement—one of the indispensable contributions of a radicalized notion of social death—is part of the liberatory work of deconstruction. As well, this sense of supplementarity is anti-ideological. It disassembles knowing and being at sites of the reproduction of forms of knowledge and modalities of the social and sociogenic subject. Death thought in *this* context, conceived in relation or in response to social death and hegemonic conceptions of life, is exterior to life, outside the economy of movement, rest, and stagnation, and is, in the end, the *removal* of breath. The lungs that breathe, the logic of *psyche*,[13] and the infusion of life with social meaning—this is what a system of social death produces as the impossibility for subaltern life. There is *la frontera*, to be sure, but that borderland is barely visible, if at all, from inside the force of systematicity and its commitment to closure. Social death must be total.

It should be said that Patterson's text does not think the death of social death in exactly these terms. The exilic subject lives elsewhere in his account. Social death is haunted by the violence of its exile, to be sure, but it is also constituted in part by the aspiration or waiting for and lingering in anticipation of life. That is, in its first iteration for Patterson, death is made by life, which means that social death is made by the desire for the social that animates, with layered despair no doubt, the subjectivity of the subaltern class. In this version of social death, death remains inside the economy of life and its anticipations because the slave wants life against death—a certain desire or longing for belonging, something that would mean the entire inversion of a given society. The revolutionary is born and borne here. This set of characterizations is necessary as an analytic precisely because Patterson needs to be able to describe both the world-making (in exilic sites and conditions) by the enslaved and the emergence of a total world at the moment of emancipation. Freedom is a crisis for the infrastructure of slave societies and the afterlives of enslavement. This is the link between critical theory and the sociological, which binds theorization to the social lives of those who lived in, through, and in the wake of enslavement.

But the slave as a *figure* in philosophical thinking is not tightly linked to the sociology of the life of the enslaved and is instead linked to the thoughtful life of thinking itself. How does the social death of a figure at the foundations—or maybe more provocatively at the origins—of thinking implicate, and therefore depend upon, an exiled absence? Not an exiled figure in struggle for emancipation, but an absence, a socially dead figure, one that has its sense of death doubled in the act of exile. This doubling of death entombs. It is not simply that there is death, but that death is buried in another movement of absence: the removal from presence as absence, the quasi-presence of the failure-to-appear. Burying the dead in this way, not in the ground under our feet but on the margins of the world, the interstices, and away from sight, seals absence in a kind of purity. Away from view, away from the world, away from a relation to center/margin, this sense of absence calls us to rethink both life and death and, in particular, the link we make between them as a temporal continuum. A radicalized notion of social death as supplementarity and the figure of the slave actually breaks time itself. *Another kind of diachrony.* I am thinking here of how Lisa Guenther remodels Patterson's key idea in order to make sense of incarceration and solitary confinement.[14] Solitary confinement, as an historical and contemporary practice of social death, isolates to the point of moving the cry of the incarcerated, the suffering of a body under carceral violence and its varied regimes, outside the space of seeing, hearing, touching, and knowing. This is a *radical* sense of the solitary, conceived not as a broken relation, but as a dislodging of the very idea of relation in the spatial move of the incarcerated outside our shared embodiment—however violent that embodiment might be—and into an impossible relation to itself. Is a radicalization of social death as supplementarity necessarily an impossible relation to self? Or does it make relation *otherwise* emerge as quiet movement in the shadow of the state, of the system, and of the abjecting work of hegemony? What remains? What persists?

Vicissitudes of the Colonial

The relation of social death to life is thus inexorably fraught and complicated. In *Slavery and Social Death*, Patterson maps out a system for thinking death and life as conjoined twins, as it were, dependent upon one another in terms of certain vital organs but also wholly independent phenomena that live very differently in the world and have their own desires, needs, and, most important, sense of place and emplacement. Inseparable but also entwined in their vital core. What is that vital core? The shared world. But it is also the case that social death marks the body and person as outside that world. This is Orlando Patterson's double session. The figure of the slave, the unremunerated and abject element in the structure and rhetoric of critical theory, gathers this double session into one moment. An explosive moment for sure, one akin to Aimé Césaire's evocation of the *morne* in *Notebook of a Return to the Native Land*: "a hunger buried in the depth of the Hunger of this famished *morne*."[15] The *morne* is destructive, but also in possession of its own unseeable world. How might this figure of the slave make and unmake the pretensions of the Western tradition with a destructive and nonvisible self-possession? How is social death as supplementarity built into the Atlantic theory tradition? And what does this mean for thinking coloniality and its afterlives?

Reading coloniality as the figure of the slave in the history of Western thought is a matter of reading for the visible: extant links to and systemic *inclusion* of what is other. Indeed, this can easily be cast as a revision of the standard critical theory trope that every social order needs its other, folded into but also out of material inclusion. Being-with without belonging. This is the first glance reading of Patterson's social death, in which the exilic is still fully visible and in dialectical relation to life. Critical philosophy of race does this so well. But it is also a matter of reading under erasure, reading in search of the quiet supplement that is spoken, almost compulsively, at key theoretical moments. This form of reading casts dialectics as a kind of assimilation to empire, a colonial gesture of adoption, adaptation, and inclusion of the socially dead in some form of life. Separation and distance from that inclusion means moving from resistance to refusal. In some ways reading under erasure is a good part of what Fanon wants from his decolonization of Hegelian dialectics in *Black Skin, White Masks* but does not yet have the methodological vocabulary to characterize and execute: delineate the limits of the logic of comparison, then open the *question* of the outside, of what does not enter into that logic, and of what it would mean to think that withdrawal and resistance in the mode of refusal. Fanon's available theoretical vocabulary is largely linked to presence, to absence as a variation on presence (nonbeing is linked to being and not yet nothing), and is therefore limited by a commitment to *only* resistance and negation. But thinking the outside as radical exteriority calls for thinking otherwise: Fanon after deconstruction, Derrida after social death. How might this outside appear as the figure of the slave in conceiving history, ethics, and propriety, as well as the afterlives of coloniality embedded in the historical experience of nihilism?

That is, what are we to make of decolonization and decolonial thinking *as* thinking?

I am reminded of one of the enduring lessons of Paul Gilroy's *Postcolonial Melancholia*: We have asked so much of the formerly colonized, but so little of the colonizer. That is, the colonized, in the moment of independence or revolutionary struggle and after, have always been tasked with the work of decolonization, to rid themselves of the structuring work of colonialism in political institutions, social habits, and cultural production. We can think here of Fanon's theorization of decolonization in *The Wretched of the Earth*, which moves systematically through the composition of the postcolonial state with the aim of total violence: destroy the colonial, let loose invention and its possibilities for another kind of world. Or Aimé Césaire's call for a humanism made to the measure of the world in his *Discourse on Colonialism*. There are so many examples. But what, if anything, has been asked of the colonizer, who lived in every aspect of life, for centuries, from the violence and abjection of the colonies? What would it mean to press the question of decolonization into *this* space? What would that do to the figure of the slave and how we read that social death supplement in, into, and through canonical texts *including those produced as subaltern discourse*?

What work can we do with absences and with what has been written under erasure?

If absence has its own quasi-life—which is the paradox at the heart of deconstructive thinking, but also the life of the enslaved as socially dead—then it opens up the question of what it would mean to *read* absences as a way of reading the life of the figure of the slave. I mean this: reading for absences, not on the model of fashioning absence as another mode of presence but instead reading absence as its own kind of style and economy with particular expressive demands. Here, I think, we see an emergent difference between what is asked of us in Derrida's text and what is asked of us by the decolonized figure of the slave. Derrida asks us to understand the inherent instability of systematicity. This is the danger of "that dangerous supplement." The figure of the slave does the same if we read the figure as a deconstructive introduction by authors of systematicity, an introduction of surplus life into the deathworld that produces abject difference. But the figure of the slave is also a moment of *refusal*. That is, absence is simultaneously, in the figure of the slave, a moment of destabilizing danger *and* a refusal to appear even as an absent absence, a moment of what Spivak describes in the example of the self-immolation of the widow in "Can the Subaltern Speak?" Reading the figure of the slave deconstructively shifts when the decolonial frame of refusal and life *otherwise* is introduced as life buried in the abject figure. How does that life speak? And what would it mean to speak but also to hear? Or to not hear, and leave on the lower frequencies in an *other* kind of ethics of difference? In the decolonial frame, and this is decolonization's conventional model and method, we move the center away from the system itself in order to catch sight of, in the reading of absences and of the unsaid in the saying, life inside or even *as* refusal. The *lower frequencies*, as Ralph Ellison has it at the close of *Invisible Man*. The doubled and redoubled discourse of blues lyrics, of jazz sounds, of vernacular speech born of violence and abjection—that refusal of presence which is the life that remains after refusal to appear except as social death, except as absence—has a sense of life that must be thought outside economies of life and death *as well as* the radical, unnamable death that haunts those economies.

The figure of the slave, liberated from its place in an economy of abjection and juxtaposition, decenters to the point of eliminating the very idea of center. Without that center, speaking and hearing is different. A new humanism fits this moment. A humanism made to the measure of the world. I think this is the moment in which the figure of the slave as a deconstructive deployment brings Derrida close to Fanon as well as to the Césaire of *Discourse on Colonialism*. Deconstruction opens possibility in its fracturing intervention, and versions of another kind of humanism reorder what it means to signify, belong, gather, know, and be. But that is to take deconstruction as a thinkerly intervention in the social and epistemological order. Which, of course, it is. There is an other reading, however, that reading under erasure which intervenes in thinking itself and in the cultivation of other sensibilities. Reading under erasure is opening itself, but also a way of attending to the counternarrative structure in *la frontera* of a given system, in particular a system dedicated to the production of social death. In this way the figure of the slave read under erasure is the shift from anticolonial to decolonial, the shift from dismantling the

Manichean fantasies of the colonial imagination and its material reality to thinking thinking otherwise. This is the enigma. Because at first glance it would seem there is no real natural relation between deconstruction, social death, and decolonial thought. My aim here is to assert and demonstrate an organic link through a consideration of the margins of nihilism. This is, for me, an absolutely essential link if we want to understand what is at stake in questions of refusal, voice, and cultural formation. What does it mean to be, to think, and to make worlds in the space/nonspace of deconstruction, social death, and what those worlds signify in their traces?

This is a particularly difficult question. To begin, what *is* the problem of decolonial thinking? I emphasize here the problem of *thinking* precisely because decolonization has such varied registers. Indeed, one of the first tasks of anticolonial struggle, which in some ways is also decolonial action, is reclamation of space. This might mean land, national borders, institutional property, institutional practice, or infrastructure. In fact, it always means all of those things. There can be no vital sense of liberation if elements of dependency and its complexes remain. But thinking is also a space with its own demands: language, poetic imagery, modes of expressive culture, and so on. Thinking is also a transcendental question, the transcendental is a thinking question, and both are questions concerned with the conditions for the possibility of thought and what comes from thought, whether that be the (re)birth of intellectual traditions, conceptual language fitted to a postcolonial imaginary, management of complexes and compulsions, and so on. There is always an "and so on." One cannot know in advance what is called for in the moment of thinking *after* and *amid* the colonization of the imagination. Fanon was right that the future as postcolonial is unprecedented. The imagination itself is colonized. Yet, thinking remains and thinks with remainders. And in spaces of refusal.

So, we can say something about the shape and contour of what the decolonial demands. Fanon's work in *The Wretched of the Earth* as well as the concluding bits of *Black Skin, White Masks* provide important vocabulary for what I am trying to do with deconstruction and social death. Colonialism, Fanon notes and returns to regularly, is structured by a relation between the metropole—the colonial center as both place (the colonizing nation) and imaginary (values, languages, institutions)—and its margins: the colony, the colonized, and the experience of subjugation and exploitation. Colonialism spatializes power and administration in both geography and the imaginary. How the colonizer and the colonized think, feel, express, breathe, and move is drawn out across center and margin in order to make power both visible and felt to everyone gathered under colonialism as a sort of *Gestell*. The spatialization of colonial administration produces the body of the colonizer, and it also produces the colonized as a deformed shadow of that body. We can think here of the close of the fifth chapter of *Black Skin, White Masks*, where Fanon quotes Mark Robson's 1949 film about the Pacific Theater in World War II, which becomes a cinematic story about being Black in an antiblack world—the United States in *Home of the Brave*, but Fanon writes it across the colonized world. He writes: "The crippled soldier from the Pacific war tells my brother: 'Get used to your color the way I got used to my stump. We are both casualties.'"[16]

The colonized are never whole. That is by design. Fanon adds his typical note of defiance: "Yet, with all my being, I refuse to accept this amputation. I feel my soul as vast as the world, truly a soul as deep as the deepest of rivers; my chest has the power to expand to infinity."[17] A particular kind of call to decolonization is in this passage, but it is also a call that comes from an ambivalent, even aporetic space that Fanon himself cannot account for. The amputated subject is somehow also a subject without limits and capable of refusal. Decolonial thought is anchored in that ambivalent space, sorting it out, as we shall see, in the interest of making other forms of being and knowing possible. But it begins with the casualty of blackness, of the colonized, and what it means for amputation to characterize *being* in an interracial, colonial world.

Decolonization as material political praxis is therefore tasked with its alpha and omega: the project of identifying, then eliminating the center. Manichean thinking is the problem produced by and endemic to colonialism, constitutive of its meaning, which means, in Fanon's wholly correct assessment, that decolonization works with, then against, existing antagonisms. The antechamber of that working-with-antagonisms is the problem of thinking and refusal. Deconstruction and social death help us see this other somewhat, if not wholly, hidden aspect of the center/margin, metropole/colony relation: the production of margins and interstices. This other aspect raises a different set of questions that, as we shall see across this project, opens up a new, enigmatic horizon in and for the work of decolonial theory. The play of center/margin is a play of life and social death. But social death is also something else. It has a halo or horizon, one in which another kind of death and still yet another kind of life lives. How does this other kind of life produce a language for itself and work, as expressive and world-making creaturely life, in a quasi-space, quasi-time prior to the work of amputation? The center/margin problematic that Fanon identifies is less the space of this question than it is the space that decolonial thinking puts in a different perspective and register. Colonialism is only the vanishing point of the world if the project of colonization is a total and closed system. Deconstruction and the vicissitudes of social death contest that sense of closure, both in interruptive work and in the identification of margins and *la frontera* of being and knowing otherwise. Fanon's vocabulary for decolonial work is the juxtapositional foreground for decolonial thinking, not the stage of its entire meaning. Deconstructive work is always fundamentally parasitic. And so we begin-with Fanon in order to begin-again.

Beginning-with in order to begin-again is the enigma of deconstruction. It is also the retrieval of the double session inherent in the work of producing social death. The intimacy of deconstruction and anticolonial-then-decolonial thought requires some creative work but is also set out quite clearly (no matter how programmatically) in Derrida's collection of essays from the 1970s *Who's Afraid of Philosophy?* These texts engage with the question of education and the place of philosophy in the French university system, and in those moments when Derrida discusses the coloniality of language we are reminded of his Algerian roots and witness to revolution.[18] Derrida takes up the question of coloniality as a problem of thinking and what he calls "the colonizing principle in general" in relation to monolingualism. The monolingualism question is important. It touches on a key structure of colonial domination, one that Fanon outlines in the opening chapter of *Black Skin, White Masks* in terms of the alienation built into linguistic practice in the colony. Fanon draws on a crucial insight common across midcentury Atlantic theory, the claim that, in Martin Heidegger's turn of phrase, "language is the house of Being." To be is to be *in* and *as* language. But Heidegger's formulation is too abstract for the colonial situation. It is not Being that is housed in language, it is Being-in-language that operates as an imperial form of civilization. "To speak means being able to use a certain syntax and possessing the morphology of such and such a language," Fanon writes, "but it means above all assuming a culture and bearing the weight of a civilization."[19] And just a few pages later in *Black Skin, White Masks* Fanon reiterates the same: "To speak a language is to appropriate its world and culture."[20] The house of Being, run through the historical experience of colonialism, becomes a carceral experience, effect, and affect, setting the Black speaker in relation to whiteness in the mode of inexorable alienation. Fanon is clear about this across his early work, especially in its most pessimistic iterations. Language and colonialism set the Black subject in relation to whiteness as *destiny*. And this is a destiny that epidermal racism denies. Not deferral. Just impossibility. This is one modality of social death. To speak as a colonized subject is to speak as socially dead, to speak toward a destiny that is blocked by the incarnate, political meaning of antiblack racism. Yet, there is the plodding work toward that destiny, saturated with nihilism and nonbeing. *Social death as the only life available to the colonized*. Indeed, Fanon will describe this zombification of the colonized as "more terrifying than colonists."[21] The colonist can be resisted, overthrown, but the zombified colonial subject is forever dead inside the system of colonial life and death.

If we read the question of monolingualism in this frame, then we can see why Derrida so readily characterizes monolingualism—the insistence on a single language that works its hegemony without constraint—as a form of mastery and that deconstructive intervention against it is a form of anticolonial critique. Perhaps this is an anticolonial critique that makes decolonial thinking possible. But to get to the moment of thinking, there is first the question of passage—identifying the possibility of passage and clearing the space to navigate the thorniness of any and every path. Language is passage to, but also into the interstices at the outer reaches of, the limit.[22] Derrida writes:

> Every monolingualism and monologism restores mastery and magistrality. It is by treating each language differently, by grafting languages onto one another, by playing on the multiplicity of languages and on the multiplicity of codes within every linguistic corpus that we can struggle at once against colonization in general, against the colonizing principle in general (and you know that it exerts itself well beyond the zones said to be subjected to colonization), against the domination of language or domination by language. The underlying hypothesis of this statement is that the unity of language is always and vested and manipulated simulacrum.[23]

Here, Derrida is making a broad and important claim concerning language, theorizing hegemony in terms of how language reduced to the monolingual enacts violence at every turn. Fanon, paired with Heidegger's key insight, stages the colonial importance of language, but Derrida's appeal to multiplicity as the counter-narration of Being's house shifts away from the Manichean world of colonialism's total project and toward surplus possibilities inside colonial essence. Colonialism fights against multiple languages, from the beginning. In this way, Derrida's remarks on monolingualism and the multiplicity of codes can be read as an iteration, with different sites and citations, of his broader account of supplementarity. If monolingualism is a reduction or leveling of language, then what would it mean to reintroduce the baroque character of Being's house? To embrace rather than make abject the multiplicity of sounds, beings, expressive culture, and chaotic models of belonging? That baroque character supplements the closed system of monolingualism. It also suggests that decolonial thinking, in the antechamber of the question of language, speaks or *ought* to speak the mixed languages of Gloria Anzaldúa's *la frontera*. As well as all the other mixtures that remain unassimilable and undigestible in the logic of colonial Manichaeism. Passage to the limit. Passage into the interstices of life at the limit. There is always excess of excess.

This begins to tell us a story about the relationship between deconstruction, social death in colonial language practice, and the possibilities at work in multilingualism. This is a multilingualism, it must be said, that for Derrida is produced by the dismantling of the unity of language. Contesting it from the inside of the monolingual, perhaps, but also from inside the possibility of language itself. Monolingualism is both intractable and negotiable. Whatever the possibilities *otherwise*, the monolingual is the lifeblood of the colonizing principle. Derrida writes:

> The monolingualism imposed by the other operates by relying upon that foundation, here, through a sovereignty whose essence is always colonial, which tends, repressively and irrepressively, to reduce language to the One, that is, to the hegemony of the homogeneous. This can be verified everywhere, everywhere this homo-hegemony remains at work in the culture, effacing the folds and flattening the text. To achieve that, colonial power does not need, in its heart of hearts, to organizes any spectacular initiatives: religious missions, philanthropic or humanitarian good works, conquest of markets, military expeditions, or genocides.[24]

This remark initiates passage to the limit of the monolingual and toward a multilingualism made possible by deconstruction's commitment to a *first structural opening*, then later to cultural and political practice. Derrida's *Monolingualism of the Other* is such an interesting mix of theorizing the supplement with the cultural-political framing, a sense of the supplement's resonance across subaltern quasi-life. In that way, this moment of opening is the moment of *possible* practice. A decolonial opening that works without the presumption of a center. That opening is fraught, as all things always are in Derrida's work. He remains (rightly) insistent that we speak only one language, which draws us back into the ambivalence of deconstructive argument. We are always entwined with that from which we most want to distance ourselves. Or is it rightly the case, always? Perhaps in the move from center/margin to the margins life of *la frontera* we discover composite, creolized, and chaotically mixed relations to self, other, language, and world: a multilingualism made to the measure of the world. What would it mean to move so dramatically from margin/center to thinking *otherwise* that the very notion of margin/center seems less the work of hegemonic monolingual practice, more the practice of spatiality and time as and from the outside?

The decolonial move against the idea of center, against the Manichean structure of the world introduced by the colonial order, is a move toward extant practices in those interstitial spaces of colonial, postcolonial, and post-Emancipation life. The very idea of those spaces needs decolonization. Fanon could not see it in *Black Skin, White Masks* when musing on the colonial meaning of speech and speaking, but, already inside the colony as part of its broken border structure, language itself refused the monolingual. *Refused.* We know that what most interested Fanon is resistance; in that way, *The Wretched of the Earth* is the clearest expression of his philosophical values. Manichean structures are important to Fanon precisely because they crystalize, then agitate, the necessity of radical resistance and purposive violence. Refusal, however, is another mode altogether. Refusal is the withdrawal of engagement in contested space—in this case, withdrawal from the monolingualism of colonial social and cultural space—in order to make meaning in *another space* and to make that meaning in languages and identities thought *otherwise*. Margins of philosophy. The interstices. When Fanon turns to the internal differentiation of French in Martinique (and by extension the francophone Caribbean more widely) in his observation that alongside the colonial language the colonized also speak pidgins and creoles, he draws back from any approach to speech that would affirm such language(s) as refusal or world-making practices. Part of this has to do with Fanon's inability in *Black Skin, White Masks* to imagine Black subjectivity outside the white gaze, a structural question that underscores the fundamental pessimism of that text. But it also speaks to a broader question of colonial world-making, its scope and its power. Colonialism is a total project, in Fanon's hands characterized as one massive global modernist text. But is the colonial project ever total? Is the aspiration and audacious claim to closure actually the fantasy of the colonizer and of the colonizer alone? If colonialism produces any form of narcissism, it is likely this one: that colonial power has such reach and power over totality.

This is the question that animates the decolonial moment at the intersection of deconstruction and social death. My excursus into Fanon here is less about Fanon-commentary and exposition and more about how his case in *Black Skin, White Masks* is symptomatic of modernity's commitment to system integrity and the politics—conservative or radical—that follow from such a vision of colonial world-making. The figure of the slave looms large over Fanon's early text, infusing his account of pidgin and creole with the abjection proper to the figure. That haunting presence of the figure of the slave does not appear inside Fanon's frame, even as that ghost appears as an absence that makes the assertions against pidgin and creole possible; the abjection of both turns on unremunerated terms inside the argument. And that tells us a lot about how Fanon understands systematicity. Systems, as we learn later in *The Wretched of the Earth*, are precisely what is contested in revolutionary violence. Systems need to be ruptured from the outside, from actors inside the zone of nonbeing who are also animated by the righteous rage of *les damnés de la terre*. In that accounting and existential-political exhortation, Fanon describes both the limits and possibilities of systematicity. Systems are vulnerable to revolutionary action, and such action is critical for the liberation of those oppressed by colonial systems. But it is important to note that he also understands systems to be closed and without fracture, fissure, openness, or the possibility of even partial exit. There is no sense of margins, interstices, or internal differentiation on Fanon's account, which is why the abjection of pidgin and creole is inevitable for his thinking. If the system is closed, then what is produced inside that system cannot be a site of liberation. The center determines the meaning of the margin. Liberation from that center/margin system can only come through the destruction of the system: anticolonial revolution as the elimination of Manichaeism. Fanon's apocalyptic thinking.

Now, it is worth saying that Fanon is plainly right about this. There is no liberation without the end of colonialism, the return of land and institutions to the colonized, and the decolonizing work of culture and nation building. Those ends begin again with the question of the new. New humanism. New postcolonial statecraft. New knowledge. New being. But his frankly modernist vision of colonialism also underscores what is so important about the intersection of deconstruction and social death. Deconstruction, when thought between Derrida and Patterson, is the elaboration of supplementarity as the opening of the system at the very same moment of its closure, anchored in forms of social death that exceed the life/death play inside the system. So, if we configure interstitial space as the production of subaltern subjects in the mode of *refusal*, the move away from engagement with the system and toward the commitments of world-making *otherwise*, then we see how that revolutionary vision of Fanon and others has to imagine a different relation to past and present as it imagines a liberated future. Another beginning, after colonialism, to be sure. But in that beginning, there is also the persistence of the remainder. The persistence of the remainder is the antechamber to decolonial thinking and its capacity to facilitate passage to the postcolonial, as well as through the anticolonial. Anticolonial struggle, the work to liberate from a total system, is a struggle against a form of genocide. In the postcolonial moment, though, deconstruction crossed with social death draws the remainder of the system back into its presence to itself outside colonialism's production of presences and absences. And *that* life must be kept in the postcolonial future. For centuries, it has done its own kind of decolonial work.

I am reminded here of Patrick Chamoiseau's short novel *School Days* and how he writes about the anxious specter of loss. Loss in *School Days* is the loss of creole language and identity in the departmentalized postcolonial state, a state aspiring for the new but one that risks forgetting the remainder, letting slip into oblivion what was produced and lived in the margins of plantation life and its aftermath. Early in the novel, Chamoiseau's protagonist is summoned to write his name on the board in a classroom. The classroom is conducted in French—Martinique is an overseas department, after all—but contains Creole-speaking students. The boy pauses while writing and is sent into ontological reflection: "He saw himself there, captured whole within a chalk mark. *Which meant he could be erased from the world!* Pretending he wasn't scared shitless (which would have tickled Jojo), he began to copy out his first name a thousand times, in order to proliferate and avoid genocide."[25]

Avoid genocide. This is such a provocative remark by Chamoiseau. But for all its literary indulgence and drama, it captures something really important about the matter of life, death, and presence in the world. Heidegger was right: Language is the house of Being. Fanon was right: To speak is to appropriate a culture and world. In *Black Skin, White Masks*, written from the colony, this means the impossibility of appropriating that which alienates, but in *School Days*, composed in the postcolony, it is a reproach to neocolonialism—the presence of French as the executive and institutional language of Martinique—and also a report from the interstices that are, in the postcolony, navigated through the center, the margin, and in the space between. That is, in *School Days*, we can begin to see how the reproach to social death is already there. And in this way we do not need a *new* new humanism. We need, instead, the chalk mark rewritten in pencil (not pen, for multilingualism maintains openness to radical revision) so that erasure *at least* requires struggle-against rather than a simple swipe that produces quick invisibility. Chamoiseau's proposal in this scene, writing in chalk as an ontological event, tells the entire story of the precarity of refusal in a hegemonic, monolingual shared world. But even if the subaltern cannot speak under conditions of coloniality, that does *not* mean that the subaltern is condemned to oblivion of its own terms of life outside social death. Rather, there is an/other form of life. Creole life. Patois life. Vernacular life. Situated on the hither side of the supplement.

This is why it is so important that Derrida's late work returns to the problem of monolingualism. Monolingualism is the first and the last horizon of coloniality. To contest it is to contest the conditions of social death; Fanon's insight into the fate of colonized French speakers, especially around the question of diction, is such an important stage for thinking deconstruction with social death. But the monolingual is always already an illusion that sustains delusion, the idea that through acts of essential colonial violence one could eliminate or fatally obscure the surplus that lies outside the monolingual. If it is an illusion-delusion, then monolingualism can only proceed as contingent on the supplement of what-cannot-be, of radical absence that makes the play of presence/absence possible. All of those deconstructive motifs played out in the coloniality of language, culture, and world. The socially dead also have ideas.

When we read for absences, we read under erasure. Social death meets its explanatory limit in this reading. Another world is possible because another beginning has already happened.

2
Racial Formation and the Remainder in Baldwin's Nonfiction

> There, in that absolutely alabaster landscape, armed with two Bessie Smith records and a typewriter, I began to try to recreate the life that I had first known as a child and from which I had spent so many years in flight.
> —JAMES BALDWIN, "THE DISCOVERY OF WHAT IT MEANS TO BE AN AMERICAN"

What is racial identity? How is blackness produced both by and outside the white gaze?

These particular questions sit at the center of James Baldwin's nonfiction from the very outset. The earliest Baldwin essays collected in *Notes of a Native Son* document the vicissitudes of blackness, lived at once on the periphery of American society and in the immanent objectification of the white gaze. That spacing of life will prove existential. It is a matter of identity, not just political geography. We can also think of the close of Baldwin's writerly career, and how his last work of nonfiction from 1985, the largely underread but utterly profound *Evidence of Things Not Seen*, offers a long reflection on the Atlanta child murders and returns again and again to the production of blackness by the white gaze. So much of his work between reckons with protest, exile, and the persistence of Americanness in spasms of violence only to return to his animating question: what does it mean to say *Black*? Or, in the vernacular of his moment: Who is the American Negro? Across these decades of writing and threaded through his various concerns and obsessions, we see how Baldwin deepens and nuances his understanding of racial formation. Racial formation is largely concerned with the complexity of "the Negro." What does it mean to live as a Black person in a country that does not want you, that has never had space for your belonging, and is structurally and institutionally committed to the reproduction of that ghettoization? Baldwin's characterization of "the Negro" circles around this tension of nonbelonging. But in his expansive and expanding vision he returns again and again to the same site of reflection, asking us again and again how white violence makes racial identity. Identities forged in violence raise complex and urgent ethical and epistemological questions because, grounded in racial terror as a sociogenic principle, the labor of identity-making precedes agency and human *poiesis*. What does it mean to *be* and to *know* in this space of identity-making? Is anything *otherwise* possible? Or is the possible ever actual? What words, if any, might we have for this *otherwise*?

Baldwin's long engagement with the white gaze underscores with increasing urgency how that gaze carries with it a profound and immovable sense of innocence. Or, importantly, how it imagines *itself* innocent. Moral autoaffection of the worst and most dishonest kind. All of the violence and abjection that results from the white gaze registers, for the white people formed in the enactment of that gaze, as a series of surprises, shocks, and exceptions. As we will see, Baldwin's conception of racial formation articulates and explains the everyday experience, destructive and cruel, of we have come to simply call *white innocence*. How could atrocity occur simply by the *fact* of whiteness? The gaze and its violence is (putatively) *never* intentional. The gaze (allegedly) *never wants* to inflict its harm. Putatively, allegedly. That is, white people, as a matter of identity formation, imagine themselves wholly outside the economy of violence and all of those attendant forms of premature, extrajudicial death and killing. *Racial terror is reserved for the Klan. It's always those other whites, I swear.* This is also part of what it means to, say, blame Black people for conditions of poverty and abjection or what Baldwin calls, again in the vernacular of his moment, *the ghetto*. Innocence is imagined inaction and untraversed distance from the world. Innocence therefore operates—that is, it hopes and it imagines that it operates—outside the kind of identity work done by racialized and racializing social forms. And here we have to understand *imagined* in the most expansive sense. For Baldwin, racial fantasies are not belief states or types of consciousness alone. Although they may also be characteristics of ethics and the psyche, what is *active* in terms of transforming bodies, lives, and communities is that racial fantasies are firstly imaginary in the strongest sense, namely, in the sense that Édouard Glissant gives to the notion of the imaginary: a total vision of what is both possible and impossible. To produce the ghetto while simultaneously displacing the origins and hard racializing work of that abjection on to those subjected to its violence is plenty testimony to the force of the imaginary and its commitment to white innocence. *Watch whiteness work.*

The ghetto is therefore no mere social phenomenon. That is, the ghetto is not simply a political construction that exploits and abandons an entire population, nor is it simply an externalization of what the white gaze makes of bodies, lives, and people. Though it is all of those things, for sure, the ghetto also sits at the center of the formation of racial identities in the United States. In this way, the ghetto is *necessary*. The ghetto is not only a world in which the abjection work of the white gaze confirms itself—the fantasy of blackness made material and complete—but also a *relation* that makes white identity what and who it is. One of Baldwin's important contributions as a thinker is how deeply and emphatically he thinks identity formation as a question of relationality. Rather than conceive racial abjection and subjugation as economic interest, sadistic practice, or historically sedimented belief structures—though it can also be all of those things at the same time—for Baldwin it is a question of how the *habitus* of interracial relations produce, in that relation, the structure of being and beings. The process of making racial identities is fundamentally dialectical, and that dialectic resolves into robust, clear, and difficult if not near impossible to dislodge, senses of identity. The strength and resilience of those identities comes less from enforcement by various repressive state apparatuses than from the intersection of historical sedimentations of meaning (the *habitus* of interracial life) and constellations of external manifestation of that meaning, whether impoverishment, linguistic and other notions of the proper, epidermal racial signification, or practices of criminalization and incarceration. In each iteration at this intersection, racial meaning is reproduced without alteration of the base structure of social life: antiblack racism.

Racial dialectic is nothing like a representation of a deeper genesis of meaning. Which is to say, racial formation for Baldwin is not something like a static visual meaning that confirms beliefs. The ghetto, for example, does not merely function as visual confirmation of white racist beliefs in the inherent incapacity or inferiority of Black folk. Rather, racial dialectics make and remake meaning in dynamic, conflictual, and often if not always violent confrontation, producing and reproducing the racial order in moments of active production of, say, poverty, criminalization of it, resistance to it, and activation of the repressive state to stall or eliminate resistance. All of this converges to produce a spectacle in which white racism is able to manufacture its own superiority and all along maintain its innocence. This is an entire world. This is *the* entire world. Indeed, the whole of the argument Baldwin makes about the formation of racial identity is that it makes a world in which each racial identity always already knows its fate and that each fate has violence built into its very being: subjection to premature death or executor of factors that manufacture premature death. Death is the sociogenic agent in making us who and what we are as Americans. *Deathworld as genesis.*

Still, there is life. Life persists, produces meanings, remains obstinate inside death. How is this world possible and in what ways does it exceed the deathworld into which we are all born? How does Baldwin's work both surface the structures and affective life of social death, affirming them as elemental to the structure of being and beings, and also supplement those structures with anarchic or even rooted possibilities? Or, in a dialectical frame: What is the outside or exterior of this dialectic, the surplus in the essence of its violent dynamic of production and reproduction? And how does exteriority interrupt Baldwin's work, perhaps in or perhaps against his own pen?

In thinking through the structure and significance of racial formation and its dialectical structure, we can begin to see the system of racialization as Baldwin sees it. Or, as he might want us to put it: *that to which Baldwin's writing bears witness.* Witness obligates. Obligates to outrage and defense, of course. But also, in a deconstructive framing, witness obligates us to the other of racial formation, the antidialectical remainder. What and who is this remainder? How does social death operate inside Baldwin's account of racial formation, how does that figure of the slave carry supplementarity with it and, at the outer boundary of his account of deathworld, open the system in a passage to the limit?

The Natal Pessimism of Black Life

Raoul Peck's 2016 documentary film *I Am Not Your Negro* was a monumental event. Whatever one's feelings about this particular portrait of the author, the film reinscribed Baldwin's work in our contemporary consciousness and conscience in important ways around questions of racial outrage and racial justice. Reinscription folds time, marking how our moment and a sequence of formative moments from the past create a sense of unbearably awful inheritance. The film invited this reinscription with its invocation of struggles for racial justice around the Movement for Black Lives and the #BlackLivesMatter movement and their direct confrontations with police. In that way, the temporality of *I Am Not Your Negro* is its own theoretical event. After a series of murders of Black men and women by the police, these movements rooted themselves in a message and demand as blunt and clear as the "I Am a Man" signs that dominated the sanitation workers strike in Memphis, Tennessee in 1968. The signs—placards, songs of protest, hashtags, posture in the street— all say something blunt and clear: Black lives deserve recognition and respect.

The simplicity and minimum of the demand and articulation of deserts is its own kind of troubling of the national conscience, if in fact there is one in the United States. The demand of #BlackLivesMatter and "I Am a Man" is straightforward: recognize our humanity. Recognize our possibilities. Recognize our lives. We can imagine Baldwin's question, one generated by the violence of the dialectic of racial formation: *recognition on whose terms?* This was also Frantz Fanon's question at the close of *Black Skin, White Masks.* It is the question raised by anyone who takes inheritance seriously. Recognition comes with conditions: conditions under which humanity is possible, conditions for the possibility of being human. What does it mean to want that recognition, to be seen under those possibilities as a human? How do adjudicate the legitimacy of humanism? This is the decolonial question par excellence.

But just as much, if not more, *I Am Not Your Negro,* like the Movement for Black Lives and #BlackLivesMatter demonstrations, is about outrage and rage. To be sure, in the moment of mass protest in the mid-2010s media outlets in the United States were quick to offer glossy, high-end photography portraits of the movement founders and laud the innovations of it all, from questions of gender and sexuality to the use of social media for mass mobilization. And those were exceptionally important elements of the moment. Indeed, the spectacle of revolt shifted the terms of what revolt looks like and, along with that shift in optics, expanded the program of liberation struggle. Sexuality, race, class, nation, anti-imperialism, regional needs, global demands—the folds in this moment were stunning and very much needed. Overdue in a history for which liberation struggle was often as much a conservative gender project as it was a justice project. Ecstasy and joy were for that reason alone no small part of protest. *But if God got us then we gon' be alright.* At the same time, the moment was drenched in rage. There is a reason why the right wing panicked when seeing protests on their television screen. Rage is terrifying, especially when one knows the collective guilt borne by this nation. Terrifying for white Americans, anyway. With terror comes claims of innocence in order to blame and castigate the enraged for their rage. It is a logic as old as the founding of the United States. But it is also a moment in which the imaginary of white innocence is brought out into the open and put under critical scrutiny. White backlash is part and parcel of race, protest, and demands for the recognition of basic humanity.

For Baldwin, and Peck understands this so well in his film, the question of Black rage is therefore not simply a matter of affective response and political orientation—though of course it is also both of those things. Black rage is to be read as *symptomatic.*[1] That is, for Baldwin, rage functions as a formal indicator of a wider structure of the world, both in terms of the being of subjects in the world and the character of that world itself. Baldwin does not explicitly use the language of epistemology and ontology, but this sense of being and knowing intersecting as indicators in the affect and political orientation of rage is central to the organization of his nonfiction. Rage is the story of so much of Black life; the violence inflicted upon every aspect of Black life, from the psychological to the broadest material conditions, writes politics and affect on the body. But for Baldwin the body itself, what it feels and knows and reckons with as an orientation toward an antiblack world, is *itself* a kind of indicator even as it is a word and world unto itself. What is registered in the body, in the skull of the Black person subjected to the history of antiblackness, forms one's sense of subjectivity and, in that formation, points to the structure of the political world in which that subjectivity comes to be. A certain kind of sociogeny, perhaps. In that sense, to know what Baldwin calls "the Negro" is to know the United States in the present, in the past, and at the crossroads for a future. These terms of rage could not be clearer from the first screens of *I Am Not Your Negro*, where the opening text is critical:

In June 1979,
acclaimed author James Baldwin
commits to a complex endeavor:

tell his story of America
through the lives of three
of his murdered friends:

    Medgar Evers
    Martin Luther King, Jr.
    Malcolm X

Baldwin never got past
his thirty pages of notes,
entitled: *Remember This House*[2]

This text alone tells so much of the story of not only *I Am Not Your Negro*, but also Baldwin's work in its bleakest registers. I am always struck, each time I watch the film, by how clearly Peck sees Baldwin's pessimism, nihilism, and despair. The bleaker registers emerge in the link Baldwin draws, both in this quotation and in his broader project *Remember This House*, between murder and America. To be sure, Baldwin's work is always about *Americanness*, even when he writes of exile, travel, and being a foreigner in a foreign land. All of those exilic meditations return to the nation of his birth, a place he insists, across all paradoxes, on calling *home*. But here Baldwin is talking about America—and not Americanness, which is something importantly different—as *murder*. The murders of Evers, King Jr., and Malcolm X are America's story, not an exceptional moment and not a deviation from what it means to *be* this place. Ontology as violence, violence as ontology. A most painful form of sociogeny. Necropolitical praxis.

Peck is characterizing Baldwin here, of course, paraphrasing and drawing out a general lesson from the unpublished work as an introduction to the film, but he could easily have turned to Baldwin's own text. We can recall, for example, the utterly devastating letter Baldwin writes to his nephew, which serves as a sort of prefatory note to the published version of *The Fire Next Time*. The nephew, who was a child at the time, is both Baldwin's kin and a portrait of what, if anything, remains of the category "child" in relation to African American reality. White innocence and white violence initiate Baldwin's most troubled and troubling comment, which is also his most incisive and, for me, most enduring expression of the nihilism that sits at the heart of his account of racial formation. In that letter, Baldwin writes:

> This innocent country set you down in a ghetto in which, in fact, it intended that you should perish. Let me spell out precisely what I mean by that, for the heart of the matter is here, and the root of my dispute with my country. You were born where you were born and face the future that you faced because you were black and *for no other reason*. The limits of your ambition were, thus, expected to be set forever. You were born into a society which spelled out with brutal clarity, and in as many ways as possible, that you were a worthless human being.[3]

One can only imagine the nephew reading this letter. That is, one *can* imagine the nephew receiving this letter and reading it across the years of his life, discovering at each moment how a world awaits Black bodies, anticipates the transformation of lives and people. It is the body that awaits: "because you were black and *for no other reason*." But one also *cannot* imagine the nephew except as an iteration of America itself, his singularity as a person absorbed into the cruelty of the world that generates the conditions for being itself. The unspeakable. The unimaginable price. This is the generative moment of interracial social encounter, stretched across time and mediated by our incarnate being in the production of being as a death sentence. A death sentence at *some level*. How do we measure that level?

Measuring the death sentence, the intention that the nephew should perish as a matter of the being *of* the world and of him being *in* the world, is simultaneously a question of ontology, epistemology, and the shadow that nihilism casts over both. The very being of the world is, for Baldwin, a condition of the nephew's death sentence. He was born *into* a world and that moment of birth, the natal relation, is animated by the figure of the slave made embodied. The should-perish natal subject performs unremunerated labor in the production of white identity, which, in the social death lived from the moment of first breath, also produces generational rage. Born as and borne by the world's first breath, at and as the origin of the nation, it is also the condition of the production of Black experience and then in some measure the identity of blackness itself. Let us come back to this in detail, but it is important to first understand how, for Baldwin, should-perish subjectivity is laboring as an active/passive category in the dialectic of racial formation. Not as an efficient cause, strictly speaking, nor as an element in dialectical motion. Rather, it is the absence at the heart of the production of presence: the self to self, the self to other, and the other to self, all of which proceed to presence with a haunting absence. *Specters of the deathbound subject.* Knowledge of self and world, the structure of subjectivity itself, is in this way a modality of social death in the sense of blackness appearing in Baldwin's work *as* social death, but also, in a double session of death-absence, social death as a condition of social death. Baldwin's documentation of themes of shame and doubt—the psychological effect of ghettoization and exclusion from most forms of civic and economic life—tracks the inner life of should-perish subjectivity through symptomology. Affective life, the life Baldwin characterizes in his nonfiction and explores at great depth in his fiction, is not the *meaning* of racial formation and its infrastructure. The dynamics of that formation are much more complicated and in many ways much bleaker than the collage of symptoms that begin to tell the story of ontogenesis. Natal pessimism, rather than the pessimism of the social and political world, names this complexity and locates origin before all other origins. *It intended that you should perish.*

All of this work of natality and being operates under the shadow of a robust nihilism. That much is clear and needs detail. To be sure, it is a nihilism that has provocative countermeasures (though never fully curative) of persistence, resistance, and, at its most minimal, forms of life made in/as survival. To measure nihilism with resistance and resistance with nihilism is to measure "America" in its most fundamental, base structure. Now, it is a not uncommon trope about Baldwin's work to say that he engages in a sort of American "exceptionalism." Honestly, I have always found this trope problematic in terms of its wider resonance, which in its original formulation is a characterization of global political economy and imperial ethics—matters that set the United States outside the rule of law and the ethics of common decency, leading to what we have known, globally, since the 1950s or so, as the impunity of American political hegemony. Applying such a characterization to Baldwin's work is odd and misleading. Baldwin does not speak to this issue at all, and in fact there is no indication that he was interested in excepting the nation from any of its sins, domestic or international. Quite the opposite, actually. America is impugned.

But what Baldwin *is* attentive to is how the United States has its own particular internal racial dynamic; every nation has this kind of difference, and honest, probing analysis of such structures *should* be exceptional. History and memory are not abstractions. They are the substance of social, cultural, political, and existential life. In the case of the United States, dynamics of racial formation and identity work are rooted in one of the two founding wounds of the nation: plantation slavery and its long afterlives.[4] Long afterlives, sedimented in memorial and historical structures and reproduced in the *habitus* of everyday life, transform extant hegemonies into natal violence, deathworlds, and senses of ontogenesis that make whiteness and blackness variations of one and the same story of catastrophe. Like all sites of antiblack social and political formation, the United States—what he always just calls "America"—has its own structures that are both visible and intuitive. Baldwin documents these structures in his fiction and nonfiction in order to make them visible, but it is the intuitive dimension that is particularly interesting. That is, for the American reader of Baldwin, his descriptions of interracial experience are no revelation, but rather appear as vivid depictions and clarifications of the racial everyday. Baldwin led a compelling and unique life in many ways and he speaks from interesting locales with quirky tales here and there, but his accounting of the racial everyday is just that: everydayness as critical theory. Everydayness as critical theory documents the vicissitudes and various cruelties of antiblack racism, racial formation, and white obstinacy in order to make the intuitively obvious into something conceptually clear, troubled, and troubling. What is the world of interracial life? How can we adequately describe it in order to understand the production of should-perish subjectivity?

Racial Formation and Deathworld

It is the question that really haunted Baldwin: What is "the Negro" and how did this identity come to be? The question haunted Baldwin because it has no easy answer.

Narratives of race and racial inheritance did a lot of work in the history of the concept of race, turning to essentialisms of one sort or another—biological, climatological, questions of sedimented and immovable cultural forms, and so on—in order to explain how someone in, say, Kinshasa, Congo, might belong to the same identity grouping as someone in Sacramento, California. It really is that crass and blunt, but also urgent and important. Diaspora needs some sort of narrative of unity across difference, always. To be sure, many explanations from the long history of theorizing race look absurd from our contemporary viewpoint, but it is also true that we often inherit at least the *aspiration* of this kind of thinking. We still use the concept of race and imagine that the concept names something, rather than working as an empty signifier of anything except historical meaning. This is no shame on us for operating with a strong language of race. It is morally imperative, in many ways. Indeed, we imagine that race names something real for good reason: Race has visceral, material effects on our social, cultural, and political worlds unlike near any other operative concept in the social imaginary. Without biologism or strong cultural determinism, we are left with the fact that racial identity, in terms of its metaphysical status, is fictive and both produced and reproduced through social form and force. That form and force has metaphysical effects and affects. Reality itself is ordered and reordered on the grounds of racial meaning.

How do we explain this formation of racial identity when "scientific" explanations have all been debunked and exposed as political atrocity? We can think here of the particularly rigorous and important approach to thinking about the relationship between social-political reality and racial formation in Michael Omi and Howard Winant's argument, developed across their various works on the production and reproduction of race in the United States. Their work is wide-ranging and ambitious, worthy of an entirely independent treatment, and so I am invoking it here only for the resonance of a claim made in their centerpiece chapter of *Racial Formation in the United States*. This claim summarizes their work on the relationship between racist practices and theories (from folk to scientific) of race: "Race, therefore, is *more* than racism," Omi and Winant write, "it is a full-fledged 'social fact' like sex/gender or class. From this perspective, race shapes racism as much as racism shapes race."[5] *Racial Formation in the United States* is a long, deliberate, detailed elaboration of this description of race as a social fact. Not just a social fact, but one that is *full-fledged*, meaning that it does the work of racial essentialisms without the terrifying pseudoscientific accounting for identity. Crucial for understanding race as a social fact, as the centerpiece of what is for Baldwin the deathworld and should-perish subjectivity, is the zigzag movement between racism and race. The racialized experience of social death, the deathworld for African Americans, is a world of atrocity and cruelty, but also a fully developed lifeworld—always held in relation to the production of various forms of death, animated by the figure of the slave—for white Americans. The social fact is in that way lived as embodied nihilism and its companion piece embodied privilege. The absolute inseparability of Black and white experience in the deathworld is paramount for Baldwin. But is race inseparable from racism? What would it mean to try to keep them at some distance?

In thinking through and framing how Baldwin's work on race accounts for origins and production-reproduction, it is helpful that Omi and Winant narrow their inquiry to the United States, keeping the account of racial formation site specific. If we delink the language of race from any variety of essentialisms, then we see how intimately the formation of whiteness as a racial identity works with not just the formation of the racially other, in this case Black or African American (the difference matters), but also the entire formation of a society. This is what we mean by the phrase *racial state*. The racial state is a state that organizes its key social structures and components of identity around racial distinction. Omi and Winant write: "The theory of racial formation suggests that society is suffused with racial projects, large and small, to which all are subjected. This racial 'subjection' is quintessentially ideological. Everybody learns some combination, some version, of the rules of racial classification, and of their own racial identity, often without obvious teaching or inculcation. Thus are we inserted in a comprehensively racialized social structure. Race becomes 'common sense.'"[6]

What Omi and Winant show us in this passage, and indeed across much of *Racial Formation in the United States,* is that we cannot think racial identity without national context; ideological formation is site-specific and subject to the institutions and *habitus* of place. But what I find striking in this passage and across their book is how Omi and Winant describe racial difference without employing an equivalent of social death. To be sure, they understand the scope and effects of antiblack racism—even as the book is about race as such, and not specifically or exclusively about blackness. Their neutrality in theorizing race as produced by institutions clears out the central role of atrocity and its repetitions; sociology meets its limits and needs witness. Beginning *with* witness, beginning with the representation of the ghetto and the world it renders with such clarity, underscores the role of abjection across the work of racial formation. To wit: If race and racism are not inseparably and intimately entwined, then abjection is an accidental or secondary feature of race. Baldwin affirms the sense that race *might* mean something other than the production of racism, but that hesitation is rooted in a deeper and primary account of how the national specificity of producing blackness as a racial category is tied to the specificity of antiblack racial terror. That terror is at the end of a gun or a whip, but it is also at the end of the landlord's lease and the mass dispossession of Black communities by white mobs—vigilantes, businessmen, bankers, property owners, the police, and the justice system. And whiteness too is generated in these moments.

With Baldwin and Omi and Winant, we can see the movement between identity formation and the national-social context. Institutional habits, policies, and the like serve as both creative forces in the making of racial identity and evidence of identity's legitimacy. In terms of the *doxic* features of our founding wound, everyday speech around race at times stand at some distance from racism. Perhaps it is this distance, distance that helps make sense of affirmative notions of racial identity and culture, that leads Omi and Winant to partially cleave race and racism. Certainly, something of our everydayness is reflected in that cleavage. Critical theoretical approaches, however, raise different questions inside a hermeneutic of suspicion. Baldwin theorizes inside that hermeneutic and, from that critical position, articulates the ghetto as ontogenesis, rather than as one institution among others. The should-perish subjectivity of social death reframes Omi and Winant's framing with the problem of abjection. Not just in terms of the inextricable link between blackness and abjection—though Baldwin surely shares *a good bit* of that characterization with Afropessimists—but also in terms of the genesis of white identity. White identity shares a fundamental dependency upon the abjection of blackness. This mutual dependency carries with it its own kind of pain, making blackness unreconcilable with a *pure* version of what W. E. B. Du Bois described as "our spiritual striving" for self-understanding. The impurity of identity is at once the melancholy of being and the echo of the supplement. It is also true, because the identity formations are essentially tied to social processes, that whiteness is bound to abjection as the contamination of innocence and the presence of atrocity inside the very notion of *that* modality of being. Race ceases to be what Omi and Winant describe as common sense in this moment, transforming, in the relation of mutual dependency, into haunted affective and ontological space. An anxious relation.

In the essay "Notes of a Native Son," Baldwin describes this anxious relation as what draws Black people to a terrifying figurative crossroads: amputation or gangrene. Two compelling ways to express the nonlife of social death, whether dismemberment or slow but deeply painful deterioration of the body. Unnecessary disabling of the body or poison and agony? How are we to figure social death as embodied? This gruesome physical metaphor, which is barely a metaphor given the totalizing effects and affects of racial violence, raises the question of how to reckon with the *racism* lies at the root of this conception of racial formation—*pace* Omi and Winant. The metaphor matters. It speaks to the visceral foundations of racial identity, embedded in nihilism and cruelty. Baldwin writes:

> This relation [of Black and white Americans] prohibits, simply, anything as uncomplicated and satisfactory as pure hatred. In order to

really hate white people, one has to blot so much out of the mind—
and the heart—that this hatred itself becomes an exhausting and
self-destructive pose. . . . One is always in a position of having to
decide between amputation and gangrene. Amputation is swift but
time may prove that the amputation was not necessary. . . . Gangrene
is slow, but it is impossible to be sure that one is reading one's symptoms right. The idea of going through life as a cripple is more than
one can bear, and equally unbearable is the risk of swelling up slowly,
in agony, with poison.[7]

This passage has multiple twists and turns, beginning with Baldwin's sense of refusal. The exhaustion produced by hating white people is itself a form of white oppression, so the distance taken from that relation (refusal of hatred) is a critical sense of care for self and self-value. It is also an early expression of Baldwin's long-standing quarrel with the Black radical tradition around questions of rage and hatred of the oppressor, a quarrel that is not firstly about hope or imaginations of another future, but always and more provocatively about the refusal to let white people so intimately inside the heart of Black life. The fact of interracial space, however, is the terror from which there is no exit. A certain Black nationalism would cleave and discard white people, yet Baldwin sees what would be cleaved and discarded as an ontologically necessary (though not sufficient) condition of racial formation. "And the trouble, finally," Baldwin writes, "is that the risks are real even if the choices do not exist."[8] Thinking trouble in the same moment as racial formation is to think social death as a constitutive element of American life. *If trouble don't kill me, I believe I'll never die*. American life, our bound and complex finitude, is unimaginable without the fatal trouble of social death and its production of racial identities.

To be sure, the complexity and, for some, even objectionable character of Baldwin's position here lies in the claim that Black identity is entwined with white racism. That is not an entirely inaccurate assessment. This is where Baldwin's conception of racial formation is a story of social death and also a story of how identities were made in the United States under conditions of catastrophe rather than cultural exploration, *poiesis*, and collective freedom. Peck's film helps us see the contours of Baldwin's nihilism and pessimism with particular clarity, and these are its best and most ethically and politically productive roots. It is also true that Baldwin will elsewhere argue for a more complex sense of Black life, but only as a moment *outside* the dialectic of racial formation that begins and passes through this entwinement: the Negro as an enigma of exteriority, the question of the supplement that haunts the passage to the limit. More fundamental to this issue, though, is Baldwin's commitment to thinking *Americanness* as more than a place and project, and rather as a critical concept and ontology. That is, for Baldwin, Black Americans are precisely that: Black *Americans*. The ethnic character of his vision of Black Americans both surmounts any robust concept of race—he is no thinker of Négritude, even if he adores and shares their sense of the beauty of blackness[9]—and, in so many ways, *replaces* race as an identity cornerstone. Or perhaps ethnicity is Baldwin's way of naming the particular forms of abjection that attend to the production of racial identity, saturating, at the origin, the meaning of race with racial violence. Which is to say, ethnicity—Americanness, in this case—so saturates the language of race that black Americans are all but, and maybe precisely and exactly, their own *people*. Baldwin's long meditations on the ghetto and other forms of the *habitus* of antiblack violence draw us into this ontology and, when that ontological element is linked to the specificity of place, produces a description of the being of a collective that is akin to, if not precisely and exactly, a nongeneralizable sense of subjectivity. Should-perish subjectivity is social death. Social death is the beginning of peoplehood identity in an antiblack world. And, of course, that should-perish subject, the ethnic and racial and *particular*, is haunted by its supplementarity. Discerning the function of that supplementarity in the production of ethnicity, the absent shadow of abjection, is the work of exiting the system of racial formation and dialectics.

The signal of this ethnicity is carried in some of the strangest and most unexpected encounters documented in Baldwin's work. Witnesses witness, even when that witnessing is prompted by surprise and generates an unexpected discourse. I am thinking in particular of his essay "Encounter on the Seine," in which he offers a long meditation on exile and racial difference. In that way, it is like most of Baldwin's nonfiction. But "Encounter on the Seine" shifts a bit of emphasis by theorizing race and identity in a diasporic context: fellow people of African origin in France. One might expect fellow-feeling and exuberance, yet Baldwin in this essay is struck by his failure to *feel* and *experience* a sense of inextricable connection to Africans in France. He writes: "They face each other, the Negro and the African, over a gulf of three hundred years—an alienation too vast to be conquered in an evening's good-will, too heavy and too double-edged ever to be trapped in speech. This alienation causes the Negro to recognize that he is a hybrid. Not a physical hybrid merely: in every aspect of his living he betrays the memory of the auction block and the impact of the happy ending."[10]

Baldwin here draws our analysis to the hyphen in our contemporary vernacular of African American, the linking, both precarious and robustly ontological, of the African and the American. Hyphens both keep separate, marking social death perhaps, and conjoin around shared features, identities, and places. That is, the hybrid or combinatory relation of the hyphen produces, on the page and in our readerly eyes, a sense of being and not a mere aesthetics of existence. And so Baldwin writes further, confirming just this, that the alienation manifest in this gulf-ridden encounter between the African and the African-American is not a sense of lost identity, but instead that it is "this depthless alienation from oneself and one's people is, in sum, the American experience."[11] This lands Baldwin's theorization of the blackness of Black Americans somewhere between melancholy, pleasure, ennui, and a very specific, particular sense of painful history. A painful history of dislocations that then relink should-perish subjectivity to spaces of social death as home. A cruel but productive paradox.

Perhaps the most peculiar twist on this insight lies Baldwin's reversal of identification, which he notes across his nonfiction and with particular directness in "The Discovery of What It Means to Be an American," an essay written as a first wave response to the experience of exile. Baldwin anticipates his own (and certainly anticipates our) response to his exile as a moment of relief, a moment of retrieval of a more authentic sense of self, or even an immersion in the life and lives of his exilic locale. And that is certainly the case for those moments in which he remarks that exile provided some breathing space after a suffocated and suffocating life in the United States. But in "The Discovery of What It Means to Be an American," he invokes "any Texas GI" to underscore a difficult insight into interracial exilic life. Baldwin writes;

> In my necessity to find the terms on which my experience could be related to that of others, Negroes and whites, writers and non-writers, I proved, to my astonishment, to be as American as any Texas GI. . . . Like me, they had been divorced from their origins, and it turned out to make very little difference that the origins of white Americans were European and mine were African—they were no more at home in Europe than I was. . . . And it also became clear that, no matter where our fathers had been born, or what they had endured, the fact of Europe had formed us both, was part of our identity and part of our inheritance.[12]

Here inheritance appears as the unexpected link and *need* of relation between white and Black Americans, as well as the shared experience, however asymmetrically experienced across history and in the contemporary moment, of alienation from origins. Europe forms both Black and white Americans. This is the strangest of shared estranged and estranging origins. But that formation in Europe is nothing like a *root* for identity formation. Rather, the inheritance of what Europe did to identity turns attention to the dialectical relationship between Black and white racial formation in the United States. This is not a diasporic story. It is, rather, entirely a relationship of negative dialectics, producing a remainder but also producing a deep, resilient commitment to *not* reconciling difference in any sense of values or human decency. Social death is both the energy of the dialectics of racial formation and the product of it. Antiblackness consumes and makes.

Baldwin's notes on the mutual dependency of white and Black Americans for a sense of identity opens up a strange and compelling dialectic of racial formation, and he of course wants to emphasize, always, that this dialectic is never one of reconciliation. It is, rather, a dialectic that produces abjection in a twofold structure: the abjection of the white gaze and the production of an abject class or caste. The white gaze reproduces abjection, whether the gaze comes from the interpersonal or from the embeddedness of that gaze in institutions and social and political *habitus*. In its abjection, identifying the bottom of the well, whiteness as an identity is both created and calcified. Baldwin writes in "Princes and Powers" that the United States is a society in which

> nothing was fixed and we had therefore been born to a greater number of possibilities, wretched as these possibilities seemed at the instant of our birth. Moreover, the land of our forefathers' exile had been made, by that travail, our home. It may have been the popular impulse to keep us at the bottom of the perpetually shifting and bewildered populace; but we were, on the other hand, almost personally indispensable to each of them, simply because, without us, they could never have been certain, in such a confusion, where the bottom was.[13]

This is one of the most important and striking passages in Baldwin's nonfiction. First, he links the wretchedness of possibilities that define Black life in an antiblack world to birth; social death is not an accomplishment, but a natal condition. Second, he asserts with no small bit of painful paradox or irony that this wretched space is also *home*. The dialectics of racial formation is painful for this exact reason: They produce an ontology of self and place. If racial identity aimed only at alienation and estrangement, then racial formation would foment a sense of revolt and marginality inside the process itself. But the question of home changes so much of that, generating the paradox of African American claims to place in a place that makes no space for Black life as life. And, third, in linking natal pessimism to the painful sense of home, Baldwin underscores the *need for* and *dependency on* the abjection of blackness for white racial identity. It is not the case that white Americans appear with a preformed identity or root any sense of identity in Europe; Baldwin's brief remarks on the Texas GI reveal so much. Severed roots and beginning again mark Americanness with Americanness, and inside this horizon is social death.

This dialectic produces a world.

How should we think of this world in Baldwin's work?

I think Edith Wyschogrod's work on deathworlds, as a conceptual companion piece to Achille Mbembe's work on necropolitics, is particularly helpful here. If we recall Baldwin's letter to his nephew in which he writes that the world into which the nephew is born is one that wants, plans, and desires him to perish, and set it alongside this articulation of need for and dependency on abjection for identity formation, then we start to see how he conceives the world as a space of death and death-making. There is the haunted and haunting figure of social death, of course, but also the invocation of material violence that operates as a buttress and reinforcement for social death as a figure of ideology and political world-making. Baldwin's remarks on should-perish subjectivity and the dialectic of racial formation serve to underscore the affective and structural elements of our *shared* world as oriented around the death of Black bodies, lives, and people. Wyschogrod's conception of deathworld enhances our insight into this phenomenon. Though *Spirit in Ashes*, the work in which deathworld is developed as a critical concept, is largely concerned with the Shoah and its impact on theorizing the human and community, Wyschogrod is also and importantly making a wider observation about the nature of white Western ideology and world-making. In that wider observation, her conception of deathworld becomes a compelling vocabulary for comparative study. She begins with a characterization of the *life*world and how it is transformed by forms of mass death. Wyschogrod writes:

> All sociocultural forms of existence "live on" or express this fundament although no *specific* pattern of culture is endemic to the lifeworld as such. The structure of experience is perceived by way of cultural forms; it is clothed in some cultural expression, but at the same time this foundation allows these forms to emerge. Prior to the appearance of slave labor and concentration camps it was possible to imagine the destruction of the life-world, but it was not possible to imagine the paradox which arises when human life perdures but the life-world as we have described it ceases to exist.[14]

In this passage Wyschogrod is already engaged with the logic and broad ontological economy of Patterson's notion of social death. Indeed, what I find so important and interesting here is how this notion of the lifeworld in crisis fumbles around in search of words for the phenomenon described, that impossible space of the destruction of the discursive and symbolic orders that sustain life, yet life persists in the ruins, on the ashes, or after the drowning of memory left at the bottom of the sea. Destroying the lifeworld as we know it, what we know about how it functions across cultural and civilizational differences, is not the same as death itself. This is an ontological shift in which Being is fundamentally altered and, in that alteration, produces different kinds of beings.

Ubiquitous and obstinate, the post-lifeworld world, a world that produces a different kind of Being and beings, is as familiar as it is unthinkable in its horror. And yet we need a name for this opposing social arrangement. For Wyschogrod, naming begins in the death camps of Nazi Germany and totalitarian Soviet Union, but we can see how that version of deathworld had long been the characteristic of south Atlantic life and indigenous life across the Americas for centuries prior. Being already had the lessons at hand for *that* and *those* murderous totalitarian forms, which Aimé Césaire to bluntly noted in *Discourse on Colonialism*: The death camps were a European practice long developed as a procedure for control and domination in the colonies.[15] That construction of a world is an antilife version of world; the opposition of this lifeworld, and indeed what renders it both decrepit and only now a remnant of another era, is *deathworld*. Again, Wyschogrod writes: "The world of concentration and slave labor camps as concrete actualities emerges from a systematic effort to deconstruct the life-world—the sphere of micropractices which make human existence possible—to dismantle it and not mere compress its range. Here a space is created in which is changed not mere this or that component of experience . . . but the scaffolding of experience itself."[16] In both of these passages, Wyschogrod's allusion to slave labor refers only to Soviet-era gulags and related places of catastrophic political violence. It is a feature of the analysis that limits its scope (and reveals profound Eurocentric boundaries around the rhetoric of the unprecedented), but as interpretative readers we can see its resonance across theories of social death and the history of slavery and its afterlives. The deathworld is an *event*. Wyschogrod is careful to note that the space of the deathworld creates or changes a sense of world that makes "the scaffolding of experience itself," made from the ground up and then back again. An infrastructural claim, then, this notion of deathworld configures identity production in the seat of the worst imaginable violence. A violence that makes identity out of the Manichaeism of colonial and enslaving death: the identity of the killable class and the identity of the class that kills. Mbembe's iteration of this kind of world, a necropolitical world, clarifies the kinds and types of subjectivity that emerge out of death, noting how necropolitics scaffolds being and knowing *in the deathworld*, but also occupies the political imagination and any sense of thinking otherwise. Social death is not a merely feature of the world. It organizes being itself, experience itself, and therefore the meaning and experience of subjectivity. A dialectic of asymmetrical violence, producing asymmetrical identities out of and in one and the same world.

If we frame the necropolitical and its companion notion biopolitics as variations on deathworld, then I think the notion of deathworld is well fitted to Baldwin's thinking of economies of life, death, and racial formation. Baldwin is surely not drawing a portrait with a view toward something like the biopolitical precisely for the reasons Mbembe gives in distinguishing between necropolitics and biopolitics. Biopolitics is fundamentally about legislating the terms of life, how life and death *both* are parceled out in the management of populations. This is a productive model for understanding certain forms of antiblackness, but, like Mbembe, Baldwin is more concerned with how interracial space is organized around death than with the relationship between life and death. From the *white* perspective, it makes sense to understand the production of white identity as biopolitical; it is, after all, how white people give themselves life. White people would be lost without their dialectically produced class "Black" as a measure of the bottom of the well—the argument Baldwin makes in "Princes and Powers." But for what Baldwin calls "the Negro," the bottom of the well is not *only* a figure of the slave or a logic of opposing (or offsetting as marginal) to life, but also (or as a result) the existential experience of exposure to premature death and extrajudicial killing. So, this sense of vulnerability and the experience of death *suggests* a necropolitical reading; in Baldwin's most pessimistic moments, we can see resonance with Mbembe's description of the necropolitical as the "primary and absolute objective the enemy's murder."[17] At the same time, Baldwin's account of the dialectics of racial formation *needs* Black people in the very same measure that it needs white people. Extermination as the end of terror, the purpose and goal of terror, would only set white identity adrift and make it lost. Deathworlds *need* and *want* the social other in the same way that Patterson's account of social death needs that other. The world functions *as* death only—or, perhaps, most efficiently and cleanly—when the socially dead tarry alongside the living and occupy the mixed space between life and death. This is the paradox of eliminative racism. "Although the mode of temporalization in the deathworld closes off the future of its inhabitants," Wyschogrod writes, "its aims are often in the interest of another quite different future, that of the collectivity from which its inhabitants are excluded."[18]

Deathworld and dialectic: Baldwin's account of racial formation turns on the work of abjection and its ability to produce whiteness and blackness, which, in turn, reproduces a particular kind of deathworld. In the *movement* of racial formation's dialectic, we have to stay attentive to the residuals and elements of refusal. Is dialectic ever pure? Of course not. And so what is supplementarity to racial formation and abjection?

The Negro Remainder

If we think about racial identity formation as a dialectical process initiated and structured by the white gaze, then we have to shift our idea of what systematicity looks like. Dialectical racial formation, even in its truncated phase or modality, is identity in motion and in tension, vibrating with the fraught terms of relation, their politics, and their violence. Systematicity is therefore less a (putative) accomplishment of thought and the social order that reproduces it, and more like an aspiration or desire. We can see the aspiration or desire of the dialectic of racial identity in the truncation of that dialectic: white and Black identities calcify. That calcification reproduces one and the same society at some base level. Racism and race are actually inseparable.

How, then, does a truncated system open or show itself vulnerable to supplementarity?

In this context, we might theorize racial progress against claims of a closed system of social death and antiblack racism, something that, in his more optimistic turns, fascinates Baldwin. I am thinking here of Baldwin's repeated insistence that while someone like Malcolm X or the Nation of Islam widely is surely right about white people—the claim that whites are the devil, agents and perpetrators of the worst evil—he is also wrong. There is also another kind of white person for Baldwin. Or at least another *possibility*, the kinds of fleeting glimpses and hints we get in a novel like *Another Country*. Inside the deathworld that produces social death, such possibilities are limited and only seen in gesture or inside the jazz club or in a flash of intimate exchange, but these moments suggest, if one is looking for such a thing, a future that might be different. A sort of moral twist on his account of seeing the Texas GI abroad in "Encounter on the Seine," perhaps, but here writ large to the arc of interracial life in the United States. This is to read the question in terms of an emergent, nonexploitative sense of comparison and relation. Compelling, yes, in terms of imagining a revolutionary future, although such imagining is never quite Baldwin's temporality. Rather, there is for him first the question of remainder, the sense of the Negro, in Baldwin's vernacular, that *is* outside dialectical formation and, in that exteriority, a sign of the noncomparative.

For Baldwin, the enigma of this noncomparative identity—or maybe, better put, a sense of the humanity both outside and inside the infrahumanity of the socially dead—lies in the problem of signification itself. We do not really have a proper name for this identity and humanity. Fanon stumbled upon a similar enigma in his theorization of a new humanism and the strange temporality of the unprecedented future. Baldwin's temporality, however, is not oriented toward the unprecedented, but instead toward the remainder and its capacity to have *already* fractured the edges of the closed system—and then fabulated a sense of life in that borderlands. "Fracture" resonates in two ways. First, fracture works to name the insecure boundaries of a system's limits, which can be conceived as the result of resistance and revolutionary work or as the function of refusal inside the terms of antiblack worlds. Second, and entwined with this, fracture is the critical conceptual component of the secret life of refusal, a secret that secretes humanity outside the closed system and, in that secretion, marks *la frontera* of deathworld with possibilities *otherwise*. Between or in the milieu of these two resonances of fracture is the broader deconstructive sense of passage to the limit and the opening of the system. What is the surplus of humanity in the essence of social death and its deathworld?

This opening of the system of antiblackness, the grounds for the dialectic of racial formation, is already present in Baldwin's earliest bit of nonfiction. I am thinking of the close of his discussion of Richard Wright's *Native Son* in the 1949 essay "Everybody's Protest Novel," a strange and allusive piece that, in the end, amounts to calling Wright and Bigger Thomas the slur "Uncle Tom" by literally linking the character, and the author's vision, to the literary figure. It is a provocative claim that stings even in the twenty-first century, but the essay is not merely polemical. Baldwin's reflection on Wright makes a straightforward claim, one he makes multiple times across his nonfiction and always with the same insight: Bigger Thomas is the production and product of the white gaze and represents a sense of Black identity fully and wholly formed by that gaze. Uncle Tom is a distortion of the human person, even if, in Harriet Beecher Stowe's hands, he is intended to evoke sympathy. On our most generous reading, Stowe can be read as producing a figure of abjection in order to ask us to ask ourselves "Is this what our racist world has made? And how can we make things otherwise?" In that way, Wright's writing Bigger Thomas as the dimension of Uncle Tom that unleashes the rage produced by his abjection at the hands and eyes of whites is just an iteration of the same degradation. It is an iteration of the same degradation because it fails to take account of any difference between Bigger as seen and worked over by whites and Bigger as a human being with a complex inner state. That is, Wright fails to see Bigger's humanity—the supplement to the antiblackness that produces Bigger, to the antiblackness that produces Uncle Tom—even in the moment of profound, violent, and uncomplicated resistance. What does it mean to cast resistance without humanity? It means to always render Black life as social death and inside the carceral work of the white gaze. How does Baldwin navigate this space of resistance and the problem of humanity?

On a first reading, Baldwin's "Everybody's Protest Novel" simply wants to underscore how the protest novel as a genre—a genre to which both Stowe and the Wright of *Native Son* belong—is inextricably bound to the production of Black degradation. Degradation makes sympathy possible. Or so the protest novel would hope. Stowe and Wright, however different their approach to writing the affect of politics might be, share an approach that generates sympathy, not with a spectacle of shameful violence and death, but by folding Uncle Tom and Bigger Thomas into the familiar and the everyday: the deathworld. Deathworld is not *outside* Tom and Bigger. In fact, both are inside that world and produced by it; to be the character of social death is to be in and of deathworld. Baldwin likens this to a theology, which, in the context of "Everybody's Protest Novel," is the language of both creation—deathworld creates abject Black subjectivity—and of persistence across time, as if it were a metaphysical fact—deathworld is reproducible in its everydayness and familiarity. Baldwin writes:

> For Bigger's tragedy is not that he is cold or black or hungry, not even that he is American, black; but that he has accepted a theology that denies him life, that he admits the possibility of his being sub-human and feels constrained, therefore, to battle for his humanity according to those brutal criteria bequeathed him at his birth. But our humanity is our burden, our life; we need only to do what is infinitely more difficult—that is, accept it. The failure of the protest novel lies in its rejection of life, the human being, the denial of his beauty, dread, power, in its insistence that it is his categorization alone which is real and which cannot be transcended.[19]

Baldwin's remarks here are admittedly programmatic, writing a kind of promissory note to and toward an arc of thinking to come. A promise that, written inside this total and closed system—*a theology*—helps us begin to discern a sense of humanity that labors against social death and its deathworld. Laboring: perhaps only just a little, but also not nothing. Indeed, we can read so much of Baldwin's nonfiction as one long meditation on this closing remark to "Everybody's Protest Novel." What is the humanity of the inhuman? How is humanity possible in a world that only wants to see you perish?

Just two years after the publication of "Everybody's Protest Novel," Baldwin revisits the stories of Aunt Jemima and Uncle Tom and gestures toward a response to exactly these questions. The response requires sensitivity to supplementarity, to life outside the very dialectics of racial formation that underpins so much of his work—a key moment for seeing how Baldwin's understanding of the opening of the antiblack system of social death is built into, while also exterior to, that system. In "Many Thousands Gone," Baldwin revisits his critical remarks on Wright in the context of narratives of racial progress. What is the emergent and crucial difference between antebellum blackness and midcentury revisions of racial meaning from the perspective of Black people themselves? This is less a question about rights and institutions for Baldwin, and more a question about the fate of the racial imagination after Emancipation. Baldwin notes all the senses of progress, how the "almost as dark, but ferociously literate, well-dressed and scrubbed, who are never laughed at, who are not likely ever to set foot in a cotton or tobacco field or in any but the most modern of kitchens"[20] live in a world unrecognizable to Jemima and Tom, and how the world of that mythic pair seems so distant, so abject compared to their own. On this reckoning, progress shows up aesthetically and, in turn, existentially. How one is seen and how one imagines oneself being seen is central to racial self- and collective transformation—even as there are "others who remain, in our odd idiom, 'underprivileged.'"[21] What does it mean to see Jemima and Tom from this perspective, from the perspective of a thoroughly modern life? This is precisely how Wright sees Bigger: a remnant of an older era, but also someone hauntingly present, in his absence, in our thoroughly modern, post-Emancipation world. We can think here of Bigger's rage at his mother's comfort with abject poverty in the opening of *Native Son*, in which she scolds him for reacting too violently to a rat inside the home—a symbol of that abjection of Black life and Bigger's fury in confronting it, which then cleaves his relation to his mother and marks a difference Wright *imagines* makes all the difference in the world. Bigger sits *between*. Sitting in that between, functioning as the protagonist of Wright's most important work, Bigger reproduces precisely what he wants to eradicate: abject blackness. *Native Son* in that moment becomes a protest novel that indulges its other too intimately, too consistently, and perhaps too uncritically.

But in "Many Thousands Gone," Baldwin answers the critical question left open at the close of "Everybody's Protest Novel": What would it mean to affirm and explore the humanity of the abject, rather than let that abjection sit as a moral lesson? In other words, what if figures of social death were read-dressed as *humans*, as figures socially dead under the white gaze and its world, but also human *inside* and *at the margins of* social death? The should-perish subject is dead, yet also supplemented by a secret, then secreted, kind of humanity. The secret is critical here. Aunt Jemima and Uncle Tom, like Bigger, are humans and lived lives, like all of us, that are complex and also social—however hidden inside the folds of their unremunerated labor. That is, in their sociality *as* sociality, each is socially dead. What of the complexity? What of their origins, where they come from, and that exterior space in which they imagine their lives and those lives take on meaning? These questions are incompatible with the desire—righteous as it is—to consign both to the morally and politically distant past. Jemima and Tom appear to us in the closed system of antiblackness as unwitnessed. Abjection is by definition too much horror to behold. Jemima and Tom are present in body, of course, but the abjection that produces their social death buries their humanity so deeply that their very names trouble us. In fact, those names are no fun to even type. They signify social death in a failure to signify life. J̶e̶m̶i̶m̶a̶ and T̶o̶m̶ in the zone of nonbeing.

If the names Jemima and Tom are written in order to be crossed out, a gesture of sociometaphysical honesty, then we can understand the impulse and desire of Baldwin's ferociously literate, well-dressed, and scrubbed African Americans to excise the abject name and character from the imagination. This performs a kind of social death double session in which the remainder of dialectic is crossed out in order to double the absence of the socially dead. The margin is erased in the moment of folding it back into the center and its prerogatives. The consequence of this second erasure is the promise of an untroubled future, disentangled from the past and its persistence in the presence. But Baldwin demands that we trouble ourselves and our conscience with these questions anyway, whatever the discomforting effect. In "Many Thousands Gone," he asks simply and directly: "Before, however, our joy at the demise of Aunt Jemima and Uncle Tom approaches the indecent, we had better ask whence they sprang, how they lived? Into what limbo have they vanished?"[22]

This is such a complicated question, but asked by Baldwin with utter clarity and precision. The demise of the aunt and uncle as Aunt and Uncle is certainly to be celebrated. Those figures served the white gaze as both its production and a key site of the reproduction of white supremacy. Those figures also served a role for African Americans, as Baldwin points out here. Perhaps we could say that just as Black people served, for white people, as a sign of the bottom of the well and the measure of their own superiority, Aunt Jemima and Uncle Tom served as an opposition to remind a new generation and its sense of righteousness of what, for all the struggles undertaken from the streets to the bookshelves to the boardroom against white violence, they are not. That is, the decency of self-understanding and self-worth makes clearest sense when set in contrast and opposition to the indecency of Aunt and Uncle. The demise of their indecency is a marker of a certain kind of progress, but also a moment of forgetting of humanity at the margins of nihilism and complicity with the prerogatives of the center. Baldwin wants to remind us of just this in his revisiting of Jemima and Tom, and then, in that reminder and revisit, jolt our conscience.

What jolts our conscience? What is our forgetting?

Their life is set in limbo. They are Black and that sense of "Black" is produced by the worst kind of violence accumulated in and to their names. They are not condemned to some sort of hell because of their self-articulation; emerging as quasi-objects, saturated with absence mandated by our deathworld, Jemima and Tom cannot speak in any interracially common word. They are the subaltern in a most straightforward kind of way. It is important to always know that both were produced by the white gaze and that our ignorance of their life is a limit imposed by that gaze and our internalization of it, rather than through a flattening of their personhood by Aunt and Uncle themselves. Who sets and then keeps them in limbo? And how might that setting and keeping draw us into a relation of complicity with the white gaze and its methods of reading the Black body as a flattened signifier of nonlife and socially dead (anti- or ante-) personhood? Baldwin's reflection on this sort of signification will always remind us of the spectacle of abjection and how that spectacle overwhelms and structures even our resistance to it. This is Baldwin at his most nuanced, and also at his most troubling and intimately disruptive. It is worth quoting the key passage from "Many Thousands Gone" at length, where Baldwin writes:

> However inaccurate our portraits of them were, these portraits do suggest, not only the conditions, but the quality of their lives and the impact of this spectacle on our consciences. There was no one more forbearing than Aunt Jemima, no one stronger or more pious or more loyal or more wise; there was, at the same time, no one weaker or more faithless or more vicious and certainly no one more immoral. Uncle Tom, trustworthy and sexless, needed only to drop the title 'Uncle' to become violent, crafty, and sullen, a menace to any white woman who passed by. They prepared our feast tables and our burial clothes; and, if we could boast that we understood them, it was far more to the point and far more true that they understood us. . . . This was the piquant flavoring to the national joke, it lay behind our uneasiness as it lay behind our benevolence: Aunt Jemima and Uncle Tom, our creations, at the last evaded us; they had a life—their own,

perhaps a better life than ours—and they would never tell us what it was.[23]

This is a classic conceptual and affective move by Baldwin, a feature of his theorizing across the critical nonfiction. He begins with a rehearsal of scenes of abjection, but returns the gaze that makes the abject figure with a critical, gaze-reversing epistemological question: *Do we know them? And do they know us?* This question of knowledge gathers everything to it. It asks us why our gaze has so fixed their lives as abject that we do not see their exteriority, even in its elliptical indication. What does it say about *us* and the absorbing force of deathworld that humanity hides itself from us in the unremunerated work of absence in the dialectic of racial formation? It says to us that scenes of abjection, spectacles of the disgusting racial other, form subjectivity itself through active and passive acts of knowing, being, judging. We encounter our own violent, and troubling sociogeny. And we see the moral urgency of another kind of reading. What if we read abjection under erasure?

This sort of movement, the shift from what we know to what we cannot know but is indicated in an elliptical sense, is in many ways a simple affirmation of Black *humanity*. In the deathworld of antiblackness, however, such affirmation is neither straightforward nor intuitive inside our acts of knowing, being, and judging. Indeed, Baldwin's work is deeply dedicated to seeking and hopefully finding words for this affirmation, a discovery that is elusive precisely because the antiblack deathworld is a closed system. We ought not be able to see or know or describe life at the margins of nihilism. How might we see and know otherwise? That is, if we want to understand the humanity Jemima and Tom, even in their literary and dialectically racially formative rendering as abject figures, then we are asked to *think* outside what is made present to us. What is exterior to abjection? How can we figure, configure, and think that exterior? How does it interrupt social death in these important ways from both inside and outside the system of racial abjection?

Epistemology and ontology at the margins of nihilism asks us to ask otherwise.

Let me make and abrupt shift to an example outside Baldwin's texts, but inside this question of the margins. These critical questions about how to read absences, how to read under erasure, get important and relevant cinematic treatment in Cheryl Dunye's 1996 pseudo-documentary film *The Watermelon Woman*. Dunye's film focuses on an imaginative, embellished treatment by the film's main character Cheryl of a fictional character, presented in the film as a real historical actress and character named Fae Richards. Richards is depicted playing the role of a mammy character in the fictional movie *Plantation*

Memories—Dunye's film within the film. Though fictional, *Plantation Memories* and Richard's character in it could be drawn from nearly any actual cinematic work about the antebellum period. The depiction is simple, even comical, and it evokes all the tropes of midcentury American cinematic representation of Black women: exaggerated accents, pleading submission, loud and overspoken platitudes. It is entirely a repetition of the literary-cultural figure of Aunt Jemima and the cinematic paradigm *Gone with the Wind*. The representation in the film within the film is ridiculous, but in a way that really underscores the absurdity of the original figure of Aunt Jemima and the paradigm of Margaret Mitchell's story and Victor Fleming's direction. On the one hand, it is entirely ridiculous to believe that such a character could exist in a popular film. The portrayal in the film within a film is such an extreme caricature that it is both embarrassing and politically outrageous. On the other hand, it is entirely ridiculous to believe that such a character could not exist in popular film. The Watermelon Woman in *Watermelon Woman* is so exactly a copy of the American race movie and its political imagination that the film within a film is both familiar and ideologically affirming of the nation's history. Cheryl wants to know who this Fae Richards woman is and was, but no trace of her seems to exist outside the film. Richards and the mammy character are the abject other whose life makes *Plantation Memories* work, but that life inside (the character) and outside (the actress) the film eludes discovery, knowledge, and representation. Cheryl cannot know what she wants to know, which is the life that cannot be. What to make of this figure of the slave, doubled by the fact of representation (Richards plays an enslaved woman) and the absence that surrounds her presence in *Watermelon Woman* (the name and history of the actress are lost, even in the most obscure of archives)?

Against the abjection of Fae Richards, Cheryl, the main character who is herself an aspiring filmmaker, becomes obsessed with knowing the *true* story of Richards and the truth about the *woman*, her sexuality, and her blackness; Cheryl intuits, somehow, that there is a *secret* to the actress. Well, it is an intuition, yes, but Cheryl claims to sense that there is a secret—and it is somewhat comically played this way—rooted in the fact that Cheryl finds the actress sexually attractive. Is the attraction just lust? Or is it an indicator of something else, an epistemology embedded in Cheryl's Black lesbian gaze that is able to see more than what merely appears on screen as a flattened image? "Something in her face, something in the way she looks and moves, is serious, is interesting. And I'm going to just tell you all about it."[24] A suspicion. A desire. A comic start to what is a rambling comedic film. Cheryl's intuition-that-becomes-insight is a question of the namability and perceivability of Richards's double meaning, a meaning forged in the act of refusal that hides inside the representation of abjection. The actress *plays* a mammy, but Fae Richards is not herself a mammy. Is Fae lesbian? Does Cheryl *see* something secrete in the image, a secret in the image that somehow signifies in what is otherwise a socially dead figure? What would that mean, both in terms of how we look at and know Fae Richards—a figure modeled on Aunt Jemima—and how we remember her world and community—the signal of humanity inside absence? This problem of seeing, of reading at once for presence and for radical absence, initiates the film's narrative thread, a funky combination of documentary style and romantic comedy: Cheryl attempts to make a film about Fae's story, her Black lesbian community, and the secrets and corners of Philly club life. The problem is that there is no readily available information about Fae Richards *as* Fae Richards, only the representation of her as the essence of Aunt Jemima's abjection. No one can remember much about her. There is no existing narrative to revisit or revise. So, *The Watermelon Woman* unfolds as a story about Cheryl's discovery of what it would mean to tell this story without presence. Critical fabulation, perhaps, one that aims at articulating humanity in absence.

The key scene in *The Watermelon Woman* watches Cheryl visit the one archive she suspects holds helpful information: the archive at the Center for Lesbian Information and Technology, abbreviated with much humor and delight as CLIT. The archive is at once everything and nothing. It contains what little, almost nothing remains of Fae Richards's memory and, as trace memory with only the slightest of hints toward a path, leads Cheryl to the name of June Walker. Cheryl finds a photograph of Fae with June, her friend and lover, who is still living and tracked down at the close of the film. In lieu of meeting in person, June passes along a letter to Cheryl asking for the story of their relationship to be told. "You know, I thought it was going to be easy. I thought I was going to be able to use the camera to document my search for Fae, but instead I'm left empty-handed except this package from June."[25] The traces arrive, unsigned and without voice, so how can Cheryl tell this story? What can be made out of the small bits and pieces of memory, guided by intuition? In part, the answer is a cinematic form of critical fabulation; indeed, what the short bit of Cheryl's documentary film shows us is an *imagination* and *embellishment* of what fragments were available. It is precisely the availability of fragments and only fragments that marks the ultimate significance of Cheryl's to-come documentary and also the work of Dunye's film: what does it mean to tell a story when the archive turns up only silences and, at best, elliptical indicators? How does one read for absences? How does one make and create under erasure? "To me, a 25 year-old Black woman, it means something else. It means hope, it means inspiration, *it means possibility*. It *means history.*"²⁶ History, *histoire*—the science of storymaking *before* storytelling.

Reading for absences and storytelling or making under erasure is nothing other than the enigma of language: How are we to speak without presence? How do we conceive this space in which we must fashion and fabricate a story where a space of social death—the space of common evidence, of what is permitted to be said, in which social death evacuates meaning rather than produces it—makes very little, almost nothing available to us. Dunye instructs us: Cheryl's research fails and, in that failure, another film becomes possible.

The private and what is absent from the archive possess an important and deconstructive kind of opacity, an opacity that seals absence into itself yet also articulates, in its refusal of the play of presence and absence, a sense of the exterior. There is a story between or outside what can be told as life and what can be told as social death. This is a remainder or foreign element in the system that is also not in the system. Baldwin forces us to see ourselves in the abjection of Jemima and Tom for this reason; we are the Aunt and the Uncle qualifiers, even in our resistance to the grotesque racism that gives their abjection shape. Our gaze—and the *our* is an interracial one, clustered together in a moment of commitment to social death—qualifies their names with their position inside Being. But Baldwin *also*, in the very same gesture of nihilism, forces us to see that another story is in the archive of their lives, traces that we can glimpse but which need, like Cheryl's telling of Fae's life, critical embellishment and imagination. A double session that invites fabulation. The fabulated story, born out of the double session of nihilism and its unnamable margins, is *otherwise* than being and otherwise than the deathworld's construction of the zone of nonbeing, *otherwise* than hegemonic conditions of narration and the denial of full presence in the story that is the inexorable end of the socially dead. The dialectic of identity formation has its remainder, a nondialectical element that is not a negation of dialectics, but a fully exterior element. Derrida is particularly precise on this when he writes in a discussion of the deconstructive work of the secret: "If we take, for example, that which makes a dialectical process possible—namely, an element foreign to the system that transcends a group of categories . . . an element more or less than a table or series of categories—this foreign element, more originary than the dialectic, is precisely that which the dialectic is to dialectize, taking it into and including itself. . . . The non-dialectical does not oppose the dialectical, and is a figure that recurs continually."²⁷

It is this refusal to *oppose* that complicates the process of any dialectic. Dialectics work from opposition, after all; the entire work of dialectic is to overcome opposition. But this is not just a remainder or lost or left over and discarded element in sublation. It is the refusal of appearance, refusal to enter the order of being, and the refusal to comply with the logic that invariably produces social death. Derrida's description of the foreign element, the nondialectical and nonidentity element, is not resistance, but rather an exterior that recurs as supplement and, in its recurrence, performs as opacity and exteriority par excellence.

The difference between an opposition to dialectics, which is always subject to dialectical reclaiming, and the nondialectical foreign element is the difference between resistance (always subject to the logic of sublation) and something else—refusal, writing under erasure, the unrepresentable, the subaltern, and so on. It is the difference between, in this context, what Baldwin calls "the relationship that Negroes bear to one another" or the fabulation work Cheryl does in *The Watermelon Woman* for documentation of the lives of the socially dead and the economy of Being itself. But the logic of dialectics is forbidding. Forever voracious as a matter definition, dialectics is structurally impossible to evade. And yet there is refusal. How to imagine refusal of dialectics? This is the question of the nonstructural and the opening of the system. Nondialectical elements present an enigma by naming exteriority without entering into being and the possibility of a relation of negation. In configuring radical exteriority, spatiality *is not* and *cannot be* the language of configuration. Space, after all, marks a traversable distance. Rather, and this is one of the enduring insights of Emmanuel Levinas's work that Derrida picks up in his later writings, we must instead turn to time and its diachronic, dephasing anti- and ante-structural possibilities. Exteriority belongs to a different time, a time split off from the time of social death, unremunerated work made present, and the figure of the slave. In this sense, it is the time of the supplement lived as *world-making*. A formal consideration of time is crucial. We can think here of how Derrida works to delink phases of time, where he writes, "This dislocation of the present, which renders the present non-contemporary to itself and these people non-contemporary to one another, without that relationship with history and time which classical philosophies thought they had. These contemporaries are thus not contemporary at all."[28]

Temporal gaps are also more than formal consideration. Indeed, the deformalization of time in interstitial worlds, *la frontera*, and the space of the historical imagination is critical for self-understanding and meaning making—the very elements denied inside deathworlds and, as denial, the conditions of social death. Thinking deformalized time, diachrony, and *la frontera* as lived space also requires us to read under erasure, to see absence where and when it cannot be seen. Read with urgency, but also with critical attentiveness that eschews the need for presence. Jemima and Tom appear as social death when our gaze appends "Aunt" and "Uncle" to the first name. Their humanity is written under erasure.

Derrida is particularly interesting on this point as a theorist, specifically his work on the secret and its secretion. The time of the secret diachronically interrupts dialectics; secrets belong to time and dialectical relation as the nondialectical, the foreign element, the absence outside the play of presence and absence. But the time of the secret is also leaky. The secret shows itself to those who know how to *read* for the secret, whether that is Baldwin's evocation of vernacular life—named but not made transparent—or Dunye's character Cheryl responding to the archive that does not speak with her fabulation work inside cinematic language. The refusal of thematization by the unthematizable becomes withdrawal from presence. Yet, the unthematizable, the radically nonpresent, has its own mode of speaking, showing, and making and sustaining life. Derrida links this enigmatic mode of life to the logic of the secret as the ante- or anti-space of the thematizable, writing, "If I am to share something, to communicate, objectify, thematize, the condition is that there be something non-thematizable, non-objectifiable, non-sharable. And this 'something' is an absolute secret, it is the *ab-solutum* itself in the etymological sense of the term, i.e., that which is cut off from any bond, detached, and which cannot itself bind."[29]

This is such an important critical frame for understanding the elliptical indication of Aunt Jemima, Uncle Tom, and Fae Richards. While Dunye's film takes a step further than Baldwin's reckoning in "Many Thousands Gone," both arrive at a limit. The texts make passage to the limit of the secret and do not imagine limit to be the limit of their own intellects, creativity, or researcherly selves. In fact, it is very much the opposite. It is important that Cheryl dedicates all of her time to finding whatever can be known about Fae, but that, after gathering all that is and can be known, concedes that she knows very little, almost nothing *about Fae*, but, in that absence, knows something about herself and what it means to make this film as a fabulator of an impossible life. Baldwin cannot tell us what Jemima and Tom knew, felt, lived, and hid from us, but in that failure to tell or know, there is also the glimpse of humanity as a possibility, however inarticulable it is inside the structures of saying and naming we have available. *Absence as a kind of fecundity. Perhaps the most fecund fecundity.*

What is being asked of Baldwin and Dunye in this moment, and so what is being asked of us on the other side of this shock of the nonidentical?

In some ways, the passage to the limit and the fracturing of the boundaries of the closed system of racial formation bring us back to the strange space, which is actually time, of Jemima and Tom. An unthematizable and unnamable space, place, and time, to be sure, but we *can* name its site and citation. We can imagine the kitchen, after service hours, in which Jemima and Tom speak to one another. Their speaking manifests a relation that lay hidden in the interracial world of daily life, a life of social death and abjection. Unhidden, secreted and no longer secret, there is another kind of language. What did they say to themselves? What did they say to one another? What did their language do to make a world? It is another kind of language because Jemima and Tom do not have words for one another in their humanity inside the language of the racial everyday. They speak in the kitchen. A hidden, private, secret room. They speak as aliveness, not as social death and also not as the aftermath of white recognition. But they speak in ways that we cannot comprehend. Borderland language is not the nation's language.

This kitchen is between racial formation as we know it and a humanism made to the measure of the world. Between the colony and the emancipated postcolonial. Their language *otherwise* is between, what Baldwin described as a kind of limbo. A speaking in the antechamber of the decolonial. A speaking at the margins of nihilism.

3
Nihilism and the Refusal of Refusal in Wright and Fanon

What generates nihilism inside the Black intellectual tradition?

This question sits at the heart of the Black Atlantic tradition in its reckoning with centuries of enslavement, colonialism, neocolonialism, segregation, and all the varied forms of antiblackness that animate our world. Animation of the world is the condition of our very being, how we know, and what it means to live and breathe in common places, saturating life itself with a profound sense of meaninglessness at its center. A zone of nonbeing that makes being possible. Nihilism is at once an ontology, an epistemological claim (or protoclaim), and an affective regime. That is, nihilism in the tradition forms multiple senses of being, whether the being of subjectivity, the being of our intersubjective life, or the being of the world in its difference and indifference. Nihilism is in this way a form of knowing in a pair of intertwined senses: something that one knows from the experience of racial nihilism (it is a kernel of insight that shows up in order to produce experience) and something that requires a certain relation to blackness in order to know in the deepest and most expansive senses (a condition for knowing rooted in a relation, derived from historical experience, to the being of the world). And, perhaps most importantly, racial nihilism is an affective regime in the sense that affects of despair, rage, resignation, shame, hopelessness, and melancholy work as symptoms of a larger infrastructure of the world and of relationality as such. If we conceive nihilism in this way, drawing our clues from the symptomatic witness and testimony of the tradition, then it is clear that the sense of the meaninglessness of life and world is not a concept that supervenes on a more generalized structure of being, but is instead a foundation of the world itself. Nihilism as a cornerstone element of sociogeny. We have already seen an iteration of this conception of world and nihilism in the treatment of James Baldwin's descriptions of the ghetto and should-perish subjectivity. The deathworld is a variation, whatever the important, nuanced differences, of nihilism, which in context is a kind of witness to the manifold senses of atrocity in Atlantic world history.

In this sense, we can say that the nihilism arising from the experience of antiblack violence(s), a characteristic of being and world, is an entire system. The ontological and epistemological resonances of nihilism gesture at this feature, shifting and moving our analytical attention away from the characterizing nihilistic *elements* of social and political arrangements as structural elements and toward the symptomological work that sees what appears as a *feature* but is in fact an *indicative manifestation* of a base structure of being and world. Historical experience and its capacity to forge and remake being itself is crucial here. The atrocity structure of the Atlantic world sediments in memory, shaping how we anticipate the world's meaning, significance, and ritual unfolding, but that sedimentation also, and perhaps firstly, touches being itself. Who and what we are is generated *from* atrocity structure(s). If we begin here, which means beginning at the origin of the Atlantic world, then we begin with an important affective embellishment of what Frantz Fanon described in his account of sociogeny. Sociogeny, the generative function of the social in forming subjectivity and its various expressions, is not a bare or bland fact of the world. Rather, it saturates the world, subjectivity, and intersubjectivity. That saturation seeps into the body and its nervous system, forming and reforming the incarnate psyche in the modality of nihilism. From being to beings and back to being. A total vision of nihilism. This makes nihilism and its antiblack racist infrastructure a closed system—or, at least, a system that *wants* to close itself and envelop within it all human possibilities. In this way, racial nihilism performs important, even base-structural ideological work in both producing and reproducing a society that makes sense of self, other, and the moral-political imagination *as* this nihilism. Reproduce the social, reproduce being, reproduce world, reproduce subjectivity. Antiblackness therein appears as a quasi-metaphysical fact in the process of reproduction precisely because it structures the world while also remaining invisible as a social fact.

But social reproduction is still social, which means that the structure of this form of alienation and violence is simultaneously vulnerable to rupture—revolutionary action, radical interventions of all sorts—and comprises boundaries made of human meaning, racial formation, desire, despair, resistance, and hegemony. All hegemonies are vulnerable. This is a basic insight into the structure of worlds open to change and accounts for the persistent and ever-present call for radical action. The roots of a society can be uprooted. Something new can be made *after*. And so in the remarks below, it will become ever more apparent why Fanon is a key figure: nihilist in diagnosis, revolutionary in action.

But is revolutionary action the only rupture in the boundary of a closed system? Closure is a word for and characterization of the aggression of atrocity's repetition, compromising and collapsing time into itself in order to render the victims of atrocity in a state of torpor and secure the cycle of reproduction pending apocalypse—political or otherwise. And here is where the thought of the supplement and social death are particularly revealing. Supplementarity and social death, thought at their crossroads, open up a sense of dimensionality in being or, perhaps more radically, expose the borders of being to be leaky and fractured by what remains unthinkable inside closure. How does the system of racial nihilism, produced and reproduced in the manufacture of the socially dead, depend upon something with which it cannot quite reckon, that trace of the system that structures the system? Where is the deconstructive moment? What is the dimensionality of the unremunerated element and moment? The figure of the slave appears here as a ghost, a specter haunting post-Emancipation life as the troubled and troubling presence *and* complicated nonpresence of vernacular life. Vernacularity, as we shall see, is that enigma inside *and* outside closed systems of atrocity which exposes the leaky and fractured character of the margins thought as margin, *pharmakon*, and difference. A critical theoretical approach to vernacular language and culture, one that sees it both in presence and an absence haunting presence, helps us see how fraught the question of cultural production is under conditions of antiblack racism and its nihilistic effects and affects. Fraught, that is, in terms of how vernacularity is contingent upon abjection and also how that abjection is transformed in vernacular culture's practices of everyday and metatheoretical refusal.

And so, across the reflections that follow, I want to explore how vernacular life is represented under erasure in Fanon, as a deep ambivalence in Richard Wright, and how it works as an ontological and epistemological subversion of both. In this way, I want to show how vernacular life functions as the supplement to the system of racial nihilism, which means, in this context, that the very system that produces the pain of antiblack racism and the sadistic pleasures of white supremacy *also* produces a world generated in and by the work of refusal. This concedes at a certain level that refusal is embedded in and contingent upon practices of antiblack racism. Such concession embeds the question of the vernacular inside the very discourse it disrupts, which situates critical discursive intervention as immanent critique. Critique from inside the urge for closure, not outside systematicity and its hegemonic fantasies. *Margin as exterior in the system of nihilism.* This embedded moment therefore calls for a double reading, one that revisits the scene of abjection in order to chart the subversive path of vernacularity that is simultaneous with its contingency. That refusal, which is very different than resistance and revolutionary action, *appears* in Wright and Fanon, but, in its mere appearance and ghostly force, cannot find voice amid their pervasive and foundational apocalyptic tone. It cannot find its voice because, in their refusal of refusal, Wright and Fanon envision the only exit from the system as either submission to racial nihilism or the complete destruction of the world in search of the new. Defeat or apocalypse. And, in a certain register, that makes perfect sense. Resistance and revolution are of course warranted, urgent, and, one would hope, inexorable; the humanity of the infrahuman secretes in *la frontera* of refusal's life, but also bursts forth with destructive, revolutionary force in what Geo Maher has called *anticolonial eruption*.[1] But, refusal is nothing like a survival strategy or resilience practice that lets empire flourish. Refusal makes worlds at the margins of nihilism. What would it mean to think refusal *on its own terms*, rather than as a pause before or a survival strategy in lieu of revolutionary action? What would it mean to see refusal as a twist and variation on Baldwin's sense of secret lives and their secretion in order to catch sight of what cannot make sense, what cannot appear as a world, and what cannot be rendered on empire's own terms inside the frame of racial nihilism? Thought as the exterior in that frame, the contours and complexities of social death enact radical deconstructive practice.

    This movement in and out of racial nihilism shifts the grounds of being and knowing. Such shifts alter our imagination of subjectivity and its possibilities: how we imagine ourselves, how we bear a relation to time, and how social death is a phased element in the lived experience in and exterior to interracial life. Subjectivity, it must be said, is inextricably comprised of relation. No subject is an island, and we have meaningful senses of personhood inside terms of relation to others and the world we make, share, and negotiate. The consequences of this are both nihilistic and, under erasure, open to the *otherwise*. Antiblackness produces subjects, then through its institutionalization and *habitus* in everyday life reproduces the same essential social form. Is there surplus in that essential social form? What might the exterior to that system produce, in terms of the possibilities of imagining relation and the self? Relation is a matter of knowing in the sense of how conditions of knowing are constructed in an antiblack, racially nihilistic world and how subject position in that world make certain kinds of knowledge possible. Antiblackness produces subjects who know their own subjection, who know the world as social death and its flattening of existence. But what *other* kinds of knowledge are embedded in vernacular practices and traditions? How do those practices and traditions address the complexity of exteriority, the supplement, and life/death outside of the production of social death?

Richard Wright and Frantz Fanon are especially compelling figures and sites for thinking this set of problematics. Wright and Fanon are deeply, perhaps irreversibly, nihilistic thinkers. This is certainly not a controversial statement about Wright, who from the beginning wrote the most terrifying aspects of Black existence into fiction, but it is a more complicated claim in the case of Fanon. For both, the facticity of interracial life is the irrevocable and recurring condition of social death. There is no authenticity to Black life in the world as we know it nor in how the world knows us. Sociogenic conditions create Black life in an antiblack world, which forms the relation of Black self to self as well as interracial relations out of antiblack terms, conditions, concepts, and imaginations of possibility. That shared assessment in and of itself is no particular outlier in the Black intellectual tradition. Most honest reckoning with historical experience arrives at some variation of this conclusion. But what is striking about Wright and Fanon and why they are worth reading together around the question of nihilism is how they both embed nihilism inside the very structure of the world and subjectivity, an embedding that renders all possibilities impossible. Social death appears as the immovable fact of Black life. A metaphysical and ontological claim. Nihilism is therefore not simply a feature of the world or of Black subjects subjected to and subjugated in that world, but instead a closed system of possible modes of being and knowing of all beings who come to be inside that system. Being and knowing, then, become variations on antiblackness and movement or agitation. To exist other than under white hegemony is fatal. This is another version, we could say, of Baldwin's description of should-perish subjectivity and of the dialectical work of racial identity formation. How is this nihilism accounted for in Wright's and Fanon's work? And, in that accounting, what signals—however quietly, however nascently, however enmeshed in the secretion of secrets—fissure at the boundary of systematicity, at the margins of nihilism? What is the trace-life of *la frontera*?

The Spatial Ontology of Nihilism

Richard Wright's short story "The Man Who Lived Underground" is an astonishing journey into racial nihilism. Published in the collection *Eight Men*, the short story—which was published six decades after his death as an incomplete but fully reedited novel[2]—tells the story of Fred Daniels, a man, per the title, who lives underground. Or flees underground in search of something other than social death. The other short stories gathered in *Eight Men* take up the complexity of Black manhood in a world of antiblack racism and interracial—and then, for Wright, intraracial too—misandry. Melancholic and angry stories, all of them. But the rage that secretes from the pages of these stories is wrapped in existential reflection, simple prose, and a clear (if at times overly blunt) vision of Black life in a world that renders that life, from its first breath, as some form of social death.

It is no provocation to say that Wright's writing is broadly speaking obsessed with social death, nor is it particularly edgy to note that his writing holds fast to irreducible truths of antiblack violence. Witness, in Wright's pen, is layered with significance, especially around the vulnerability of the body's visibility and the estranged relation that that vulnerability, folded as it is into a terrifying past, bears to time. That is, the sustained engagement with social death we find in Wright's fiction is inextricably and irredeemably linked to nihilism and its closure of futurity. As we see in the reflections below, the temporality of his critical intervention is immensely important for thinking about the intractable, closed character of nihilism and its (putative) foreclosure of an outside. For now, however, it is enough to sit with how Wright is our most visceral witness to this sense of death and nihilism, infusing it with existential meaning that exceeds mere institutional or psychological content. The entirety of the world bears on the Black body and on the spirit of his protagonists. The entirety of the world. A world with no escape.

We see this first in the 1940 novel *Native Son*, of course, which has been treated above in terms of how it is theorized in Baldwin's conception of death-world and the possibility of exit. The weight of nihilism is also present with particular cynical force in Wright's 1953 novel *The Outsider*. In *The Outsider*, a rambling, in some ways understructured, but philosophically compelling reflection on violence, race, and existential meaning, Wright describes with intense detail the life of Cross Damon and the search for some anchor of a meaningful life in Chicago. Religion, nation, and politics all fail to give life substantial meaning, leading to what Abdul JanMohamed in his masterful work *The Death-Bound-Subject* describes as Wright's temporal twist on social death: All action, all contemplation, and all struggle is ultimately oriented toward a *nihilistic* encounter with one's own death as brutal and without mediation or redemption. One's own death as a *Black* person, of course; Wright is no thinker of the generalized human condition. What we learn from Jan-Mohamed's study is that the death-bound-subject is nihilistic across the entire stretch of existential time: natal, irruptive, fatal. Birth, life, death. Damon's murder at the end of *The Outsider* is in that way no shock at all, not because Wright has foretold his death, but because what we understand not only in the 1953 novel, but also in *Native Son* and most of the serious fiction that follows, is that social death is natal. From birth, toward death. What binds the Black subject to itself and to its world is the persistent presence and haunting threat of premature, random, cruel, unforgivable, extrajudicial, and inexorable death. Violent death. Unprompted and unnecessary death. This is the unflinching witness in Wright's work, attuned to the cruelty of the interracial world and without the pacifying pleasures of Black joy, resistance, or refusal. Nihilism takes up all of the space in Wright's fiction and forms the entirety of the meaning of subjectivity. Cross Damon says as much when he notes, reflecting on himself and his life, that he "was not really in the world; he was haunting it for his place, pleading for entrance into life."[3] Life as a plea rather than struggle or even defeat—Wright is here articulating a sense of nihilism that is both the condition of living in an antiblack world and that saturates the antechamber of existence. Nihilism stains even the desire to be. As well, this description of social death as a haunting presence in the world—both outside it and desiring a place—spatializes the existential subject of Wright's nihilism. It is not simply a question of the broader structure of the world or of modernity or of the age of technology. Estrangement and death are intertwined, showing in that mixture how life itself has no place for Black people and that Cross Damon, along with so many of Wright's characters, will show us what it means to be a subject subjected to this intensity of natal alienation. Plea. Haunt. A zone of nonbeing before the play of being and nonbeing.

What I find compelling about Wright's literary treatments of social death, especially in this spatializing configuration of life and death, is how the possibilities of life *as* life—that is, not socially dead and wandering or haunting in search of place—emerge only when *not* being seen. Invisibility and illegibility are where Black life becomes imaginable, even if not possible in any kind of sustained way. This runs so counter to so much of our contemporary vernacular around liberation struggle. Our common language for liberation often sees heightened presence and voice as the key to freedom and recognition. Invisibility is a condition and effect of subjection, violence, and erasure. But for Wright, and he names something incredibly important and enduring here, visibility itself is the threat, the problem, and thus the condition of social death itself. Wright understands, as did Fanon, that the white gaze is not only an imperial power, but also, perhaps firstly and most profoundly, necropolitical opticality. To be seen is to be subject to death. Being-seen is a synonym for a death-bound-subject. The Black *body* is vulnerable and the site of the erasure of Black *people* and Black *life* through mass violence and natal alienation. Little of *people* and *life* are visible targets—collective personhood and life hides inside the body, is situated as invisible bonds between persons—but the mere presence of the Black body is simultaneously a threat and, as we see in "The

Man Who Lived Underground," a fatal necessity. Whether the murder of Fred Daniels in "The Man Who Lived Underground" or the slow legal death of Bigger Thomas in *Native Son* or any of Wright's other eruptions and interruptions of social death with death's finality, social death can only be supplanted or overturned by our incarnate mortality. Social death is not a form of life but instead a suspension of life in the prefiguration of the body as already dead. Extrinsic to the time of living, the figure of the slave is the worst kind of zombie, one who does not even have the common grace of indefatigable pursuit of revenge. For Wright, then, Black people either live haunting life and plead for place, or they leave this worldly world after subjection to anonymous social murder. "He sighed and closed his eyes," Wright writes, describing Fred Daniels's death, "a whirling object rushing alone in the darkness, veering, tossing, lost in the heart of the earth."[4]

In the interest of thinking of this plea for place, let us consider Fred Daniels's life underground as *living* underground. What are the existential stakes of the spatial schematization of Black life? What does it say about Wright's conception of nihilism and its place in the formation of a subjectivity fated to death? The collection *Eight Men* is arranged, in terms of its ordering of stories, according to its own kind of dramatic fashion, framing "The Man Who Lived Underground" with the problem of life and masculinity in the just prior short story "The Man Who Was Almost a Man." This latter story focuses on a young male character, Dave Saunders, who, for all of his particularity, manifests a broad claim about and figure of abjection in the rural South. Dave's abjection is not irreducible but instead felt and then resisted. The son of sharecroppers who is faced with the meaninglessness of life under the Jim Crow regime, Dave becomes fascinated with the gun as a sign of power, masculinity, and, as a consequence of entwining power and manhood in his moment, his total vision of personhood. Wright begins the story with a series of emasculations, whether generated from the conditions of sharecropping and its extension of slavery into the contemporary or from the intimacy of family life. Again, as in *Native Son*, the maternal serves as a site of clarification of abjection (the mother character is presented in order to be viewed with disgust) and a reproduction of it (she makes demands on Dave that thieve his manhood). Between the mother and Jim Crow, Dave's body is spatialized to the point of rupture and fragmentation; he cannot retrieve his manhood because the whole of his self is either invisible or rendered inoperative. Invisible, inoperative, or figuratively (and perhaps literally) impotent, the short story unfolds as a dramatic of self-making, but self-making on the model of the ideologically reproductive conditions of necropolitics: To be is to take life with violence.

Or at least possess the capacity to take life.

Possibility *is* subjectivity in the necropolitical order, but that is possibility in which the killing class asserts a sense of life while rendering the killable or disposable class socially dead. Dave is socially dead, which is the condition of the Jim Crow south for southern Black people. But Dave *wants* his full humanity. That humanity is tantamount to liberation from the nihilism of the everyday, animated and anchored in "The Man Who Was Almost a Man" through desire and fantasy. Yet, he cannot see or imagine that humanity outside of the capacity to take life, which anchors desire and fantasy in the social-political imaginary. Necropolitics lived as liberation theory. As a sign of his abjection and desire to reverse the political order of things, the gun, a contrast point to his abject condition, becomes Dave's object of erotic fascination—the sublime to his lived negative sublime. That is the gun's promise. Wright describes this first as a possibility, a dream, a fantasy: "When his father and brother had left the kitchen, he still sat and looked again at the guns in the catalogue, longing to muster courage enough to present his case to his mother. Lawd, ef Ah only had tha pretty one! He could almost feel the slickness of the weapon with his fingers. If he had a gun like that he would polish it and keep it shining so it would never rust. N Ah'd keep it loaded, by Gawd!"[5]

So much of Wright's work on Black masculinity turns on this question of courage and "The Man Who Was Almost a Man" draws that question back to its most difficult moment: the South and the family. How does one imagine a moment of self-possession and full subjectivity in a necropolitical world, a world designed only for Black death (social and material) that is also entrenched in feelings of inferiority and natural submission grounded in more than three centuries of enslavement and its aftermath? That is Wright's existential question, rooted in the intersection of the historically impossible and the politically necessary. And here, on the question of courage to *be* or *make one's self* a man, we can also think of the juxtaposition of desire and abjection in the opening scenes of *Native Son*, where Bigger Thomas's willingness and exuberance around killing a rat makes him the exception in his family home, setting the mother as the masculine other—something made even more explicit in the 1951 film adaptation of the novel, starring Wright himself in the lead role. In both the film and the novel, Bigger, like Dave in this passage from "The Man Who Was Almost a Man," is marked in his difference by a desire to kill. The skillet in the novel, then the gun in the short story, is that figure. It is also what discloses with particular clarity the conditions of social death. Bigger's mother seals the characterization. "Sometimes you act the biggest fool I ever saw," his mother complains after Bigger kills the rat in their apartment. And then, doubling the violence against Bigger's violence: "We wouldn't have to live in this garbage dump if you had any manhood in you."[6]

The gun signifies the fault line between life and social death in a very particular context: the necropolitical order. The necropolitical order identifies not only the structure of worlds organized around the production of a killable population, but also the terms of the experience of freedom over self and world in the population politically authorized to kill. "To kill or to allow to live constitute the limits of sovereignty," as Achille Mbembe puts it in his famous essay.[7] In "The Man Who Was Almost a Man," Wright makes it plain that this is exactly what structures Dave's imagination of liberation:

> The first movement he made the following morning was to reach under his pillow for the gun. In the gray light of dawn he held it loosely, feeling a sense of power. Could kill a man with a gun like this. Kill anybody, black or white. And if he were holding his gun in his hand, nobody could run over him; they would have to respect him. It was a big gun, with a long barrel and a heavy handle. He raised and lowered it in his hand, marveling at its weight.[8]

This is an immensely important passage for understanding not only Wright's political imagination, but also how deeply nihilism runs across his fiction. The natal scene of social death is repeated here in the moment of waking up from a night's sleep, literally rebirthing the day and life's possibilities. The new that is each morning is revised by Dave as the possibility of the possibility of violence. Not yet violence, here, because the act of killing remains at the level of desire and fantasy. Rather, the gun's presence under the pillow *promises*, without surety of fulfillment, power and sovereignty. A promise because the necropolitical is more than just a feature of the world. It is, rather, an entire orientation of thinking itself. How to think in the necropolitical is folded by Dave, and so by Wright, into the question of the desire to kill.

The wake of obtaining the gun is no dream fulfillment, however. The enormity of the plantation space, complete with beasts of burden and the big house, humbles Dave's imagination. Sovereignty cannot *be* on the plantation because its system of social death is closed. No matter his contempt for her, Dave concedes to his mother's racial-political realism: Social death is not a negotiable feature of the plantation-sharecropping world, but rather a condition of being in that world and landscape itself. Social death diverts the fantasy of claiming and reversing a sense of necropolitical power, redirecting the critical gaze back to the conditions of being and time. In *this* time, the time of the plantation past folded into the present, the gun is not manhood. And so Wright closes the story with an evocation of the time of nihilism, the indefinite and elliptical deferral. He writes: "The cars slid past, steel grinding upon steel. Ahm ridin yuh ternight, so hep me Gawd! He was hot all over. He hesitated just a moment; then he grabbed, pulled atop a car, and lay flat. He felt his pocket; the gun was still there. Ahead the long rails were glinting in the moonlight, stretching away, away to somewhere, somewhere where he could be a man."[9]

To be sure, Wright is in many ways just documenting the great migration here, with its painful, yet immensely pleasurable moment of decision. Fleeing the terror of the South held *promise* for African Americans, promise of a sovereignty that would not be linked to the gun. But rather than imagine that imagination of the future, the time of the promise, Wright places the gun in the position—literally and figuratively—of the phallus. It draws power from the body's figuration of manhood, yet that power proves fleeting, illusory, and subject to the very nihilism that made it *seem* like a necropolitical iteration of liberatory possibility.

The sequencing of stories in *Eight Men* is either a wonderful coincidence or nice bit of editorial craft: "The Man Who Lived Underground" follows immediately after "The Man Who Was Almost a Man." The latter ends with the evocation of an elsewhere. We do not know if that elsewhere is pure fantasy and escape from nihilism or the very real possibility of another life. That is the story of the great migration and the story of Wright's own escape from Mississippi—only to be decimated by the variants of nihilism in Chicago, then Harlem. It is also, in that way, the story of hope in an antiblack world. *Perhaps this new moment will prove to be everything we wanted and for which we hoped.* But, as we discover in "The Man Who Lived Underground," for Wright nihilism is a foundational structure of the world. It is not something to escape. Rather, nihilism is in time itself. What kind of time? And how do we make sense of that time?

If "The Man Who Was Almost a Man" lays out the spatiality of the imaginary of life-as-social-death in an antiblack world, moving from the rural South to an elsewhere negotiated by the gun and its phallic power, then "The Man Who Lived Underground" adds dimensionality to that geography in its documentation of the psychic resonance of escape—Wright's writing of a sort of urban *marronage* at the level of the imagination. Fred Daniels, Wright's protagonist in the story, takes flight from the police and, after spotting a manhole cover, sneaks into the underground in order to avoid arrest and physical brutality. The movement underground is an escape from the direct violence of threat, but also from the persistent, relentless, and decimating violence of visibility itself. To be visible is to be exposed as the killable class; necropolitics and visibility, configured as above- and underground, go hand in hand. Escape from threat is escape from a certain political reality and ontology of the Black subject. Self-erasure, the disappearance of the self from all modes of appearance (while underground, Daniels is invisible to everyone except himself), is the condition of the experience of freedom. A radical experiment in autoaffection. And the terms of this experience are blunt and straightforward: To be is to *not* be, or to be in such a modified form—ephemeral, fleeting, ineffectual—that it barely if at all resembles subjectivity. Who is Daniels underground? We can discern a bit of that *who*. What is Daniels underground? There is no name for this kind of being except what is, for Wright, an impossible phrase: *Black and free*.

In the underground, Daniels's voice is the author's voice, surveying so many of Wright's personal social and political journeys, criticisms, and anxieties. I am thinking here of two examples in particular. Daniels comes across a cache of money and, while gazing at the bills, he shifts back and forth between fascination with their very presence and bemused contempt for their illusory meaning, responses that reflect Wright's time and experience as a communist. The meaning of money as not just a system of value, but as a fetish commodity reveals something absurd about the conditions of antiblack oppression and exploitation—from chattel slavery to wage slavery—as well as the kind of aspirations the talented tenth have for themselves and the other ninety percent. Instead of a pound of flesh, a portion of excess wealth accumulation. More money, more illusions. And troubles. And exploitation. And cruelty. There is also Daniels listening to and witnessing a church service, which he finds absurd, sad, and worthy of nothing but pitiful contempt, a response that mirrors Wright's own critical confrontations with his religious background and the place of Christianity in an antiblack world. So, when he writes of Daniels that he

> edged to the crevice and saw a segment of black men and women, dressed in white robes, singing, holding tattered songbooks in their black palms. His first impulse was to laugh, but he checked himself. . . .
>
> Just singing with the air of the sewer blowing in on them. . . . He felt that he was gazing upon something abysmally obscene, yet he could not bring himself to leave.[10]

The abysmal obscenity of this religious service tells us a story about Wright's critical sources—both Karl Marx and Friedrich Nietzsche—and also his own fascination with what Black life has wrought from its pain. Wright's ambivalence here is not a hesitation before critique, but instead a manifestation of Daniels's lingering doubts and his early acclimation to life underground. The story is in some ways really just an account of that acclimation and how at each turn Daniels, like Wright himself, comes to see the aboveground world, the world in which we *actually* live, as abject and both morally and politically reprehensible. Unlivable in every measure. Absent of hope. Nihilism without margins.

All that Daniels sees underground is a remnant or signal of racial nihilism. What is wrought from the pain of Black life is animated by the trace forces of that pain, rendering expressive and material life nothing more than a modality of social death. We can think here of the abject choir singing while awash in sewer fumes or the deranged and delirious vison of a drown corpse of a baby—surely an evocation of Nietzsche's three stages of the self in *Thus Spoke Zarathustra*, underscoring for Wright how Black childhood, unlike Nietzsche's white figure of self-overcoming, arrives dead in the world. Evoking Nietzsche's figure of self-overcoming and rethinking it as the most abject image, a dead baby, seals Wright's account of nihilism in the most graphic and visceral way possible. Natal alienation, natal nihilism. It is this overwhelming sense of nihilism, even in Daniels's line of flight and his underground *marronage*, that compels him to exit. Daniels's exit from the underground is a concession to all of this. Concession, that is, not in the sense that the aboveground is somehow different after his shadow experience of freedom, but because the inevitable is just that: inevitable. "The spell was broken," Wright writes. "He shuddered, feeling that, in spite of his fear, sooner or later he would go up into that dead sunshine and somehow say something to somebody about all this."[11] At the exit, his reentry into the meaning of aboveground and its fatal vulnerabilities, that space of social death as the mode of being and being of the world, is as clear as dead sunshine. Three police surround Daniels and shoot him. As he dies, Wright seals nihilism as a necessity.

"What did you shoot him for, Lawson?"
"I had to."
"Why?"
"You've got to shoot his kind. They'd wreck things."[12]

I had to. This is Wright's deepest characterization of nihilism. Sealed in necessity with no exit. An exit into the abyss. "He sighed and closed his eyes," Wright writes as Daniels fades into his own death, "a whirling object rushing alone in the darkness, veering, tossing, lost in the heart of the earth."[13] Nihilism is a cradle to grave *lieu commun*.

In Fanon's first work, *Black Skin, White Masks*, we see a parallel account of racial nihilism and social death. Fanon does not spatialize nihilism in the same ways we find in Wright, which probably says as much about the difference between Caribbean landscapes and rural/urban geographies in the United States as it does about genres of theoretical writing. Rhetorically there are immense differences, and rhetoric is critical for argument making and phenomenological demonstration, to be sure, but the sense of nihilism lurking around every corner of Black life inside interracial space is similarly relentless. *Black Skin, White Masks* begins with the terms of this nihilism: The fate of the Black subject is to be white. An impossibility, and this is an impossibility with expansive catastrophic consequences. To be in interracial space is to *not* be. Belonging in that space as a Black would require self-erasure, to cease being Black—an impossibility, for Fanon, according to the terms of his description of racial identification as an epidermal schematic.

We can think here of how Fanon describes interracial desire in the second and third chapters of *Black Skin, White Masks*. These two chapters are often clipped off from the rest of the book, segmented for independent considerations of Fanon, gender, and feminism. However, rather than boutique concerns or extended excurses, they are actually crucial chapters for the book's larger argument that colonialism's project is so total and so comprehensive that not even the most discrete desires escape colonization. Colonialism is seated in the most intimate, private reaches of our consciousness. Desire is not a mere psychological state for Fanon, but instead a spatialization of the internalization of antiblack racism in the desiring body. How do I desire? And what is it that satisfies, or could satisfy, that desire? Fanon's example and most racially fraught site of reflection, interracial desire and sexuality, is political in the broadest sense of colonial hegemony. Sexuality is the transformation of the psyche from the inside, spatializing desire across bodies that manifest, in touch and pleasure, the worst of colonial oppression. Fanon writes, in a vaguely lecherous passage:

> By loving me, she proves to me that I am worthy of a white love. I am loved like a white man.
> I am a white man.
> Her love opens the illustrious path that leads to total fulfillment . . .
> I espouse white culture, white beauty, white whiteness.
> Between these white breasts that my wandering hands fondle, white civilization and worthiness become mine.[14]

Far from a particular anxiety around interracial sex, these remarks are crucial parts of a larger systematic claim. In particular, this passage recalls Fanon's remarks on language in the opening chapter of *Black Skin, White Masks*, remarks in which he describes the act of speaking in the very same terms. To speak a language is to take on an entire civilization, to enter its world, to be enveloped, in some way, by the closed system of its meaning. But this entry into and taking on is only an iteration of natal alienation and social death. The cruelty of diction as a colonial practice marks the limit of possibility. Black speakers of French are never *French*, but instead always and only *Black* speakers of French. That gap, that reversal of meaning through a point of emphasis, is the color line: Black, not French. The epidermal racial schematic is made interior in acts of speaking, hearing, and the racial taxonomic practice that quietly embeds in both. And so in theorizing the anxious state of interracial desire, the white woman functions as that same figure for Fanon. Her body, an object through and through, functions as a hopeful idol, gathering to it all the magic and magisterial of whiteness and its promises. Fanon puts this bluntly: It is a matter of a "desire to be suddenly *white*" and a "want to be recognized not as *Black*, but as *White*."[15] Recognition is the critical term here and sets in motion an entire revolutionary position.

When Fanon reverses gendered positions, which in some ways draws out by contrast his particular and troubling instrumentalization of women's bodies, his analysis follows the same nihilistic racial logic. The Black woman seeks recognition in the only possible space of recognition: whiteness as measure and comparison. Mayotte Capécia's novel *Je suis martiniquaise* grounds Fanon's analysis and his nihilistic conception of desire, but the preformed conclusion of his engagement foregrounds the entire critical reading. In this way, Fanon's chapter on the Black woman's racial aspiration might *appear* to be a literary study focused on texts about interracial and mixed-racial anxiety, but he is clear from the outset that the novel is interesting to him solely to the extent that it demonstrates how "because the black woman feels inferior that she aspires to gain admittance into the white world"[16]—Fanonian nihilism, from the beginning. This admittance to the white world, he claims, is negotiated and manifest in "affective erethism," a bridge between the affective life of antiblackness and the spatialization of desire. Quite literally, Fanon locates the aspiration for admittance to whiteness in the genitals and, through sexual intercourse, in the kinds of relationality they can form. Or *have formed*; a passivity of embodied contact incarnates desire, incarnates subjectivity's aspiration, incarnates sociogeny, and therefore incarnates colonial history and memory. This is not a question of desire and arousal. This is a question of relation between bodies that is, in the first and last of it, a question of sociality, historical memory, and ontogeny generated in and by an antiblack world. Further, because Fanon identifies it with erethism and not something more bluntly material like touch or reproduction, it is important to note how deeply transformative racial bodies in contact are for him; because the erethic manifestation of desire is precisely an *overexcitement* of the genitals, theory must reckon with what initiates and sustains excitement. Interracial contact is so animated by the colonial that pleasure itself appears differently. Overexcitement is, in the end, nothing other than a sensitivity to nihilism made spatial, moving antiblackness and alienation from the psyche to the genitals to the other, then back again. The zigzag movement of sex—literally the motion of intercourse and figuratively the ideological need inside desire—transforms the entire world into an intimate, historical, and memorial orgasmic spectacle of alienation. That's really, really bad sex.

In many ways, the spatiality of desire, which is no space at all but instead the collapse of social death onto itself, is just another example of Fanon's remark in the Introduction to *Black Skin, White Masks* that there is only one "destiny for the black man. And it is white."[17] Fanon links ontology to sociogeny from the outset of the text, marking the link between being and the social, which, when also linked to racialization as embodied (the epidermis, speech), means that the entirety of psychic life is generated by a prior traversal across social and political space. The psyche enters a relation to itself and the world and is bound, in those relations, by the system of antiblackness simply by the fact of embodiment. This genealogy of the subject makes questions of race and colonialism inseparable from questions of the being of beings; the sociogenic principle embeds racialization and its colonial resonance inside the terms of relation of self to self, then self to other. Fanon's broader story of liberation takes root in this alienated space of nonbeing, the space of psyche and world and all the constitutive racist, colonial relations, and thus a space that is embedded in ways that make history and memory a *prison*. "Disoriented, incapable of confronting the Other," Fanon writes, "the white man who had no scruples about imprisoning me, I had transported myself on that particular day far, very far, from my self, and gave myself up as an object. . . . I wanted quite simply to be a man among men."[18] The desire to be a man among men, to participate in a humanism made to the measure of the world, is both an anticipation of an unprecedented future and a melancholic commentary on the fate of desire. Heterosexual and interracial desire, the occasion for reflection in the second and third chapters of *Black Skin, White Masks*, becomes, in this short comment, the homoerotic political desire of the alienated for their own alienation. There is no movement outside of the zone of nonbeing. Social death secures this immovability, and the cruelty of the violent colonial world buttresses the figure of the slave—namely, its unremunerated work of making the colonial world function as colonial. Nihilism is atmospheric in Fanon, and its resonance is in every corner of every example.

In both Wright's and Fanon's texts, then, we see the fate of Black bodies and Black people—though perhaps not Black *life*—in an antiblack world: social death and a life that when living, in however a zombified form, is not oriented toward a proper sense of death. Rather, death is only a variation on social death, a kind of conclusion to what already is̶. What was socially dead can only die as a finality of social death, not as the transition from life to death. This is exactly what Fanon means when he says that the destiny of the Black man is to be white. That destiny and the social form of social death it initiates robs the colonized of authenticity even in the most intimate of acts, from sexuality to death itself. Colonialism is a total project. Nihilism is a total experience. Totality as a closed system, which then raises the question of supplementarity: Where is the surplus in the essence of colonial nihilism? We catch sight of this supplement in the movement of nihilism across epistemological and affective registers, registers in which refusal becomes *possible*, but only possible as the *otherwise* and the *exterior*.

Affective Regimes and Their Outside(s)

What does nihilism do to knowing? And how is knowing conditioned by both the historical and lived experience of nihilism? How does nihilism register as affective life?

For Fanon, the question of knowledge, the epistemological register, is looped through ontology: Is it possible to know myself? Fanon's description of the destiny of Black subjectivity as whiteness answers that question with the total system and total experience of nihilism. Self-consciousness itself is structured by nihilism; this is the price and purchase of sociogeny, while also in response issuing the call to revolutionary, apocalyptic action. Unless the world is torn apart and begun again, the ideological production of Black abjection reproduces itself and the social order on which it depends and for which it does deep constitutive work. This is the straightforward story of a political metaphysics. The complex question lies in the matter of self-knowing, namely, how nihilism blocks the work of self-knowledge from inside subjectivity. In this way, Fanon's account of the anxieties of Black being or being itself rehearses (albeit with important differences) W. E. B. Du Bois's notion of double-consciousness. Rehearses, that is, not as a matter of influence, but as a confirming witness to the effects and affects of antiblack racism on/in matters of self-knowledge. Du Bois is particularly sharp and compelling on this when he writes:

> After the Egyptian and Indian, the Greek and Roman, the Teuton and Mongolian, the Negro is a sort of seventh son, born with a veil, and gifted with second-sight in this American world—a world which yields him no true self-consciousness, but only lets him see himself through the revelation of the other world. It is a peculiar sensation, this double-consciousness, this sense of always looking at one's self through the eyes of others, of measuring one's soul by the tape of a world that

looks on in amused contempt and pity. One ever feels his two-ness—
an American, a Negro; two souls, two thoughts, two unreconciled
strivings; two warring ideals in one dark body, whose dogged strength
alone keeps it from being torn asunder.[19]

Wright's protagonists, whether Bigger or Dave or Fred or Cross, articulate the visceral work of resistance from behind the veil. Not in terms of a second sight and *its* knowledge like Du Bois, but rather in terms of the affects that attend to the experience of being sealed behind the veil, outside the (interracial) world proper. In that way, Wright locates rage in what Fanon calls the zone of nonbeing—a locating description that is essential for what Fanon later develops as revolutionary consciousness in *The Wretched of the Earth*. The revolutionary ~~is~~ the zone of nonbeing, emphatic and erased, yet must also be capable of the rage necessary to intervene and destroy the colonial world as we know it. Fanon struggles to account for that possibility, but Wright's literary exploration of affective consciousness behind the Du Boisian veil helps us see how self-knowledge, in its split and fracture, can be animated by struggle and warfare. The extension of self-knowledge as knowledge of struggle and warfare into anticolonial and antiracist resistance is the work of revolution. It is also confirmation of the founding work of nihilism. Everything is animated by nihilism, including reactive consciousness behind the veil.

Social death is the term for this animation. Inside social death is the complex intersection of self-knowledge as resistance and self-knowledge as internalization of the social construction of a nihilistic world—and this is something for which Wright is particularly helpful. Two warring ideals indeed, necropolitical war. One of the striking features of "The Man Who Was Almost a Man" is how Wright describes the meaning of the gun. Dave's masculinity forms the crossroads of the story, literally and figuratively. Wright concludes the story with Dave standing at the edge of a new horizon, which is at once the promise of The Great Migration and, more deeply, the possibility of another positioning in the necropolitical order. His fascination with the gun is a fascination with the possibility of killing, a fascination with violence that takes life from another in order to give life and sovereignty to himself. A curative for social death, perhaps, inside the logic of necropolitics. But Dave is also constrained by place. The farm and its surrounding farmland are nothing but landscapes of social death and their persistent visual, ideological, and ontological threat of white violence. For Dave, the crossroads is an ethical and psychological one—miserable submission or seizure of the capacity to kill—while also a geographic one manifest as the lure of the train tracks, departure, and another beginning. At this crossroads, the gun is the *feeling* of necropolitics. Phallic, destructively masculine, but, perhaps for that reason, thoroughly necropolitical. The *felt* relation to necropolitics is simultaneously the transmission of knowledge of being and knowledge of the conditions of both knowing and being known. To be and to know as the killable population is to have an affective relation to self and world. A desire to escape the killable class is escape from social death, but the racial reproduction of the conditions of social death make that escape a matter of abstract, unprecedented possibility. Necropolitics as social death is a total project. Nihilism is a closed system.

Dave's encounter with the gun, a phallic moment and figure in a story about masculinity, is entirely a felt relation, a transformative moment for his affective life. Indeed, even those three terms—"his," "affective," "life"—must be revised *after* the gun. The masculine pronoun is inverted, shifting from the neutered, emasculated condition of social death to the swagger and possibility of a new sense of manhood. Affectivity itself is fundamentally different; Dave's body is repeatedly described in relation to the gun and his embodied relation to the world—vulnerable, subject to white violence, suppressed by the family—is still shaky, underdetermined, but deeply transformed by an emergent sense of power, manliness, and the capacity to take life. Taking life is the surmounting of or at least counterrelation to social death. Wright closes the story with Dave peering at plantation owner Jim Hawkins's "big white house"— an iconic intertwining of racial identity with plantation imagery—and declaring to himself: "When he reached the top of a ridge he stood straight and proud in the moonlight, looking at Jim Hawkins' big white house, feeling the gun sagging in his pocket. Lawd, ef Ah had just one mo bullet Ah'd taka shot at tha house. Ah'd like t scare ol man Hawkins jusa little . . . *Jusa enough t let im know Dave Saunders is a man.*"[20]

This passage is Dave's entire affective journey in "The Man Who Was Almost a Man," which is as much a flight of fantasy as it is possibility, bringing his embodied relation from submission to "stood straight and proud," a transformation of self, life, and relation that is rooted in the necropolitical order. A defiant declaration from behind the veil. Against the veil, but behind it. No mere gun is sufficient for inverting or eradicating the work of social death.

We can also see the affective life of abjection behind the veil in Wright's treatment of mothers in both *Native Son* and "The Man Who Was Almost a Man." In the short story, Dave's mother appears again and again as an emasculating force on two fronts. First, she is a figure of submission and resignation to submission—as opposed to, say, Dave's flirtation with death in his fantasy of shooting at Jim Hawkins's house—who cannot see another possible life. Second, she denies him access to a gun, which, given the phallic significance and signification of the pistol sagging in Dave's pocket, is a gesture of deep psychic emasculation and resignation of her own son to the economy of social death. When Dave asks his mother for two dollars to buy a gun, Wright writes her response as an emasculating scold:

> "Git outta here! Don yuh talk t me bout no gun! Yuh a fool!"
> "Ma, Ah kin buy one fer two dollahs."
> "Not ef Ah knows it, yuh ain!"
> "But yuh promised me one–
> "Ah don care whut Ah promised! Yuh ain nothing but a boy yit!"[21]

To be sure, Dave wears down his mother with his plea, but she is quick to qualify her concession and consign him to emasculation. The gun will belong to the father, ostensibly a man but also a man whose life has aged into and through social death, which shifts the meaning of the gun from an intervention in necropolitics alone to also an act of parricide. Heightened stakes. "Ain nothin wrong, Ma. Ahm almos a man now. Ah wans a gun," Dave declares, reassuring his mother. She replies: "Ah'll let yuh git tha gun ef yuh promise me one thing. . . . Yuh bring it straight back t me, yuh hear? It be fer Pa."[22] Emasculation and the family theatrics bury social death inside the home. Every closed system deploys clever tactics to keep the boundaries safe and secure.

Fanon's phenomenological treatment of the Black body in *Black Skin, White Masks* takes up many of these same thematics, with particular interest in how something akin Du Bois's veil and double consciousness—in Fanon's terms, an existential phenomenological account of being-for-others—manifests the white gaze inside the body. The epidermal schema is the key to understanding Fanon's conception of race, as well as how he imagines surmounting racism and the white gaze, but what stands out in the fifth chapter of *Black Skin, White Masks*, titled "The Lived-Experience of the Black Man," is how the epidermis is always more a figure than material example. Fanon theorizes the epidermal schema as the immovable presence of the Black *body* in front of the white gaze, a presence that blocks the possibility of being seen as a Black *person* or *subject*. Being in the world *as such*, not as an assertion or resistance, is already a fatal compromise of subjectivity. "I hailed the world," Fanon writes, "and the world amputated my enthusiasm." This evocation of amputation also closes the fifth chapter, where Fanon writes: "The crippled soldier from the Pacific war tells my brother: 'Get used to your color the way I got used to my stump. We are both casualties.'"[23] Amputation is an important image here, marking subjectivity in an irrevocable disability, incapacity, as a condition of presence to the world. In that way, the white gaze is not an interruption of life, but instead the very condition of life itself. Amputation becomes a form of social death in the modality of melanated embodiment. Wright's emasculation is Fanon's amputation, and both configurations of the Black body in the world align subjectivity with the terms of social death, racially exclusive life, and a veil of abject difference. Fanon's innovation is to locate the key aspect of abjection, the color of the body as a sociogenic fabrication, in the visual field. Visuality triggers the entire racial imaginary, opening the terrifying space of passive ideological reproduction. "'*Sale nègre!*' *ou simplement: 'Tiens, un nègre'*" introduces the chapter "The Lived-Experience of the Black Man" for good reason.

What does it mean to live as amputated subjectivity, vulnerable and exposed in the ideologically rich visual field, and without the animating counterdesire of Wright's newly armed Black subject? Part of the affective significance of the gun in Wright's "The Man Who Was Almost a Man" lies in its modification of the body; jostling in Dave's pocket, the gun functions as a phallic prosthesis in order to give the *appearance*, visually and then consciously, of a different kind of presence to the necropolitical world. Fanon's affective subject in *Black Skin, White Masks*, however, lives without prosthesis, without body modification in the visual field. Affect and amputation operate at the level of color and how color structures life, as social death, outside and inside the veil. That is, the epidermal schema operates at the level of the being of the world and the inner life of subjectivity, ordering affects and orienting a sense of being in the world. *The white gaze internalized.* Fanon writes: "Shame. Shame and self-contempt. Nausea. When they like me, they tell me my color has nothing to do with it. When they hate me, they add that it's not because of my color. Either way, I am prisoner of the vicious circle."[24]

The place of nihilism in this passage is important to discern and elaborate. Shame and self-contempt name the internalization, living and affecting behind the veil, of what lies outside: the white gaze, the amputating function of the epidermal schema, and the ideological production and reproduction of blackness *as* antiblackness. Fanon embellishes this with an important modification of Du Bois's image of the veil. This is no soft, semi-opaque blockage for Fanon. It is, rather, a prison, something Du Bois himself notes when he characterizes the "stranger in mine own house" as "the prison-house closed round about us all."[25] *An incarcerating blackness.* The carceral function of this affective modality of interracial life, social death lived in the world but also inside the psyche as a form of both incarceration and blackness, seals nihilism inside the subject and the subject inside nihilism. Fanon writes further: "A feeling of inferiority? No, a feeling of not existing. Sin is black as virtue is white. All those white men, fingering their guns, can't be wrong. I am guilty. I don't know what of, but I know I'm a wretch."[26]

Fanon's invocation of guilt as a precondition of blackness-in-the-world, an entirely ontological condition lived as affects of shame, inferiority, and self-doubt, links his thinking with the existential dimensions of Wright's fiction. Bigger Thomas and Fred Daniels are guilty simply by the fact of their existence; *Native Son* and "The Man Who Lived Underground" function as literary treatments of Fanon's phenomenology of the Black body in an antiblack world. The question of guilt and wretchedness as natal phenomena, predating active and acting subjectivities, opens up the complex sociogenic temporality of nihilism that is also an utterly straightforward rendering of time: The socially dead exist outside time as becoming. Fixed in being, which is to say, fixed *in* and *as* nonbeing.

Being, knowing, and creating are drawn into this closed system of nihilism. We can think here of Fanon's remarks on blues music in his 1956 essay "Racism and Culture," delivered at the Paris Congress of Black Writers and Artists. I mention the occasion for that essay because it underscores the gravity of the essay's broad statement. The 1956 Congress was dedicated to articulating the terms (or exploring to determine if such terms even exist) of a strong sense of diasporic link between African civilization and the diasporic cultures dispersed across the South and North Atlantic worlds. Aimé Césaire's piece at the Congress is particularly important on this theme; "Culture and Colonization" argues for a resilient historico-social sense of African civilization and for a weak sense of diasporic cultures, configuring the latter as a broken space and the former as its curative moment of aesthetic intervention. But it is important to note that Fanon does not take up this position or a variation of it; along with Wright and George Lamming, he is a dissenting writer at a conference dedicated to retrieval of the past and the redemption of that retrieval. Fanon is no theorist of diaspora. At the 1956 Congress, Fanon develops a new path into a familiar theme in his work, one that would be most emphatic in *The Wretched of the Earth*: the new. In order to claim the necessity and urgency of the new, in "Racism and Culture" Fanon pauses to disparage vernacular cultural formations. This is remarkable move, not only departing from the problem of diaspora but also declining to emphasize cultural formation in lieu of the curative work of civilizational force. But that was not an emerging new feature of his work. After all, Fanon had dismissed creole and pidgin in *Black Skin, White Masks* as variations of the deficiency model of seeing and knowing a Black person (self-knowledge and social knowledge both). Fanon describes speaking these languages, a shorthanded French (pidgin) or a composite of unproductive linguistic forms (creole), as a statement about self: "Stay where you are." Now, while Fanon *does* position this claim in relation to a complaint that white people can always speak a language poorly and it how it registers as charming or some such thing, and so how Black speakers are not granted the same grace or generosity, he nevertheless understands both pidgin and creole as signifiers of colonial oppression. Cultural forms, yes, but never capable of reconfiguring the possibilities of subjectivity *otherwise*.

In "Racism and Culture," Fanon returns this sensibility to blues music and vernacular cultural formation more broadly. It is important to note this aspect of Fanon's work because it is how he closes the system of nihilism, detecting nihilism as a sensibility in the structure of expressive life itself and thereby undermining (or so he hopes) any claims of cultural resistance and subversion. His framing of the question is important, interesting, and shows how deeply Fanon embeds nihilism in all forms of being and knowing, visually and aurally cued in every corner of the lifeworld and deathworld. "Psychologists spoke of a prejudice having become unconscious" Fanon writes, "The truth is that the rigor of the system made the daily affirmation of a superiority superfluous."[27] *Nihilism as ideological reproduction in the everyday.* As we will see, this is also the root insight of contemporary Afropessimism and, while Fanon will not arrive at the same conclusions, he does stake a similar claim that makes antiblackness inescapable and forbidding of everyday forms of resistance. And though he will contest the notion that racism is fully at the level of the unconscious, arguing instead for the constant visibility of the antiblack system, Fanon's entwining of culture and racism weaves racist violence so deeply into daily practices and habits that the distinction between the lash and the everyday vanishes. Nihilism shows up in the mode of the symptomatic—even in Black expressive culture. He writes:

> The interesting thing about this evolution is that racism was taken as a topic of meditation, sometimes even as a publicity technique.
> Thus the blues—"the black slave lament"—was offered up for the admiration of the oppressors. This modicum of stylized oppression is the exploiter's and the racist's rightful due. Without oppression and without racism you have no blues. The end of racism would sound the knell of great Negro music.[28]

This is a really striking passage and it has gotten very little, if any at all, attention in Fanon scholarship. On the one hand, it is a fundamentally *wrong* understanding of blues music and that terrible assessment is an important moment of fracture in his closure of the system of nihilism. On the other hand, it is a natural outcome of his vision of colonialism and antiblackness as total projects, projects that, for Fanon, were and continue to be deeply successful pending apocalyptic political violence. The foundational claim that makes this assessment possible is not uncomplicated: "Racism bloats and disfigures the face of the culture that practices it."[29] An entire system bears on the everydayness of life, whether the nature of our desires, as we have seen above, or even just in the commercial and expressive culture that surrounds us in our walkabout life. Neither resistance nor revolution, expressive culture is merely symptomatic of nihilism. A story told is just a reproductive act, not resistance or refusal. Certainly not refusal.

It is important to note that Wright offers us a very different interpretation of the meaning of blues and jazz music, which bears a somewhat tense relation to his understanding of African American literature. For example, his approach to understanding African American literature in "The Literature of the Negro in the United States" surfaces an important element in both Fanon's and Wright's vision of the affective life of Black people in an antiblack world. Wright's insights are varied in this essay, and he moves quickly to categorize and characterize canonical writers; taxonomical work is always rough and tedious. But there is a consistent thread throughout that leads to a crossroads of sorts and reflects the binary possibilities inherent in a closed system of nihilism: resistance literature or literature written toward the human condition as such? The latter only appears in the closing remark to "The Literature of the Negro in the United States," in which Wright addresses the reader directly and designates the thematic nature of literary production as a proper barometer of racial progress. "If, however, our expression broadens," Wright remarks, "and assumes the common themes and burdens of literary expression which are the heritage of *all men*, then by that token you will know that a human attitude prevails in America toward us."[30] If we reread the essay backward, framing the essay's earlier taxonomic and adjudicative meditations in terms of this turn at the close, then we can see how clearly Wright cleaves resistance or complaint literature (his own contribution, as well as that of the tradition) from a literature to come—a literature, to indulge Fanon's and Césaire's vocabulary, of a new humanism and of a humanism made to the measure of the world. A post-imperial, post-antiblack world literature. This is a type of literature that operates in the free expressive space accorded, in our moment, only to white writers. A postcolonial literature, in the most radical sense of the term, is a literature of the future, a literature produced from a world *outside* social death, and therefore *after* an apocalyptic event that burns the system of antiblackness to the ground. And then begins again. Another strange, eruptive and irruptive temporality.

But this configures the Black literary tradition—and, by extension, Black expressive culture more broadly—in much too narrow terms. Wright, like Fanon, levels off literary culture as symptomatic of the system of social death, one in which complaint and protest—summoned from a sense of subjectivity neither can define—is the best possibility. At least protest is not assimilation. And so on. Fanon widens Wright's comment on the literary to encompass the entirety of expressive culture. In a certain sense, that widening is simply consistent with the kind of insight both have into the relationship between nihilism and the construction of Black subjectivity. If nihilism is a feature or foundation of a system of social death, then expressive life *in* social death is contaminated with, and therefore expressive of, the terms of nihilism. Theorizing blues as a slave's lament—which is not even yet protest—stays consistent with the original theory and the purchase of sociogeny. But it is also true that in admitting vernacular expressive culture into the world of social death, we catch sight of the carriage of supplementarity in the figure of the slave, a halo around the ghostly presence of abjection and subjugation. What might vernacular cultural production say *back to* or *express otherwise than* the colonial regime of social death? How does that production operate and do important ontological labor at the margins of nihilism?

The essence of social death is the atmospheric of nihilism. The surplus in the essence is vernacular cultural formation. Vernacular culture is a *fact* of subaltern existence in the deathworld dimension of colonial and white lifeworlds, but we need not *only* understand expressive culture as symptomatic even as expressive culture is essentially related to the ambient work of nihilism. Who is the subject of nihilism? And who is the subject producing expressive life *as* life inside that nihilism, inside social death, and therefore, perhaps, in *la frontera* of deathworld's commanding presence? How might we understand the subject of vernacular culture—the producer *of* and the world produced *by* it—*otherwise*?

Refusal's Many Returns

As we saw in the previous chapter on Baldwin's work, the specter of social death shifts when we move thinking away from the Manichean world of antiblackness, the colonial world broadly conceived as a logic of psychic and political organization, and toward the interstices of vernacular culture, expressive life, and world-making. This movement is particularly compelling when it is negotiated inside the terms of catastrophic violence and social death. *Moving away as immanent critique. Deconstruction and social death.*

The discursive common space between Wright and Fanon sharpens our vocabulary for and exemplary sites of this kind of counterclaim on life. *Counter*, that is, because it is a movement against and outside *from* the outside, the exterior, and the ante- or antimilieu of *la frontera*—that space in which "languages and identities hybridize and evolve," space that is creolized and hybridized in improvisational modalities of expression, becoming, and time.[31] Fanon's example of language as identity formation and the short but decisive remark on blues music bring us to the limit of a system that Wright had marked, from center to periphery, as a visceral atmosphere of social death. The death of the Black body and the possibility of its life, for Wright. To be aboveground is to die. The death of the authenticity of desire and the possibility of incarnate being in the world, for Fanon. To have black skin is to die.

A return to the previous reflection: Baldwin's shift in thinking the space of Black life from the word to the secret—or, perhaps better, to the secretion of the word—helps us understand how vernacular life intervenes against Wright and Fanon in order to propose a different difference.

It is interesting to pause and note how Wright and Fanon propose, albeit in different registers, an irruptive exit from the closed system of antiblackness. For both, it is a question of revolution. We can see a bit of this in Wright's nonfiction, in particular his exhortation in *White Man, Listen!* for white people to grant Black people(s) the "tools" of the white West. Modernity is a virtue, one that breaks the human free of the constraints of tradition.[32] Wright asks in "Tradition and Industrialization," an essay from 1956, "How can the spirit of the Enlightenment and the Reformation be extended now to all men? How can this accidental boon be made global in effect? That is the task that history now imposes upon us."[33]

Fanon notes this passage and sentiment in one of his short pieces for *El Moudjahid* in 1959, published in the collection *Alienation and Freedom*. In this essay, Fanon reads Wright as a tepid if not wholly failed thinker of liberation. Wright's "call," on Fanon's reading, displays "an irrational, unjustified confidence in the west's 'perspicacity,' its 'generosity,'" asking in a biting concluding sentence "Has history taught Richard Wright nothing? We might be permitted to think so."[34] In light of Fanon's apocalyptic vision of revolutionary violence and its wins, this perspective and assessment makes perfect sense. But this is also a result of Fanon's entirely ungenerous reading of Wright's work generally. That ungenerous reading is rooted in an early interpretation in *Black Skin, White Masks* in which Fanon thinks Bigger Thomas "answers the world's expectations,"[35] as well as, of course, the prerogatives of Fanon's conception of liberation in *The Wretched of the Earth* as the destruction of the world through political violence and the emergence of the new. Fanon's prerogative is fitted to anticolonial struggle in his moment. Algeria, after all, was not negotiating a sense of place in interracial space. Whatever the place of the *pied noir*, Algeria was not a white-majority settler colony like the United States. Rather, the liberation movement in Algeria aimed to force out a brutal occupier in the name of Algerian land and nation rights. Wright's conception of liberation is rooted in a different kind of social and political space, one delinked from the kinds of political romanticism we find in Fanon and assessed with a kind of resigned cynicism (always Wright's motif, at some level) and with a prerogative that believes quite deeply, and not without reason, in the meaning of freedom.

The difference between Wright and Fanon, then, is a difference between an expansive and subversive sense of inclusion and a vision of another world beyond what we have known, beyond what is available to critical theory *in this moment*. But both Wright and Fanon, across such differences, are committed to a sense of revolutionary change and action that upends and destroys the world as we know it. There is no respite from violence and there is no possibility other than social death in an antiblack necropolitical order. Making global in effect or remaking the global as such—whatever the differences, the order of things ends, and then there is a new beginning and its new sense of the new. For Fanon, that is clear and visceral in *The Wretched of the Earth*, a clarity and bluntness that is in some ways only glimpsed in the more poetic and evocative modality of his earlier writings. For Wright, revolutionary sensibility is borne by the very idea that a Black person would or *could* be free, a thought that, we should always remember, set the entire nation of the United States into bloody civil war, then terror campaigns of lynching, and then the brutality of murder and mayhem in response to the Civil Rights Movement. *Pace* Fanon, history has taught plenty to Wright, including that the very idea of free blackness is already a lot of revolution. *Pace* Wright, Fanon cannot see freedom inside the imperial destiny of the Black man to be white, no matter how retooled. Both end with their own sense of apocalypse and, in the aftermath of that, a sense of beginning again.

But what is striking here is how the question of refusal and its subversive meaning never surfaces, and, when it does, it is characterized as the very abjection refusal refuses. Fanon buries expressive culture and its work as refusal inside abjection, affirming the totality of nihilism and the nihilism of totality. This is important because it shows how Fanon limits our understanding of the boundary work at the margins of systematic antiblackness. Fanon's critical remarks on blues music and Louis Armstrong's artistry are pointed examples of this limit. Wright's relationship with vernacular cultural forms is considerably more complex. On the one hand, Fanon writing that "the end of racism would sound the knell of great Negro music" is matched in sentiment by Wright's comment that if we see a Black literature that "assumes the common themes and burdens of literary expression which are the heritage of *all men*, then by that token you will know that a human attitude prevails in America toward us." For each, Black art is formed by conditions that forbid Black art to be free *poiesis*. The shared sentiment marks a common place of critical assessment: Nihilism forms expressive culture from the inside. On the other hand, and this is a crucial difference, Wright himself deploys African American vernacular speech—or an approximation thereof—in many of his literary works in order to capture something of the *life*world, and so not merely *death*world, from and toward which the fiction is drawn. It is not simply that he *uses* some form of vernacular, but rather what that vernacular is supposed to communicate: the unicity of African American *life* that is not wholly reducible to social death. This writes Wright against himself, a kind of ideological double session. In his essay "Richard Wright's Blues," Ralph Ellison captures this paradoxical relation of Wright's nihilism and the performance of his own writing. A paradoxical relation or maybe just a plain and problematic contradiction. This is invariably the space occupied by theorists struggling to account for their own position as critics and writers: How is it possible to speak outside a total and closed system, not just in order to name it from that outside, but also to articulate its life? Trace and supplementarity haunt this paradox and its contradiction. Ellison remarks on Wright the writer: "And like a blues sung by such an artist as Bessie Smith, its lyrical prose evokes the paradoxical, almost surreal image of a black boy singing lustily as he probes his own grievous wound."[36]

This is no small praise, given how Ellison understands Smith's music and its world-shifting, world-making capacity. His elevation of Wright's prose is crucial here insofar as it doubles Ellison's critical assessment of *Native Son* and *Black Boy*, moving from Wright-as-documentarian (nihilism, white cruelty, existential guilt) to Wright-as-vernacular-expression (Black life as Black life, elements of life in *la frontera* of the interracial deathworld). We can set Ellison's remarks alongside his incisive critique of Wright in "The World and the Jug,"[37] where the work done in *Native Son*, *Black Boy*, and other fiction is described as fundamentally *sociological* in its approach. Wright does documentary work, yes, but Ellison insists that he also does something more. Therein lies the paradox. Wright offers sociological discourse while at the same time indulging figures of speech, expressive culture, and African American language formation—with all of their capacity for doubled speech, lower frequencies, everyday subversion—that liberate sociology in the name of African American refusal practices. The wound, which is history. Which is Fanon's critical theory. Lustily singing and its doubled meanings, which is refusal as literary practice and testimony. Which is the trace of the vernacular at the edge of a closed system.

The question of refusal in this moment is no minor or occasional issue. In fact, in drawing out the importance and place of life in the interstices, refusal enacts a kind of decolonial thinking. This is a decolonial thinking inside the space of practice, as well as a method of reading expressive culture in relation to hegemonic forms of life and social death. This *inside* and *in relation to* is so important because it shifts and alters our sense of the temporality of decolonial work and also, because the decolonial bears a necessary relation to the systems it subverts, the time of the closed system. Decolonial work is typically, and rightly so, understood to be undertaken in the postcolonial moment; the colonizer leaves by choice or force, the state and culture enter a post- of the colonial era, and then in order to achieve or fulfill the vision of a noncolonial state and culture a process of decolonization is undertaken. This can mean a purge of former colonizers from the land in the case of settler or semisettler colonial states or it can mean a transformation of institutions, from the everyday to educational systems to the structures of economy and political representation. And everything in between. If colonialism was a total project, then decolonization is the same: answerable to the totality. Answering to totality means theorizing the passage from the space of social death to the limit of the system, then asking, in the prerogative opened up here at the margins of nihilism, how resources for thinking operate in the interstitial space at the edges of a closed system. In the fractures, in the fissures, and therefore in *la frontera* of what a closed system wants to be but cannot fully enact.

How does a sense of life at these edges of social death and its nihilistic construction of being and knowing operate? How is it generated, and, in that generation, what is the schematic of its relation to social death and the deathworld/lifeworld binary that animates racial nihilism?

The thematic of refusal is where we see the presence of decolonial work in the very same moment as colonial domination. Colonial domination creates a closed system that is undermined and destabilized by the supplement, which, in this case, is the persistence and double structure of vernacular culture. Far from the slave's lament, for example, blues music, even as it is saturated with the affects of nihilism, is about a sense of life exterior to the life/social death structure of an antiblack world. The music is not simply a sonic phenomenon. It is an existential and ontological event that ruptures the borders of a closed system. This sonico-ontological rupture in being iterates a broader, more expansive, yet also wholly in the lower frequencies form of life that is unrecognizable to the dialectical relation of white life and Black social death. The paradox of expansiveness—it encompasses a countertotality, however open, of Black living—and lower frequencies is resolved or at least best articulated as the double session of sound. Embedded in the margins of a nihilistic system, it also exceeds and ruptures while opening onto a series of alternative relations that do not return to, depend upon, or desire a place in that systematicity. This is why it remains unrecognizable inside nihilism's putative closed system. It is unrecognizable precisely because it does not enter into relation. It is not a relation of seeking recognition. It is not a relation of resistance. Rather, the refusal to seek recognition or to be recognized is a movement away from shared space, away from interracial space and its machinery of social death, that is also outside the binaries and Manichean visions that animate that space and its machinery. Fanon flirts with this insight. I am thinking in particular about his reflections on Hegel in section B of the seventh chapter of *Black Skin, White Masks*, in which Fanon theorizes the position of Black subjectivity outside the desire for recognition. A dialectics of recognition calcifies in some significant measure the white colonial mode of comparison. Thus, for Fanon, the refusal of dialectic is the refusal of the colonial economy of measure; to enter into dialectical relation is to concede at least part of the grounds of relation to white subjectivity. That concession is nothing but defeat for anticolonial thinking. And so Fanon opts for the persistent commitment to alterity, to refusal of the system.

At the same time, that refusal of the system, which we might at times call resistance, is a relation to social death that struggles *against* social death and the figure of the slave *inside* the economy that produces and reproduces the same. This is not a struggle to wrestle social death away from white people, whiteness, and the colonizer, which would then reverse or neutralize the terms of nihilism and its world constructing power. The Fanon of *Black Skin, White Masks* is not a necropolitical theorist. Rather, the resistance Fanon posits against the desires of dialectics and recognition is revolutionary in relation to and as a part of interracial space. In that way, Fanon's nihilism is shorter lived than that of Wright. Wright's characters kill and die without redemption or vision or broader political program. Fanon's intervention against dialectics of recognition does not redeem the world, but it does erupt in opposition to the fundamental element of social reproduction: the incontestable white gaze and its world-making power. *A reactive eruption and intervention*. Thus, this sense of resistance is not quite refusal precisely because resistance does not operate as or open up to radical exteriority. The radical exteriority of refusal, drawn from and drawing on the life of supplementarity, upends the very terms of dialectics with its commitment to an equally radical *indifference* rather than eruptive reactivity. Herein lies the enigma of refusal and its important nuance. This indifference is folded across the boundary lines of a putatively closed system and, in that folding, is an insurgency in its own particular sense. I am thinking here of how the very songs and moods Fanon decries as slave laments, the ones he believes to be offered as supplication to the enslaver, operate sonically and culturally both inside systems of social death and entirely outside them. The lower frequencies, as Ellison puts it at the close of *Invisible Man*, are not inaudible. They are wholly audible, loudly so in fact, but always and differentially audible in two separate registers. One that is heard by sites of production and reproduction of social death. A dialectic of recognition of humanity or a plea for recognition of pain suffered. This is Fanon's ear. This is the commercial circulation of sound that cannot discern elements of refusal and only hears expression of social death. And there is also another one heard by those whose lives have *another community* and *another world*. A world, that is, which is not just escapist or a place of respite, but an entire world of meaning and conviviality. A world, to repeat the refrain, of what Baldwin in "Many Thousands Gone" called "the relation Negroes bear to one another."[38]

If refusal produces this interstitial space and the radical exteriority of its world and processes of world-making, then we can see the antistructural consequences of a colonial logic supplemented by radical alterity: the unseeable, the unhearable, and the unthinkable folded out of the margins of a world of social death and its necropolitical actors. But also a sound in the common sonic economy. Inside and outside. Change the joke, slip the yoke. Ellison's clever title and masterful account of tricksterism, of doubled discourse, and of the secretion of meaning in measured and racially attentive acts of signification all give shape, contour, and play to what is, in its first appearance, a mimicry of the white gaze in a Black (or blackfaced) body. But this is a double session. In its second appearance, it is *this* signification, then erasure, of radical exteriority inside the system that makes that exteriority impossible and possible.

A paradox, to be sure.

But also the life and lives of refusal.

The life and lives of refusal are neither fiction nor aspiration. Baldwin's invocation of the relation between Black people—a relation that happens outside the white gaze, and therefore on vastly different terms—is a synonym for countertradition at the margins of nihilism: world-making ideas, expressive culture, and modalities of being and knowing that do not circulate in fully explicit forms in interracial space. The decolonial elements of this ante-strategy, a strategy before the full reach of white hegemony is exercised, emerges in exactly this moment. If we understand the decolonial to be a praxis committed to thinking outside the Manichean logic of colonial domination, then refusal does not move against social death in acts of reactivity and resistance but instead maintains an indifference that both creates and witnesses a world at the margins of nihilism. Refusal is not revolutionary in the sense of uprooting the entire world and beginning again. Refusal refuses. In the act that refuses, an interstitial world opens up both inside the world of social death (it is contingent, as a possibility, on that antagonism) and outside or in *la frontera* of the same. Ellison's notion of the lower frequencies names this doubled relation, testifying to a double session that is spatially and temporally distinct. Frequencies do not share the same time—even as they cross—and the lives lived in contrary or competing aural space is marked by different "territories," as it were. A radical and irreducible diachrony. We can think here of Zora Neale Hurston's well-known essay "Characteristics of Negro Expression" and its documentation of all those modalities of Black life *for* and *inside* Black life. Hurston's essay is a taxonomy of sorts, for sure, but it is in some fundamental sense not for public consumption or in the interest of making sense of expressive life for Black and white people alike. It is rather more like an intimate reflection that crosses the boundary between social death and interstitial forms of freedom in order to speak to Black people about their own lives.

And in that crossing, the movement after passage to the limit, we catch sight of the decolonial as a mode of thinking. Thinking in the lower frequencies. Thinking, not in opposition to nihilism, but outside its reach while situated at its deconstructive margins. Thinking without obsessive recurrence of the center in those margins. Thinking in the secreted space toward which the secret of the supplement, that doubled discourse of vernacular culture in the blues "lament," had always pointed while written and sung under erasure. That is the puzzle of erasure, indeed: how to read traces, how to read absences, how to read for the ghostly. Wright and Fanon *begin* this puzzle, but not in the sense of offering paths to the limit and then to the exterior and *la frontera*. The beginning of the puzzle is the marking of limits and then, in the gesture of embedding the vernacular inside the hegemonic, smuggles the supplement as surplus into the essence of the system. Changing the joke, slipping the yoke. That supplement disrupts, fissures, and fractures the boundaries of the closed system. But it also makes its sounds. "Perhaps I like Louis Armstrong because he's made poetry out of being invisible," Ellison writes. "I think it must be because he's unaware that he *is* invisible."[39] The paradox of deconstruction and social death. The sound of the lower frequencies. Refusal at the end of nihilism. Refusal as the task of decolonial thinking. Thinking refusal at the margins of nihilism.

4
The Lower Frequencies after Afropessimism

Silence is my shield
(it crushes)
Silence is my cloak
(it smothers)
Silence is my sword
(it cuts both ways)
Silence is the deadliest weapon
What legacy is to be found in silence?
What future lies in silence?
— MARLON RIGGS, *TONGUES UNTIED*

Visibility is never a curative for the kinds of harm done by racial violence, exclusion, and their cumulative effects. This is a critical insight in biopolitical theory: Visibility is a kind of confessional of one's identity, placing that identity as embodied inside the system of violence on the terms of that system. Being *seen* becomes a stage for different forms of vulnerability.

Indeed, one could argue that many of the common vernaculars of articulation and liberation like "invisibility" and "erasure"—terms deployed in an everyday sense and not in a deconstructive register—are conditions of racial violence and exclusion rather than a counterposition or counterclaim on social, political, and cultural space. We see that with such viscerality in Richard Wright's fiction on the stage of the underground, on or under which a certain trace of that disrupting phrase *Black and free* erupts but above which there is only death. We see that in Frantz Fanon's rendering of racial language as an epidermal schema, a canvas of one-dimensional coloration on which the anxieties and moral demands of colonialism are projected to the point of amputating the very possibility of subjectivity. And yet, for both, invisibility as the withdrawal from the interracial world into the interstices of the system(s) of antiblackness is no alternative form of life, but instead only a hint of escape—a sort of compromised, uninteresting urban *marronage* that bandages what is left of the body yet never restores it to its authenticity, liberated movement, or freedom.

This engagement with the epistemic and existential meaning of visibility grounds a conception of nihilism that operates in a social, political, and cultural atmospheric. Nihilism in this sense has no direct perpetrator. Rather, perpetration of racial violence is more akin to a symptom of an atmosphere that conditions blackness as the condition of nonbeing. From birth, as this body, in the zone of nonbeing. While Wright and Fanon offer a compelling phenomenology of racial embodiment and important reckoning with natal alienation, the social death documented in theorizing visibility and vulnerability appears for the reader-theorist through an account of the perceptual field. The perceptual field, and this something that the post–World War II phenomenological tradition shows with such depth, is also an incursion into ontology; subjectivity is generated in the epistemic work of perception, embodiment, and the sedimentation of history in both. To be seen is to *be*. The gaze is ontologically productive, reproductive, and creative all at once. And in many ways, we can see how this has been decisive turn in theorizing perception, race, and subjectivity at least since the opening pages of *Souls of Black Folk* and its interrogation of double consciousness. Du Bois's account of the veil and his two warring souls begins with the rejection of his blackness as being, rendering the African in him either a socially imperceptible trace or a wound of nonbeing. Then the white gaze is internalized, rendering his consciousness double in the very act of appearing as a Black body in interracial space. This opens up a profoundly rich field of inquiry, but there remains an important gap in this approach. Or at least a philosophical puzzle and decision inside this link between perception and subjectivity: asking the question of Being as such. How is Being a question outside the play between beings and how that perceptual and affective play produces identities between? How is Being a question outside questions of *intersubjectivity*? This question lies at the heart of so much midcentury European philosophy, in particular with the appearance then inheritance of the work of Martin Heidegger among French philosophers beginning with Jean-Paul Sartre and Maurice Merleau-Ponty. That shift in questioning, recast in the Black Atlantic context, appears here in a modified, politically incisive form around the question of race, the body, and nihilism. In theorizing the closed system of nihilism, how might the emphasis on questions of perception and affective life obscure the question of Being? In theorizing subjectivity as formed in acts of collaborative, intersubjective perception of the racialized body, how does that account fail to raise the question of ontological difference—the difference between beings and Being, as well as, most important, the relation between?

In the context of the European philosophical tradition, this is one of the key critical debates between adherents to Heidegger's philosophical prerogative—which works with and between the question of ontological difference—and those who return to the thick and provocative field of embodied perception. *That* context largely brackets the political significance of the question of Being in the interest of debating and establishing the terms of a robust phenomenology. Even embodiment itself is largely defanged outside of questions of gender and sexuality; embodiment is for the most part rendered as the fantasy of the body *in general* and not the body of history and memory. Empire remains forever hidden and silenced in the pages of accounts of incarnate being and of Being as such. But if we see how that same *formal* question is raised in the gap between contemporary Afropessimism, its fundamental ontology, and the theorization of the affective atmospheric of nihilism, then we can see how the *deformalization* of the question of politics returns with a particular force and transformative power to the question of Being. That is, the kinds of political neutrality we find in European theory's bracketing of the political cannot be done in the Black Atlantic context given how deeply tied matters of subjectivity are to the construction of the coloniality of Being. The Black Atlantic gaze rewrites—or can rewrite—the prerogatives of European thought, whether through aesthetic and epistemological acts of creolization or through the infusion of fundamental ontology with the political economy of history and memory. Afropessimist work is at its best when asks about Being as such and not simply subjectivities and their critical exchange in the interracial, intersubjective world of beings. Certain Black Atlantic thinkers have gestured toward this kind of work in terms of colonialism and its long shadow. Revisiting the question of nihilism inside the framing of contemporary Afropessimist ontology, however, complicates and deepens our engagement with inheritance of Being's coloniality in important ways. And it especially does so in how that inheritance shapes the world of appearance, embodiment, and social reproduction. How does the turn to fundamental ontology shift the resonance and significance of the question of visibility and invisibility? And the question of subjectivity? And so too the question of the being of beings under antiblack regimes of power?

The closure of the system is the closure of Being. In the Afropessimist recast of fundamental ontology, the closure of Being is the closure of antiblackness and all possibility. Our imaginations are enclosed in colonial enclosure. Nihilism is necessity, invariability, and inevitability. The margins are themselves elements of enclosure.

I want to ask a companion question here, one that revisits the margins of nihilism in terms of sonic and ontological variation. What would it mean to think about Ralph Ellison's appeal to the lower frequencies at the close of *Invisible Man* in the wake of contemporary Afropessimism? And to mix that sense of frequency with Marlon Riggs's riff on silence as a complex and compelling beginning for thinking politics and the politics of culture? "In the silence, baby," Riggs muses, "we could make a serious revolution. Together."[1] Silence as paradox and *pharmakon*. The antispace at the margins of nihilism. And so also, from Riggs: "Your silence is costing. Your silence is suicide." The play of voice and silence is so deeply embedded in the African American intellectual tradition, and Riggs draws on it in such compelling ways in *Tongues Untied*. Ellison, too, not only in the opening and closing bits of *Invisible Man*, but also in his work on blues music and its aesthetic—work that theorizes the music and aesthetic as an entire theory of subjectivity. How might the aural configure or reconfigure Being? How is the aural configured and reconfigured *by* Being? These are my questions in thinking about thinking between Afropessimist ontology and Ellisonian notions of lower frequencies.

In theorizing the lower frequencies inside the horizon of Afropessimism, I want to pursue pessimism as a modality of *thinking*. This is not necessarily a focus of the movement. So much of Afropessimism is, rather, a matter of assertion, provocation, and tailoring claims in light of critics who look to affects of pleasure, joy, and cultural production as counterstatements to pessimism's bleaker moments. There is a lot to the politics of this conceptual and felt space. And there is plenty of epistemology here too, especially in the Du Boisean sense of self-knowledge and its distressing link to white hegemony in shared interracial space. But that is not to render and reckon with Afropessimism as a form of thought. The following reflections on Afropessimism, then, are less interested in what has been called "Afro-optimism" and its variants—an affective counterpoint to Afropessimism's pervasive sense of despair—and more interested in how theorizing the *systematic* aspects of Afropessimist ontology and epistemology as a closed system also discloses the secret and secreting work of the supplement.

This shift is important. Afropessimism offers a serious ontology of the antiblack world and, in its treatment of that ontology, the movement (or critical sensibility) pushes thinking beyond nihilism and into another kind of temporality. That temporality has an apocalyptic tone that is worthy of careful consideration; it is by no means merely an affective series of claims. The *tone* may be apocalyptic, but the terms of thinking that underpin tone—a hint at the aural and affective dimensions of thinking—require assessment as terms of thinking (even if that thinking labors in what is, frankly, a pre-Derridean notion of ontology). Adherence to a pre-Derridean notion of ontology has important consequences for thinking critically about the horizon of pessimism, namely, in terms what it has set out as a critical program and what possibilities lie within it. In the turn to ontology, Afropessimists have been able to challenge conventional theorizing of culture and resistance by rendering both as symptomatic of Being as the antiblack infrastructure of the world. Heidegger's work is an important methodological framing here, to be sure. Heidegger's distinction between Being and beings, the key insight that underpins the project of fundamental ontology, situates the relationship between subjectivity and disclosure as intimate and inseparable. To *know* Being and to *be* is one and the same, though also a site for distinction at the level of the disclosive order. The disclosive order, on Heidegger's phenomenological treatment, places subjectivity at the center of acts of revealing but also understands that Being is the condition of beings. So, as we shall see, this means that the Afropessimist reinterpretation of fundamental ontology places the Black body and Black subjectivity at the center of analysis while also understanding that that body and subjectivity are only possible in a world structured by antiblackness. Being is antiblack, to "be" Black is to not-be. Fanon's zone of nonbeing returns here with a deeper engagement around the Heidegger question of Being, an engagement that effectively shifts the time of nihilism to the time of pessimism.

At the same time, this reinterpretation of fundamental ontology does not adhere to Heidegger's strict and at times elusive commitment to finitude. For Heidegger, and this is one of the signature claims in his post–*Being and Time* work, Being withdraws at our very approach, borne in and by names that modernity has made impossible to hear, know, see, and *think*. Being is like the Greek temple where the gods have fled, even as we still hear the rustling of absence, sit with the experience of Being's withdrawal, and respond with mourning and yearning at what Heidegger calls the *end of philosophy*. Afropessimism, however, is more confident and bolder in its treatment of the question of Being. The intensity and immensity of the question of Being moves pessimist theory away from mourning and toward melancholia and, perhaps, rage. We might interpret this as simply misreading Heidegger and the trajectory of his work *or* as a plain refusal to follow him down the path of thinking the question of Being. Both of these thinkerly dispositions are completely reasonable. One need not follow doctrine in order to draw on a thinker's insights, and in fact readerly engagement that reworks and retools is often a sign of taking an original text, thinker, and theory *seriously*. The one-dimensional, conceptually static great man theory of theory does no one much good.

But I do not think that adequately tells us why Afropessimist ontologies mark out a series of bolder claims than we find in the founding texts of fundamental ontology. In the case of Heidegger, thinking as such could, or maybe even *should*, work at a certain distance from the body and other material conditions of the existential stretch of *Dasein* across time and history. *Dasein* is in-the-world-being, yet it does not move as a body in the world, and the bearing of history on thinking does not shift the significance and signification of incarnate being. The *Da* of *Dasein* has no color, gender, or class (though it does perhaps bear the markers of nation). This is one of the important kernels of white European innocence—the invisibility of the material body in this iteration—that animates Heidegger's work and the work of so many other European thinkers. But the starting point of Afropessimism, the factical situation of social death, is visceral, embodied, social, and political as a matter of existence itself. The ontic *clue* that makes fundamental ontology work is fundamentally different: the body as a repository of memory and sedimented site of historical formation. A difference that makes a difference, the Black body and subject signals its worldliness and sense of worldhood with another kind of relation to history, a thoroughly *noninnocent* experience of history, and therefore one cannot think thinking as cleaved from the deathworlds Black people have inhabited in the Atlantic world for centuries. Afropessimism begins in this conceptual milieu. The *Da* of Afropessimist *Dasein*, we could say, is the lived experience of antiblackness as social death, a lived experience that already changes our sense of what finitude itself means, of what it means to say that *Dasein* is oriented toward a future, and so of what it means to be in the ecstatic stretch of time that makes subjectivity subjectivity. And if Being shows itself through its relation to beings—Heidegger's abiding insight across decades of work—and those beings are marked with death in a way specific to social death and its Afropessimist interpretation, then Being is disclosed *in relation to* antiblackness. What is that relation? How is Being antiblack and how is antiblackness Being? These are the questions that animate the most rigorous moments of Afropessimist thought. It is also where we catch sight of the Afropessimist imperative and method as a *system* of thought that, like all systems, raises within itself the question of the supplement. Is Being as antiblackness a closed system? If so, what are the terms of closure and the logic that demonstrably secures closure? What is the Afropessimist supplement? And what kinds of destabilization of meaning, sense, time, and Being-being as relation emerge in that supplementarity?

From Nihilism to Pessimism

The shift between nihilism and pessimism is nuanced but also conceptually important for critical theory. In our earlier examination of Wright and Fanon we saw how the relation between violence and blackness forms shape and contour of the affective, generative structure of the world. Much like the meaning of *deathworld* in my embellishment of James Baldwin's nonfiction, subjectivity itself bears all the symptoms necessary to discern, through a symptomatic reading, the infrastructure of the world as nihilism. In part, that infrastructure is signaled through the affective structure of fear and shame, both of which work emphatically inside subjectivity to fit the body as abject object in the interracial world. In part, that is the ideologically reproductive work of everything in the interracial world, ranging from the everyday labor of the white gaze to social regulations around language and expressive culture to institutional work inside political and repressive state apparatuses. Nihilism is produced by antiblackness. And antiblackness is nothing like a restrained project. Antiblackness, like Fanon's characterization of colonialism, is a total project that aims at the conversion of the inner life and institutional life of populating subjects to the logic of necropolitics. Necropolitics becomes an inheritance—it is generated by the past, reproducing itself in the everyday and shared institutional life of the present—and also a diagnostic of the lived space of social death and white life—an entire taxonomy of possibility in the world as we know it. We see this so clearly and viscerally in Wright's fiction. Nearly without exception, Wright's characters erupt in nihilistic violence, killing without purpose or vision—in *Native Son*, at the close of *The Outsider*—or suffer death for the sake of nothing other than confirmation of the nihilistic structure of his world. The police are clear when they murder: "You've got to shoot his kind. They'd wreck things."[2] That introduction of necessity into an antiblack world constructed around the possibilities and impossibilities circulated through social death closes the system of nihilism. Visibility, action, and imagination are all subjected to the same subjection: premature, extrajudicial death.

In many ways, Fanon's *Black Skin, White Masks* functions an existential-phenomenological explication of the claims of *Native Son* and other literary pieces. The sociological features of Wright's fiction are recast with such precision and insight by Fanon, filling that account of nihilism and antiblackness with a specific kind of demoralizing, excessive richness of witness. All of which is needed for the sake of understanding the compulsive and systematic work of necropolitics. "'*Sale nègre!' ou simplement: 'Tiens, un nègre*," as Fanon puts it in the opening of the fifth chapter of *Black Skin, White Masks*. The systematic work of nihilism works on the imagination in terms of both expressive culture and revolutionary political vision. We can see this in Fanon's evocation of a "term for term correspondence" between colonialism and anticolonial struggle. Both share the same desire, need, and vital sense of energy. Fanon writes, "the arrival of the colonist signified syncretically the death of indigenous society, cultural lethargy, and the petrifaction of the individual. For the colonized, life can only materialize from the rotting cadaver of the colonist. Such then is the term-for-term correspondence between the two arguments."[3]

The beginning of colonial relations is the inception of a particularly radical form of nihilism, one that not only transforms the terms of relation between the foreigner and the indigenous—colonial invasion, conquest as a form of life for each demographic in the colony, subjugation as the extension of the terms of invasion and conquest—but also the terms of emancipation from that nihilism. A terrible double session. The violence and its visceral character in invasion, conquest, and subjugation calls for the same intensity and kind. Fanon writes further that "it so happens that for the colonized this violence is invested with positive, formative features because it constitutes their only work. This violent praxis is totalizing since each individual represents a violent link in a great chain, in the almighty body of violence rearing up in reaction to the primary violence of the colonizer."[4]

Fanon's rather blunt linking of colonial violence to revolutionary or liberatory violence is striking. It is striking because it risks turning revolutionary or liberatory violence into a reactive political formation rather than an impulse (or even just animating desire) for the oppressed to be who they are outside the colonial system, whether that is a sense of who the colonized were *before* conquest or how they have created a sense of life in the interstices of the colonial system. Retrieval and refusal are suspended in order to let reactivity intervene against colonial hegemony.

The temporality of this is key. Fanon's rejection of the past is clear from the very beginning, as is Wright's skepticism around, if not outright hostility toward, tradition. For both, the past represents a nostalgia long erased (not under erasure) and, when still that past persists, a kind of dispiriting refusal to contend with how conquest and oppression have fundamentally changed the world. When Wright described tradition as a retrograde, naïve appeal in "Tradition and Industrialization," he directed it at the geography of nostalgia: Africa. But also to Asia and the colonized world more broadly. "The West," which is a vexed term for Wright precisely because colonization has in some measure made the entire world into the West, perpetrates a double temporal crime in the colonies, marking the past as abject and irretrievable *and* blocking any sense of a fully developed future. But rather than imagine modalities of retrieval or a right to tradition, Wright instead argues for the comprehensiveness of a sense of freedom. He writes: "The problem is freedom from a dead past. And freedom to build a rational future. How much are we willing to risk for freedom? I say let us risk everything. Freedom begets freedom. Europe, I say to you before it is too late: Let the Africans and Asians whom you have educated in Europe have their freedom, or you will lose your own in trying to keep freedom from them."[5]

There is only the future. The future that is *only* demands a radical break with the past and present toward a future without precedent through and through. This inexorable break with time means either death for Europe or Europe can cease being what it is—empire, exploiting hegemony, violence and degradation—and become, like Africans and Asians, something free and liberated from everything. *Including tradition.* Wright and Fanon meet in this quirky critical sentiment with profound consequences. The past or the present represent only different strategies for *failing to become*. The colonized or the Black body under antiblack regimes stay frozen in time. Becoming, for Fanon, therefore means beginning with the unprecedented: the very idea that Black bodies, Black lives, and Black people *matter* and have *life*. This generates a new humanism. While it is true that Wright does not use the language of humanism or a new humanism, the risk-everything vision of freedom represents precisely that same sentiment: There is no precedent, there is no culture or history to imitate (colonial mimicry is a graveyard of aspirations), and so there is only the new.

I rehearse all of this to underscore the visceral and difficult character of Wright's and Fanon's nihilism: Social death is an embodied worldly threat, executed by fiat and with impunity. It is necropolitical through and through. That "through and through," that total sense of command, is part of what so troubles a careful reader. Not only is the designation of a killable class central to their nihilism, but Fanon's vision of liberation, something lacking in most of Wright's grindingly nihilistic fiction but rehabilitated in some nonfiction pieces, is itself an extension of the necropolitical order. The imagination itself is colonized by the Manichean structure of the colonial logic of power and sovereignty. The redesignation of the killing and killable class both begins revolutionary action and sustains its righteous energy. Life materializes from the cadaver of the former colonial body—a body that is literal (there is warfare) and figurative (there is the destruction of the state and its political culture). Fanon's commitment to an unprecedented future is his logical critical extension of Wright's early fiction, especially in terms of political sensibility and vision, and in some ways an expression of Fanon's optimism as a thinker. But it is also a gesture of deep nihilism about the present. There is nothing for Wright or Fanon in the present that could set the terms of liberation. And the past is equally untenable and undesirable; tradition is fantasy, "the great black mirage,"[6] and impossible in existential time. That is, the past offers no instruction beyond the animating force of rage-memory of invasion and conquest, in which the rotting cadaver of the colonist settles the atrocity ledger. Not without moral justification. But moral justification is not the same as existential need and demand. Liberation is total, just as invasion, conquest, and subjugation were total. Totality means victory over the totality of time itself. Neither the past nor the present make knowledge of self and world possible in any way that is *authentic* or unmediated by antiblackness. The past is petrified and lost, only retrieved through a filter of antiblackness in the present. The present is social death, and Black subjectivity is formed and reformed, produced and reproduced, only as the figure of the slave. A complete evacuation of meaning.

But the future remains open.

In that way Wright's evocation of freedom in the "Tradition and Industrialization" essay tells a double story, demanding something unrecognizable in the world as we know it—"Black" and "freedom" are an unthinkable pairing—and calling toward the world as we know it in order to reconfigure and produce different kinds of subjects and social-political realities. As well, Fanon's description of the horizons of antiblackness and meaninglessness in the present is never quite the closed system it might pretend or want to be. Fanon's optimism or at least impulse to *know* and to *be* in revolutionary space is embedded within the present and that limits his articulation of colonial antiblackness as a closed system. This is how necropolitics bears on both the diagnostic and revolutionary aspects of Wright and Fanon. Necropolitics is not just a theory of power and sovereignty. It is also an account of how the imagination imagines liberation in the deathworld. It is exactly in this space opened up by Wright and Fanon, their nihilism and its retreat from the full implications, that contemporary Afropessimist theory takes root. But that taking root is situated in the ambiguous and ambivalent time of nihilism. If nihilism in Wright and Fanon *wants* the unprecedented, yet remains in some key ways linked to the present—the "new" in a new kind of freedom, the "new" in a new kind of humanism—and stays committed to eschewing the past, then the future is the first and the last push against the meaningless of Black time. Black time is meaningless in the past, present, and the folds between that make interracial time ecstatic. The center of nihilism and of the everyday. In that ecstatic time, Black time becomes nihilistic, evacuated of meaning, and therefore fundamentally enabling of white time's ecstasy that disables Black time's hope. To be Black in the antiblack world, Fanon notes, is to live with an amputation. The future is prosthesis. Or perhaps regenerative of figurative limbs. Perhaps a new body altogether.

Afropessimism wants nothing to do with this prosthetic future folded into the cultural and political present. Pessimism encompasses the entire stretch of existential and social time. Past, present, *and future*, as well as all of those between spaces.

It should be said, however, that the term "Afropessimism" is by no means a precise or narrow signifier. Rather, it gathers to it a whole cluster of thinkers, methods, and motifs that explore the depth of the relationship between an antiblack world and the meaning of blackness itself. Now, in many ways this is *the* question that unifies the Black Atlantic intellectual tradition and is nothing particular to Afropessimist theory. Indeed, the "Black Atlantic" is that milieu in which the term "Black" and the phenomenon of "blackness" originated, an event that structures and has structured the world for centuries around the Manichean opposition of black and white. Race birthed in this context is saturated with abjection to the point of making abjection the very infrastructure of the interracial worlds of settler colonies, slave societies, and the persistence of white hegemony and its gaze in the colonial imagination for both the colonizer and the colonized. The key shift in Afropessimism is the move away from antiblackness as a feature or decisive embellishment of elements of social, political, and cultural life and toward a more foundational account of how the world of antiblackness conditions every and all the things that might arise from that world. We can already see the appeal of fundamental ontology for theorizing this relation. Antiblackness, we might say, is like (if not near equivalent to) colonialism: a total project. A total project, in this case, in which antiblackness is identified as a structural question rather than, as is the case with colonialism, a sense of particular national or racial interest. The line between structure and interest can be difficult to discern for precisely the reasons we find in Afropessimist accounts of structure: Interests *themselves* are formed by structural components, so the independence of interests from the structure of antiblackness is rendered illusory. Racial interests, prejudices, and advocacy instead emerge as symptomatic of a wider question of the internal, infrastructural composition of an antiblack world. Ontology, social death, antiblackness, nihilism, and the task of thinking. In that composite event, Afropessimism finds its most rigorous and systemic argument and theorization of Being.

How does this shift in thinking impact theorization of social death? Social death is a question of how subaltern and abject subjects find themselves in the world. Not find themselves as a mode of entry into the world with all the dialectical and dynamic elements that would suggest, but instead as a matter of facticity. With the term *facticity*, I have in mind here Heidegger's characterization of subjectivity (*Dasein*) in *Being and Time* as already finding itself in the world in a particular kind of way. A particular kind of way that is formative of the being of beings. Heidegger writes: "In this everydayness there are certain structures, but essential ones which, in every kind of Being that factical Dasein may possess, persist as determinative for the character of its Being. Thus by having regard for the basic state of Dasein's everydayness, we shall bring out the Being of this entity in preparatory fashion."[7]

This passage tells so much of the story of subjectivity in Heidegger's early work as well as indicating the terms of the development of his thought in the decades that follow. But for our purposes here it is important to note how Heidegger describes the worldliness of the subject as always late to itself. We find ourselves *already* in the world, rather than consciously and actively entering the world and, in that activity, preparing ourselves for acts of perception and judgment. The existential stretch of subjectivity is for Heidegger worldly from the beginning; we find ourselves *already* here, in this place, and the task of thinking ontology is to re-collect and recollect the structures embedded in that place and in ourselves as subjects in the world.

In theorizing this structure of subjectivity and worldliness, Heidegger is particularly attentive to existential time and how temporality makes sense of the subject—and then how we make sense of temporality, having already been made *by* it. The next step in analysis in *Being and Time*—and this is so critical for both understanding nihilism and generating the terms of the Afropessimist subject—is linking the ecstatic temporality of the subject to historical experience. Heidegger's shift in analysis sets in motion a complex intersection of existential modes of time, beginning, as always, with how we find ourselves in the world *already*. To be in the world is to be in language. To be in language is to inherit history: word, concept, and the possibility of thinking. Facticity gathers all of this to it in a moment of radical passivity that is also the condition for the possibility of existential freedom and activity. Heidegger writes:

> "Historicality" stands for the state of Being that is constitutive for Dasein's "historizing" as such; only on the basis of such "historizing" is anything like "world-history" possible or can anything belong historically to world-history. In its factical Being, any Dasein is as it already was, and it is "what" it already was. It *is* its past, whether explicitly or not. And this is so not only in that its past is, as it were, pushing itself along "behind" it, and that Dasein possesses what is past as a property which is still present-at-hand and which sometimes has after-effects upon it: Dasein "is" its past in the way of *its* own Being, which, to put it roughly, "historizes" out of its future on each occasion.[8]

Heidegger's link between facticity and history or historical experience in this passage is absolutely indispensable for understanding the Afropessimist subject. In terms of figures in the Afropessimist movement, this is especially important for understanding Calvin Warren's work, as well as Jared Sexton's rewriting of psychoanalysis in a pessimist frame. For the former, Heidegger is the locus of *Ontological Terror* and its myriad claims about the relation between Being and blackness, in particular how Warren works to recast Fanon's zone of nonbeing in Heideggerian terms. For the latter, it is the presumption of the account of the libidinal subject, namely, that claim that subject inherits the historicity of racialized experience in the structure of desire. So, for Sexton, the way in which we find ourselves in a libidinal flow is couched inside the being of *Dasein* as an ecstatically stretched cluster of impulses and desires that are so deeply entwined with history that the libidinal subject becomes something like a cluster of symptoms and racial pathologies. These are the very terms and signs of inheritance.

There is a lot to say about the meaning of Being and the question of blackness and Warren's work will prove especially helpful in this regard. But for the moment, I want to underscore how the question of history, subjectivity, and time in Heidegger's work marks a very different relation to futurity. The future is folded into the past and present, rather than standing apart from it as an open and therefore potentially unprecedented possibility. This is not any kind of historical determinism, of course. For all of his conservatism and of course also fascist politics, Heidegger understands the possibility of historical shift and change in important terms. In fact, that is part of his (shameful, murderous) interest in National Socialism at the beginning of the regime: the promise of another future for Germany. The unprecedented can be radical in myriad ways, of course. Yet, the primary lesson, as it were, of Heidegger's conception of the temporally ecstatic subject and the relation of time and subjectivity to history is that we cannot make the future *without* the folds of past and present. The future is in some significant measure already written, at least in the factical terms of grasping subjectivity as a temporal phenomenon. What we *can* do is seize upon what is given to us by history and, in that seizure, form an authentic relation to time as such and specifically the time of futurity. When we form that authentic relation to the time of futurity, we work *with* what is given and, in the genius work of the imagination and the crafting of things with the tools of history, make something *different*. The new is in that way nothing new. Or at least not wholly new. Inheritance in Heidegger both limits and makes possible all possibility. Being's historical libidinal economy. It desires its own world and remains incarnate in its worldliness.

The question is how, when redeployed inside the Black intellectual tradition, this shift in temporality also marks a key difference between nihilism and pessimism. The key difference here is the relation of the future to the present and past. Nihilism still gives hope; the meaninglessness of the world of social death bears hope within it because the temporality of the Black subject, even the subject subjected in its subjectivity, holds the future pure and open. A new humanism. A literature written to the human rather than the condition of racial subjugation. The essential difference between the future and all other modalities of time structures hope. Indeed, hope is contingent upon the cleavage of this essential difference. But if Heidegger is right about the folds of ecstatic time and is then rewritten into the Black Atlantic experience, then that cleavage is not possible with any kind of purity. If Being is a closed system and time operates inside or at least in conjunction with Being, then hope cannot take root inside that closed system. Pessimism begins in this essential *non*difference between the future and other modalities of time. Pessimism takes inheritance to be sociogenic and binding of time itself, rendering the future another kind of variation of present and past. Heidegger helps us see this and with crucial modifications of the terms of analysis—midcentury German thought is not a duplication or map of Black Atlantic experience, of course—pessimism as Afropessimism emerges as a coherent system of thinking Being, thinking subjectivity, thinking time, and therefore thinking the conditions of the possibility of thinking itself. What is the subject of this Black time? What is the subject of this Black history and its facticity? It is the story of a certain kind of terror of nonbeing, of the nothing. A thinking that moves to the furthest margins of nihilism in search of temporal closure.

From Terror and Ontology to Cultural Production

It is always worth recalling Fanon's remarks on the zone of nonbeing in *Black Skin, White Masks* and to do so here, both in the interest of what the text wants to say and how it says more than it can contain. This is a feature of great works. The brilliance of insight is not simply reducible to an enduring or timeless observation and theorization, but is also, perhaps even first, a description of the fecundity of a claim. Fanon's remarks on the zone of nonbeing are exactly that in so many ways, generating an important observation of the work of antiblackness on the body and Black life as well as a passageway from nihilism to pessimism. He begins *Black Skin, White Masks* with a reflection on "man," by which he likely means humanity (though it is also gender specific in so many ways), and the structural incompatibility of "Black" and "man." That incompatibility speaks to the problem of humanism and how notions of the human have been crafted and deployed in the interest of making blackness abject, socially dead, and incapable of a full sense of humanity. It is structural at the level of social, political, and psychological infrastructure. To be is to be subjected to social death. Fanon writes:

> What does man want?
> What does the black man want?
> Running the risk of angering my black brothers, I shall say that the Black is not a man.
> There is a zone of nonbeing, an extraordinarily sterile and arid region, an incline stripped bare of every essential from which a genuine new departure can emerge. In most cases, the black man cannot take advantage of this descent into a veritable hell.⁹

It is important to underscore the significance of this passage. Both desire and want animate the remark, noting the incompatibility of life behind the veil, to recall Du Bois's figure of Black subjectivity, with interracial life, the interracial world, and therefore the range of possibilities for subjectivities sociogenically constructed as Black. In that world *as* incompatibility, desire meets sterility, an unproductive space in which the Black subject's body is evacuated of its vitality and fecundity. Social death becomes a form of incarnate being that exposes the racialized body and makes it vulnerable to all modes of violence. Yet, there is also desire. For Fanon in his early work, this sets the tone of nihilism and stages his subject's transformation late in the book, which moves from the depths of this sense of meaninglessness to the ecstasy of an unprecedented future in the concluding remarks. The final line of *Black Skin, White Masks* pleads for the universe to make him a man who questions. Questioning, life as and in the interrogative, is the desire behind the veil made vital in another world. A rupture in and break with space and time.

But the account of the zone of nonbeing in *Black Skin, White Masks* also positions the Black subject in an impossible place, one that implicates other forms of temporality that disable or at the very least make considerably more complex the work of liberation. Fanon opens a space of conversation for Afropessimism in his evocation of the zone of nonbeing, in particular his characterization of it as a "descent into a veritable hell," but that space is limited, in Fanon's own treatment, by a lack of a rigorous ontology. That is, for Fanon sociogeny is sufficient for thinking the zone of nonbeing. An antiblack world produces that social form *nègre*, which has no place in the very world that generated it. Sociogeny, however, is structured by the time of nihilism and the cleavage of the unprecedented future from the ecstatic temporal stretch of the subject. Heidegger's claims about the structure of the historical subject—in this case, reframed as the racial subject of inheritance—lingers in the background as a critic, asking how deeply our sense of possibility (or even necessity) has been transformed in the work of history on the time of being-in-the-world. The rigorous and coherent character of Heidegger's linking of time, history, and subjectivity makes the question of Being more expansive and complex and, in that thinking, returns us to Fanon wondering how the zone of nonbeing might say more than the concluding transformation would indicate. This is especially the case when one considers Heidegger's post–*Being and Time* work and its rigorous interrogation of the question of the Nothing. Nonbeing is a rich and complicated proposition. How does a more robust ontology alter the trajectory of the thought of nonbeing? And how does that ontology shift our understanding of the time of antiblackness?

With this in mind, we can see how Warren's *Ontological Terror* is such a key moment in the short history of Afropessimism. The book is nothing like an event; it does not appropriate thinking in its shift of frame, even as it generates important new vocabulary for thinking through pessimism in a Black Atlantic context. Rather, *Ontological Terror* distills much of the conceptual direction and impulse of prior Afropessimist thinkers and reorients pessimist thoughts *inside* a deeply Heideggerian vision of fundamental ontology. Indeed, one of the first lessons of Warren's work is that the Afropessimist movement, for all of its interrogations of affect, epistemology, and the political and libidinal economy of antiblackness, has not adequately raised the question of Being as such. The question of Being is inseparable from the thinking of subjectivity and blackness. Fanon's conception of world, borne out in his theorization of sociogeny, gestures at the question of Being but always in terms of a straightforward existential-phenomenological account of the subject in relation to language, desire, the gaze, and the struggle for recognition. In each of those relations, Fanon describes how blackness is a question for *beings*. But Heidegger's work was from the outset about displacing the question of beings with the question of Being, linking the fundamental ontological question of Being to beings in a conception of ontological difference. That difference, the difference between Being and beings, is a relation of disclosure. Being is disclosed through the existential structure of beings or *Dasein*, which means, in the Afropessimist context, that the abjection of beings as Black discloses something about the structure of Being itself in relation to blackness. Fanon already indicated such a link and series of questions in the phrase *zone of nonbeing*. What is nonbeing to beings? That is the experience of the *nègre*—at one and the same time, a racial signifier and a racial slur. What is nonbeing to Being? This question is too much for Fanon's text; Fanon asks more *in the direction of* ontological difference than the text of *Black Skin, White Masks* can answer. The building blocks for this "answer," as it were, lies in Heidegger's post–*Being and Time* work, something that Warren is able to revisit and rewrite with the question of social death as its stage. From the great West Indian thinker to the great German thinker to the question of blackness in the

United States and maybe the Black Atlantic broadly. A peculiar sequence that offers the challenge for *Ontological Terror*.

This is already immensely fraught space. One of the prominent features of *Ontological Terror* is that, in the end, it is largely a book about Heidegger. Not the Heidegger of the Heidegger studies industrial complex, that is for sure. Indeed, what discussions there have been around Heidegger and race have either revolved around National Socialism and *The Black Notebooks*, around well-known passages here and there that publication of *Notebooks* largely confirmed, or energy drawn from Derrida's confrontation with Heidegger in the *Geschlecht* series. Those discussions are immanent to Heideggerian texts and their intimate horizons, whereas Warren's treatment of those texts is creative reading in the best sense: reconfiguring key phenomenological and hermeneutic insights in order to intervene in Afropessimist discourse with a genuinely robust vision of ontology. This robust vision is much needed. To be sure, key works from the Afropessimist moment have always staked out *a version of* ontology as a foundational field of inquiry, while also (and this is important) drawing on insights and methods that are one step removed from *purely* ontological inquiry: psychoanalysis, Marxism, Fanonian thinking.

In linking Heidegger to questions raised by the experience of blackness and antiblackness—the two terms are inseparable, the affirmative produced in and by its negation—Warren is able to give depth and substance to Fanon's evocation of the zone of nonbeing. The intersection of ontology and blackness becomes, in Warren's hands, a matter of the Nothing. Here, we can think of an important contrast point with Zakiyyah Jackson's *Becoming Human*, which also takes on the question of ontology. Jackson's aim is to describe and critically intervene in the space between the human and the animal, an aim that poses antiblackness at the interval between inclusion in the category of human and the abjection of blackness. *Between* orders of being. But of course orders are not innocent. Orders articulate terms of exclusion, exploitation, and violence. In this moment, Jackson navigates a passage through pessimism, marking blackness as the "exception" and "plasticity" that makes representations of the human possible.[10] There is no exit out of this impasse. The terms that make representation of the human possible, or even the *becoming* of the human possible, exclude blackness in particular ways that make "Black" and "human" unthinkable and inexpressible. In a Black Atlantic context, Jackson here approximates something like Gayatri Spivak's subaltern. The conditions for representation make representation impossible, or what Jackson calls the *exception*. Against this, and here is the exit from Afropessimism, Jackson proposes retooling the notion of the human *for* Black people rooted *in* Afrodiasporic notions of being and becoming. Not so much Fanon's and Aimé Césaire's new humanism, written to the measure of the world, but nevertheless in that horizon: an alternative sense of the human exterior to white Western racial ontologies, which also sits between the human and the animal. A certain kind of deconstructive move, to be sure, but one that positions critique wholly external to the white Western logic of humanism. A third sense of exile alongside the intrusive and extrusive modes of exile in social death, perhaps, but if read in relation to Patterson's work, this is an exile that imagines another kind of being and life as both possible and necessary.

This contrast point of Jackson's work is important because it raises the question of passage and to what extent passage to the limit of ontology and the racialized subject can be surmounted by an alternative vision of being and becoming. Jackson and Warren travel a similar conceptual path in navigating the border of ontology. For both, it is a question of the exception—though importantly not a *state* of exception—and how expression links to Being, which then renders blackness inexpressible inside Being itself. To where does exceptionality send us, conceptually, in terms of the meaning of Being for blackness? *Blackness*, always, for the very conditions of phrasing it as, say, "Black life" are erased in the act of ontological exclusion. For Jackson, this sends us to alternative traditions for configuring the human/animal relation. For Warren, it sends us to a notion of nothingness or simply *the Nothing*. And here is where Warren's treatment of Heidegger's thinking of Being in relation to Nothing offers so much promise for Black studies. In that thinking, Warren claims, Heidegger "helps us understand the relation between black suffering and metaphysics, slavery and objectification, antiblackness and forgetfulness, thinking and remembering. (*Heidegger's philosophy, in many ways, can be read as an allegory of antiblackness and black suffering—the metaphysical violence of the transatlantic slave trade.*)"[11]

There is an interesting shift here in characterization, set between two sentences. Heidegger "helps," which is the moment of creative engagement. Heidegger's work is an "allegory," which is the moment of another claim on the text. And so Warren provocatively suggests, with a "perhaps" framing the remark, that "Heidegger was *really* talking about black(ness) and black suffering all along."[12] This is no doubt a strange claim for Heidegger scholars to digest, but it is also a remark and characterization that places the crisis of white Western modernity and postmodernity in the space of mass murder, trafficking in the worst kinds of violence and the history of catastrophe. *The colonist lives from the cadaver of the colonized*, to reverse Fanon's telling of a similar story. Modernity lives from death but produces certain forms of death to which Heidegger's work can be profound witness. In that witness to that living, Heidegger becomes for Warren and others a living text for Black studies and the study of antiblackness.

This is no mere question of scholarly resource and priority. It is also and firstly a question of the meaning of ontology for theorizing antiblackness and its sense of world. As well, it is a question of the shift from nihilism properly speaking to the time of pessimism. If we return to Patterson's theorization of social death, we can see the figure of the slave and the problem of intrusive-extrusive exile appear in a bleaker, less temporally fluid frame. The social death of Patterson's notion of the slave moves, as exilic, inside the time of the antiblack world; there is a *place* in that world, albeit a place of abjection, nihilism, and radical exclusion. The ontology of exile is difficult to characterize here, but Warren and the Heidegger of Warren's reading challenge the very matter of thinking social death inside Being. Patterson describes exile as intrusive and extrusive, which doubles the meaning of blackness. It is outside the system of life and meaning. This is the exilic in the ontological sense. But exile is also *relation*, a way of being both inside Being and outside it in the mode of deficiency and erasure. But relation, always. And it is this relationality that makes alternative imaginations of the figure of the slave—whether as a subject of rebellion or a new configuration of the human/animal—possible. Warren's engagement with Heidegger and rehabilitation of the Nothing as an expression of blackness disengages social death from Being itself.

We can think here of an especially important moment in *Ontological Terror* in which Warren addresses the question of biopower while theorizing Samuel Cartwright's 1851 essay "Diseases and Peculiarities of the Negro Race." Cartwright's essay, as Warren notes, thinks race in the direction of epidemiology and away from metaphysics, which, on the face of it, would suggest an early biopolitical theorization of race and racialization. It is such an historically interesting essay for such treatment all by itself, but Warren stages Cartwright's work in order to make an important and incisive comment on the place of biopower in thinking blackness and ontology. "Our concern here is not biopower, however," Warren writes, "for the black psyche is designed not to fold blacks into humanity and the human sciences, but to situate black being outside these discourses. The black psyche is not about the manipulation of life or forced living, but about maintaining the meaninglessness of death and the obliteration of life."[13]

In many ways this remark on the meaninglessness of death and obliteration of life is a clear restatement of the guiding logic of *Ontological Terror*. But read between Fanon, Patterson, and Jackson, as well as Achille Mbembe, we can see how Warren deploys fundamental ontology and the thought of the Nothing in order to upend the discourse of social death, exile, and the impasse between the human and the animal. This closes the system of antiblackness, but in an importantly different manner and according to a very different logic. In that closure of the system, sealed in the question of Being and ~~being~~ black, social death as lived experience appears, phenomenologically, as a symptom.

Indeed, broadly speaking, this kind of expansion of the concept of social death is one of the most important innovations in contemporary Afropessimism. For Patterson, social death is a characteristic of enslavement and a property of the formal institution of slavery. The development of this notion in Afropessimist theory recasts the property of enslavement in the long, enduring horizon of slavery's afterlife. It is important to emphasize the function of *life* in afterlife, noting how that phrasing identifies slavery as operating as an active agent in the work of everyday world-making, world-destroying, and cultural and political imagination. This is one of the most difficult claims in Afropessimism, but also the claim that animates the entirety of the movement. Sexton puts it bluntly in *Black Masculinity and the Cinema of Policing* when he writes that he "takes productions of the culture industry, no less than its independent offshoots and countercurrents, as privileged occasions for thinking again about how profoundly the global practice of racial differentiation, from slavery to segregation and beyond, structures the totality of state and civil society."[14]

The stakes of this folding of culture into totality could not be higher, given how in *Black Masculinity and the Cinema of Policing* Sexton, deriving from a political insight in Anthony Farley's critical legal theory, understands the pacifying effects and affects of culture. That is, this is not merely a question of the nature of culture and its capacity to resist or refuse, but rather first and foremost a question of how cultural production—in the culture *industry*— blocks the figure of the slave incarnate, the socially dead, from dreaming and conceiving what Farley describes as a nonservile sense of insurrection.[15] Slavery's after*life* operates in this moment by truncating the cultural and political imagination from the inside, rather than disciplining it from the outside with mobilized racial violence and/or institutional forms of subjugation and exclusion. That political purchase for interracial social space is the elimination of righteous insurrection.

How should we conceive the conceptual dynamic of this blockage of the socially dead from insurrection of the material and affective sort? When Sexton writes that "blackness is not the pathogen in afro-pessimism, the world is,"[16] we catch sight of the urgency of Warren's contribution to and transformation of fundamental ontology. "World" is not a terminal concept. It is, rather, a conceptual space contingent upon and generated by Being itself. Heidegger's insight into ontological difference, into the essential difference yet fundamental entwinement of subjectivity (beings) and Being, deepens and critically widens the claim Sexton makes in "The Social Life of Social Death." To think *world* as pathogen, and therefore nihilism and other pessimistic affects as symptoms, is to theorize sociogeny in a phenomenologically naïve register. Naïve, that is, not in the sense of an empty, shallow, or uninformed claim, but rather in the sense of a claim that needs further grounding but cannot generate those grounds on its own terms. Ontology does just that. And so, in this way, *Ontological Terror* operates as a profound deepening of the troubling characterization of the world as pathogen—a theoretical rhetoric common to multiple Afropessimist thinkers and texts—and operates in order to close the system of pessimistic thought in thinking the Nothing as Black ~~being~~. To cross out is not to erase from Being. To cross out is to mark the incompatibility of blackness with Being *or* beings as well as the inarticulable character of that incompatibility. Black being literally cannot be said. The subaltern cannot be spoken *of*. This pushes the question of social death into the infrastructure of Being itself with important conceptual, epistemological, and political consequences. Dispiriting consequences, of course, always. It is pessimism, after all.

Critics of Afropessimism, especially those aimed at versions of it written prior to the publication of *Ontological Terror*, have leaned into questions of pleasure and cultural production. This is no small intervention, one that has its best moment in Fred Moten's work on Black optimism. In some ways, any radical critique of Afropessimism that posits an oppositional (or appositional) *optimism* operates, or ought to operate, in the same space of a pessimism conceived as a structure of feeling. Not quite immanent critique, but something very close to it. Whether as a ground for theory or a symptomatic moment, affective life is important for understanding Black nihilism and its transformation into an Afropessimism. So, when affective life—the pleasures of Black culture and cultural production, aspirational or grounded love of blackness as such—is gathered to sites of resistance as a response to Afropessimism, there is an intimacy of concern for and attentiveness to the varied souls of Black folk. This is why it is important when Moten writes in "Black Op" that Black optimism "is bound up with what it is to claim blackness and the appositional, runaway, phonoptic black operations—expressive of an autopoetic organization in which flight and inhabitation modify each other—that have been thrust upon it." Relationality blocks optimism yet is also the condition for the possibility of asserting the *possibility* of that optimism precisely because it is located inside the terms of pessimism itself. Thus, Moten adds that "the burden of this paradoxically aleatory goal is our historicity, animating the reality of escape in and escape from."[17]

In light of our reading of Wright's "The Man Who Lived Underground" above, we can see how nihilism itself already limits the scope of any optimistic claim issuing from an *under*, whether underground or undercommons. The allure, significance, and power of the *under* lies in its flash of the experience of the impossible: Black and free. Escape *from* the world means death upon reintroduction to that world. This is the terrifying truth-telling moment in Wright's short story. But Moten also modifies the term escape, in a funky and compelling twist on *marronage*, as an escape *in*. That escape *in* marks the fraught status of Black cultural production in an antiblack world, which for Moten is at least the possibility, if not lived actuality, of a world within a world, a fold in Being, that makes an optimism at least *imaginable* and *conceivable*. Runaway, autopoetic, and appositional—an optimism lodged inside the possibility of a cultural negation of what social death enacts, which is the negation of the life of Black life. But lodging the question of cultural production and optimism inside the structure of the world is conceptually compelling while also an utterly fraught move, especially because it is one that answers the question of social death inside the notion of intrusive exile. Sexton's "The Social Life of Social Death" serves as an important critical rejoinder to this iteration of an Afro-optimism precisely because it argues for the *longue durée* of social death.[18] To this point, Sexton writes that a "Black optimism is not the negation of the negation that is afro-pessimism." Reactive thinking is not sufficient. It is not sufficient because, on Sexton's treatment,

> black social life does not negate black social death by inhabiting it and vitalizing it. A living death is as much a death as it is a living. Nothing in afro-pessimism suggests that there is no black (social) life, only that black life is not social life in the universe formed by the codes of state and civil society, of citizen and subject, of nation and culture, of people and place, of history and heritage, of all the things that colonial society has in common with the colonized, of all that capital has in common with labor—the modern world system.[19]

It is so interesting to read this passage in the frame of *Black Masculinity and the Cinema of Policing* and the passage quoted earlier, one in which Sexton deploys the phrase *culture industry*. That phrase informs his broad assessment of cultural production and the work of reproducing, in the work of the culture industry *broadly* and also the Black culture industry in particular, the figure of the slave. An unremunerated figure that makes antiblackness work while simultaneously creating the *feeling* of remuneration, freedom, and insurgent inclusion from the margins of nihilism toward the center. But that figure remains incarnated as socially dead in pessimistic space even when it "lives" as the social life of social death—which, as Sexton notes, is not life in any way livable under the codes of state and society. Fanon's abjection of blues and "great Negro music" in his "Racism and Culture" essay shows up here in modified form.[20]

As a reply to the Afropessimist counterclaim we find in Moten's "Black Op" essay, this is a fascinating and consistent extension of the Afropessimist prerogative. Social death, de jure, cannot produce life on the model of life generated by the world that produces the death structure of social death. The de jure status of this claim is important. In a certain sense, we could argue that Moten's thinking of flight and inhabitation at the same time, the odd but necessary movement of escape in *and* escape from, gives us a language of paradox and impossible simultaneity that describes, perhaps even prescribes, the possibility of survival and more. Impossible simultaneity engages social death at the heart of Patterson's description of exile, describing manners of flight and escape *as* home in extrusive and intrusive terms. If we leave the theoretical language in the modality of world and worldhood, then Moten's intervention *might* and likely *does* suggest modalities of counterbeing that intervene against—or perhaps outside—the work of social death and Afropessimism. This is where Warren's work is crucial to secure the boundaries of pessimism against this kind of immanent critique. Fundamental ontology conceives world and worldhood as *leitfaden*, leading clues and threads that indicate formally and informally the relation between social death, pessimism, Being, and Nothing. Sexton concedes something important when he describes the possibility of Black social life in a world of social death: the *possibility* of life, however life is reconceived. But Warren's intervention alters the terms of any claim to counterbeing. The radical sense of Nothing that Heidegger develops, and then Warren embellishes in such fascinating ways with the question of blackness and Black being, renders inoperative the very terms of Moten's optimism. And it is precisely this shift that is so critical for Afropessimism. Sexton and others *need* that sense of rendering inoperative in order to maintain Afropessimism as a purity discourse. But such purity cannot be maintained without a rigorous ontology and the closed, fully grounded system it offers to thinking. If social death is a *leitfaden* rather than a sense of world and its nihilism, then impossible simultaneities *inside* social death cannot generate a sense of space for their play. The question of the meaning of Being and its cruel companion Nothing surmount the play of the world with a grounded pessimism. Impossible simultaneities become their own *leitfaden* of the Nothing. A purity of discourse, a closure of the system. The future is blended back into the space of ecstatic time. Without cleavage from the past and present—the time of nihilism—Afropessimism seals nihilism more deeply inside time and the imagination of futurities. There is no outside.

Purity discourses are always the most compelling for thinking the supplement. They are compelling for thinking supplementarity because they work in the horizon of closed system thinking without hesitation. Closure refines our theoretical sensibilities. How does the closed system of Being, ~~being~~ Black, and Nothing fracture and fissure?

Frequencies and the Problem of Totality

What stands out in Afropessimist ontology, whether in its allusory status in Sexton, Wilderson, and others or in explicit form in Warren's work, is its commitment to a sense of totality. This commitment is not just totality as a quiet habit of thinking or convention of empire but is actually the entire prerogative of the movement. Without commitment to closure of the system, Afropessimism would merely be a note on mood, which is no real pessimism at all. And, to that end, there is a reason why some of the key theoretical backbones of contemporary Afropessimism come from, however much modified, systematic thinkers like Heidegger, Lacan, and Fanon. All three offer a metanarrative of how notions of Being and world forestructure senses of desire, creation, action, and possibility. While certainly Heidegger and Fanon draw lines at the edges of their systems that open to exteriorities of various sorts—Heidegger with some intention, Fanon in his omissions and conceptual missteps—Afropessimism interest(s) in their work deploy and reconfigure the work in the interest of a pessimistic system of totality.

Totality in any system is both fabrication and vulnerability. This is the irony of thinking totality—that, in drawing the limit of the possible, other moments of the impossible emerge to disrupt boundaries drawn to close totality. One of the innovations and deep challenges of Afropessimism lies in its strategic and conceptual work around ontogeny. In moving pessimism and blackness away from their root in affect and the cultural economy of antiblackness, both of which form the real roots of racial nihilism, and into the question of Being, Afropessimism after Warren more provocatively and rigorously closes the system of pessimist thinking. If Being itself is antiblackness, then the very terms that might produce fissures and cracks in the boundary of a given system of antiblack racism and social death can be cast as already produced in the horizon of what they might want to interrupt or fracture. *Fatal contamination in the interest of closure.* This makes for an interesting conceptual reversal. Thinking totality is fabrication and therefore always vulnerable, but if Being itself is antiblackness, then the terms of resistance are themselves fabrications and vulnerable to repetition of antiblackness. This is where Fanon's remarks on blues music take hold, in an ontogenic vision of Being and antiblackness, in order to foreclose the possibility of resistance. ~~Being~~ Black, that radical sense of Nothing at the heart of Being itself, absorbs all possibilities. Including the possibility of subversion and the otherwise.

The distinction between nihilism and pessimism emerges in this moment, as well. In particular, I am thinking of how fixated nihilism is on the present and its cleavage from futurity. Wright and Fanon, as we have seen, articulate their nihilism in relation to conditions of the present. Emasculation, the police, the state, religion, and capitalism for Wright. For Fanon, language, the gaze, colonial measure, and the generalized relation between metropole and periphery. The temporality of nihilism is in the fullness of the present—certainly informed by the past and oriented toward a future of repetition and reproduction, but it remains stuck in the present as such. Fanon sees this in his later work, *The Wretched of the Earth* especially, but also in his concluding reflections in *Black Skin, White Masks* where he turns again and again to a repudiation of history and memory: refusal to be defined in the horizon of slavery, denial of reparations because we are not absorbed in or by the past, and an opening of time in(to) which he pleads to be seen as a man who questions. The opening of the future, however abstractly articulated in *Black Skin, White Masks* and however obliquely indicated in Wright's spiraling fiction, is a sign of the link between nihilism in the present and its temporal limit. Nihilism does not control the future because nihilism only controls the present in a configuration of racial hegemony that depends upon reproductive institutions and structures of thought. Revolutionary violence is violence against time itself, which is then violence against the colonial state that opens nihilism to another future. In Fanon's treatment, that opening is always a story of fiat and not negotiation of systems and their limits; the purity of the future makes possible the purity of breakage. Wright's story is more truncated and rarely imagines the future so boldly. Bigger Thomas is sentenced for murder, Fred Daniels is killed by the police, and Cross Damon is murdered. In this sense, Wright is more concerned with the impact of nihilism on Black affect and the imagination of possibility than he is with the future, although the close of "The Man Who Was Almost a Man," when Dave Saunders stands at the train tracks contemplating another beginning, does suggest another life possibility. That possibility suggests a future very much along the lines of Fanon's vision: violence as the beginning of liberation. Dave keeps his gun close, in his pocket. The reclaimed phallus, another possible future.

It is also important to situate this moment of nihilism, then pessimism, in the context of the question of language—a context that is underthematized in the Afropessimist movement with a few exceptions.[21] Political economy, social theory, and broad characterizations of the structure of slavery's afterlife are more prominent for important reasons, namely, because the nihilist and proto-pessimist figures and texts in the Black intellectual tradition provide such key resources for just those approaches. But once the question of Being emerges as not just an element, but as a ground of Afropessimist thinking, language forms a sort of halo around concepts, characterizations, and theorizations of world, worldhood, and whatever remains (or does not remain) of the socially dead subject. The question of language is important not just for strategic reasons—though it is certainly that—but also as a follow through of all the invocations of Heidegger and fundamental ontology. Language and Being are so intimate in Heidegger's work, but it is also the emphasis on the peculiarities of the word that complicate any theory that deploys that work for the sake of closure to a system. It is critical first to link the question of Being to language and subjectivity. This is one of the strengths of Warren's *Ontological Terror*, linking Being, antiblackness, and the impossibility of beings as Black; the crossing out of the being of Black as ~~being~~ Black is no mere embellishment or typeset performance. It is a way of holding writing tight to theory. Being is an event of, in, and through subjectivity; there is no question of Being outside the being of the subject who raises the question; recall the famous claim by Heidegger that *Dasein* is the being for whom the question of Being is a question. The being who raises the question raises the question as a matter of language. Language speaks Being, houses Being, and *Dasein*'s own relation to Being is navigated in or through a relation to language. That moment of raising the question is the moment of the entwinement of language and Being. History, memory, and time are important in this moment precisely because all bear on how language is and is not able to carry a relation to Being. Sometimes there is intimacy. And sometimes language falls away from Being, especially in the epoch of technology and its flattening of the world. Or colonialism and its alienation of subaltern speech.

 I say all this, but in no way want to invoke Heidegger in the mode of informal fallacy, to appeal to his authority without foregrounding theoretical inquiry. Rather, it is helpful to return, via Warren's conceptual prerogative, to one of the most important insights post–*Being and Time* as a way of reframing the problem of ~~being~~ and Black, then Being and Black. In "Letter on Humanism," Heidegger plainly and straightforwardly places Being in subjectivity, then both in the frame of language. He writes: "But for man it is ever a question of finding what is fitting in his essence that corresponds to such destiny; for in accord with this destiny man as ek-sisting has to guard the truth of Being. Man is the shepherd of Being."[22]

Language is the modality of the shepherd of Being. Language organizes and makes purposive the relation of *Dasein* to Being, absorbing both while also maintaining all essential differences. Language *houses* Being precisely in the sense that it is a home for subjectivity—there is no sense of the subject outside of language and language places us in culture and history—while also summoning Being into that shared space of expressive and thinkerly life. Thus, if language is the house of Being, then our relation, whatever it is and however we configure or describe it, to Being (estrangement, intimacy, astonishment, absorption) is inseparable from the relation of language to thinking. Perhaps this trope from Heidegger is already plenty familiar, but it is always worth quoting and thinking through in full: "Thinking accomplishes the relation of being to the essence of man. It does not make or cause the relation. Thinking brings this relation to Being solely as something handed over to it from Being. Such offering consists in the fact that in thinking Being comes to language. Language is the house of Being. In its home man dwells. Those who think and those who create with words are the guardians of this home."[23]

This is one of the most economical and fecund passages we find in Heidegger's work, drawing a clear connection between subjectivity, thinking, language, and the question of Being. The intersection of thinking and language is crucial, as well as the place of the poet as guardian—"those who create with words"—in thinking Being. Being is the event that sets the terms of the Being of beings in an epoch, forming our relation to language, world, self, and other.

For Heidegger, that eventfulness of Being is bookended with the depth of engagement from the Presocratic Greek world and its language on one end and the epoch of technology in modernity and its flattening of the world and reduction of language to correlation on the other. This is the framing of Being by beings—to think and speak in evocative relation to being but never in its totality. Framing or epoch curtails disclosure and tailors it to the being of the subject *in place*. The event of Being, as well as the event of the epoch, gives thinking its possibilities and impossibilities. We can see how this is an important tool for theorizing pessimism in the Black Americas. For the Afropessimist context, it is the event of slavery and its rendering of a zone of nonbeing out of which Black people or Black ~~people~~ (~~beings~~) *want* an exit, but, given the relation of Being to language, struggle with (or are a priori defeated by) the impossibility of the word to fashion an exit or alternative space of existence. Or is that too strong a characterization? Let us pause that question for a moment and only note, for now, that the space of Black existence is also a question of frequencies—what kind and for what ears? Here, it is not "can the subaltern speak?" but instead "can Being speak being (to) the subaltern?"

In terms of the explicit claims of the text, Heidegger's theorization of language and Being is for those who find themselves at home in a given language. This feeling of "at home" has two boundary aspects to it. First, there is the immanence to language and language practice, the intimate contact between linguistic play—the poet as the guardian of Being's home—and that subjectivity which makes cultivation of Being through the word possible. Second, and this is characteristic of Heidegger's later work, "at home" feels less like *stasis* and presence, more like mourning and yearning. The ancient Greek word functions this way for Heidegger, naming and gathering Being to itself but standing remote from modernity's approach to it. We can recall here Heidegger's remarks on the ancient temple from which the gods have fled in "The Origin of the Work of Art." That essay demonstrates the impossibility of word and world across the stretch of epochs, leaving us in a mournful relation and infused with desire for retrieval. In each case, and all those texts between that do reparative work between subjectivity and Being through language practices, language is *properly* and *politically* a home. This last part, the politics of home, is an ideological formation that hides inside Heidegger's text. It is an important formation, this sense of *hiding*, precisely because comfort with the formulation of home and language in Heidegger reveals a lack of intellectual sensitivity to colonial difference and, in turn, to how we might begin to see a point of navigation to language's movement to the interstices of speakerly life.

This is the shift that Afropessimism's turn to fundamental ontology does not make.

The relation of language, subjectivity, Being, and being-at-home in some manner or another—all of these sites of relation stage both the terms of social death and, given the porous character of language and its vulnerability to vernacular modifications, the surplus possibility in the essence of binding necessity. What Heidegger articulates so well is the condition for a *right* to nonalienation, which produces a mourning relation to loss when one is alienated from language's origins stories. But sometimes estrangement without the possibility of redemption or reconnection is entirely the point of language practices and their guardianship of Being. Fanon described this in *Black Skin, White Masks* in terms of this as the colonized's experience of European languages and practices, whether in the problem of diction—who speaks properly, who is the measure of the proper—or in the larger question of the relation of subjectivity to the Being of colonial space and time. This is the existential work of *Black Skin, White Masks* that we can embellish and deepen with the frame of fundamental ontology. Fanon draws on a thoroughly Heideggerian vision of language, place, and historicity in his assertion that "to speak means being able to use certain syntax and possessing the morphology of such and such a language, but it means above all assuming a culture and bearing the weight of a civilization."[24] This is one of the most important pedagogies of colonialism: In the elemental act of language acquisition, then use, one enters into a relation to Being as a politicized historical space. A home, perhaps. But a home that makes space for the figure of the slave, of the guardian-who-is-not-one, one who is *actually* a guardian of his own social death, and so one who only speaks as, from, and toward a condition of social death. This is Afropessimism's advance on nihilism in Fanon's text, the move to close even the future within the system of antiblackness. Fanon's insight, framed by Heidegger, generates and important and stunning claim: Being itself is one massive plantation. The plantation is not a site, but an entire ontology. An entire ontology that, shepherded by language, makes a sense of world and culture possible. So, later in the opening chapter of *Black Skin, White Masks*, Fanon adds that to speak a language "is to appropriate its world and culture"[25] and this positions the Black nonsubject as a shepherd of its own death. *To be* is to be in colonial language formations, practices, and *guardianship*. It is this latter that ties language and Being to colonial forms of alienation; the colonized are not guardians of Being as such, but, instead, guardians of the capacity of colonial Being to sustain both speaking as appropriation and social death as a kind of presence in the world. Politically, colonial Being *needs* social death in order to operate.

If we read Fanon with Heidegger, then we see how with even just this modest tweak another dimension of Heidegger's work becomes a resource for an Afropessimist argument that moves through language, toward Being, and into the fatal place—neutralizing and blending the flow of time under the regime of antiblackness—of social death in Being-as-plantation. But there is also an important difference that makes a difference. Heidegger's articulation of the relation between Being, language, and subjectivity turns repeatedly to the poet. It is the poet who crafts the word in such a manner that it can carry such an ethical and historical burden. *Crafts*. This is crucial. Guardianship of Being is the most profound task allotted to our capacities and practices. We can think here, for example, of the special place Friedrich Hölderlin holds in Heidegger's philosophical imagination. Fanon, however, does not center the poet in this characterization of language, social death, and colonial Being. Rather, Fanon centers the problem of speaking *broadly*, in terms of the sonic-grammatical (diction and the proper), and specifically speaking as a social practice and *habitus*. Speaking as such, for Fanon, functions differently than the poet's word. To speak—*parler* in each passage from Fanon—is to make language, and the body in which it takes aural forms, *public*. That publicity circulates in the interracial political-historical space of colonialism. This is why Fanon describes the adoption of world and civilization as fraught, tragic, and violent. Speaking puts the Black body in the world, in front of itself and other Black bodies as well as the white gaze and the colonial formations that animate each relation. Fanon's description of the place of language in colonial hegemony and production of social death adds, with some creative reading, depth to the problem of ontology in Afropessimist thought.

But, of course, this is also a truncated rendering of the work of language. What else is possible—and even, firstly, *actual*? If we shift from *diction*, Fanon's site of colonial pathologization, to *modulation*, then we begin to open up very different relations between language and world as well as, perhaps, the fold in Being at which Moten hints in his evocation of inhabitation. *A fissure at the boundary of the system.* But diction can never get us to this theoretical antisite and the work of supplementarity. Diction is fundamentally an adherence to sonic rules—sonic-grammatical from the beginning. The colonial listener sets the rules according to which the colonized speaker is fated to failure because of the sound of voice, the color of skin, and how the epidermal schema transforms both the visual and the aural. The visual and the aural set a hard limit on colonial mimicry. Colonialism is a total project, after all, and so it insinuates itself between the senses, making for unexpected, yet predictable, distortions of seeing and hearing out of racial anxiety. Modulation, however, is an entirely different economy, one that traffics out of the closed system of the proper and into the anarchical play of the vernacular. That anarchical play is the productive and world-building work of language. Or, with a better temporal phrasing, anarchical play is the expressive life of what *has been made* of the world in language, with language, and for those who assume its cultural space. Toward this, let us revisit Ellison's question of the lower frequencies and question of a blues aesthetic.

Invisible Man is a strange novel, innovative and elusive even all these decades later. It is at bottom a long meditation on Black life in the cracks of the interracial world, and so a sense of life that cannot be reduced, however much it bears a relation, to that world. *Written from and to the margins of nihilism.* Ellison concludes *Invisible Man* with a straightforward comment on the frequencies on which the novel has been written and ought to be read. It is an amazing comment for that reason, worth quoting in full. In a reflection directed at the reader, Ellison writes:

> 'Ah,' I can hear you say, 'so it was all a build up to bore us with his buggy jiving. He only wanted us to listen to him rave!' But only partially true: Being invisible and without substance, a disembodied

voice, as it were, what else could I do? What else but try to tell you what was really happening when your eyes were looking through? And it is this which frightens me:

Who know but that, on the lower frequencies, I speak for you?[26]

The conclusion to the novel organizes the rhetorical structure of Ellison's entire discourse. Not just the figures, the plot, the characters, and so on, but also and firstly the discursive structure of *Invisible Man*. What Ellison understands is how language makes worlds, how tropes and turns of phrase and related motifs create reality—whether alternative realities or inside the reality that we already know and live. Those tropes and turns of phrase hide inside language, write themselves and are themselves written under forms of erasure, and from that inside are generated forms of life, also under erasure, which sit *otherwise than being, beyond colonial or racial essence*. "I myself, after existing some twenty years," Ellison's protagonist declares, "*did not become alive* until I discovered my invisibility."[27] That invisibility is the life of the lower frequencies. Hidden from the hegemonic work of Being and ~~being~~ Black, but still a claim to life. Racism has no final word on Being, antiblackness cannot shepherd and cultivate Being, because Being is multiple, folded, and fissured. Social death and its pathologies, symptoms, and melancholia is the social life lived outside the fold, outside the fissure, and in the atmosphere or principle of a unified, closed world. But Being folds. Inside the folds, there are cracks and fissures that give rather than limit and extract life. Indeed, we are reminded of this at the very outset of the novel, which so evocatively recalls the aim and structure of Louis Armstrong's music. Ellison writes in the novel's prologue: "Invisibility, let me explain, gives one a slightly different sense of time, you're never quite on the beat. Sometimes you're ahead and sometimes behind. Instead of the swift and imperceptible flowing of time, you are aware of its nodes, those points where time stands still or from which it leaps ahead. And you slip into the breaks and look around."[28]

The notion of lower frequencies appears in the last lines of *Invisible Man*, but we can see how the racial-conceptual structure of that phrase was already in the novel as a way of framing the entire project: writing in and from the cracks, not out of desperation, lament, or plea, but as art and beauty as modalities and modulations of being and knowing. *You have to hear Armstrong's music. Hearing is thinking.*

If we think Ellison's lower frequencies in this frame, then we begin to see how the claim to a closed system of language bears supplementarity within itself, that something which not only destabilizes a system, but which makes other forms of life possible outside the play of possibility and impossibility. This latter feature is paramount in Ellison's novel, where language doubles itself inside Being in order to produce a sound modulation that folds the sound of social death into and out of the sound of life *otherwise*, the sound of lower frequencies. A blues aesthetic is critical for understanding the life of this *otherwise*. For Ellison, Armstrong's music breaks with the flow of time and erupts in the cracks, something you can *hear* but only with ears attuned to the kind of interstitial life at stake in that music. This is true broadly for Ellison as a property of blues music and its ability to make expression out of pain without that pain's expression being reducible to what Fanon described as the slave's lament. Indeed, Ellison famously describes Bessie Smith, his muse in all things, as "a priestess, a celebrant who affirmed the values of the group and man's ability to deal with chaos."[29] An ontological event, to be sure. Metaphysics of race, culture, and world. But this is an event *against* and *otherwise than* what we know of Being. What would it mean to take this seriously? It is not so much that Ellison argues for inclusion in Being, an uncrossing-out of ~~being~~ Black. Rather, Ellison's argument is that "the group" finds its values expressed, rendered, and reckoned with in the alternative modulations of the aural, which moves in a space and place not subject to the shared time of the interracial and of the social life of social death. The aural, as the lower frequencies, moves us into *la frontera* of this different time and different being. An African American iteration of what Gloria Anzaldúa described as the creation of new myths that make a new consciousness possible—except that, for Ellison, those myths are coextensive with the system of social death itself. Folded into being. Another consciousness signaled by the aural. *How to be with sound.*

In this way, I think we can bring the aural and the question of frequencies to bear on Warren's stylistic choice, a choice that turns out to be particularly conceptually revealing, to cross out Being and its conjugations. In the context of *Ontological Terror* and of the Afropessimist prerogative generally, writing being and Black crossed out makes sense. Crossing out Being names, visually, social death and the figure of the slave; the line through being marks the unremunerated. It builds a sense of pessimism's abyss into the most important element of language and identity formation. Ontology is fundamental. But what is important to note here, in terms of the aural and the question of frequencies, is how the crossing out of Being and its conjugations is at once a broad ontological claim and a concession to social, political, and cultural space as a totality. A closed system. And, as we have seen, the deconstructive force of the supplement lies in its ability to lodge itself, parasitically, inside the system while also opening the system to the radically undigestible exterior. When we return to Heidegger's insight into the intimacy of language and Being, disclosed through the work of subjectivity, then we already crack open or fold elements of the system that are vulnerable to language's play. In that opening of the system, the figure of the slave, the anarchic unremunerated element, becomes *otherwise*. That is, the figure becomes otherwise than that figure of enslavement, and so a sense of life imagined—and lived—otherwise than social death. Both in the past tense. We are operating in the *always already* space of witness being late to life otherwise at the margins of nihilism, now pessimism. Ellison helps us see how the aural cleaves language and time, which makes it possible to navigate the space of ontology, the time of beings and Being, very differently. Ontology navigated not necessarily to an Afro-optimism (which might just be a variation inside the system of social death), but to another sense of life forged and produced by aurality and its life as alternative frequencies. Moten's evocation of inhabitation begins to resonate with a new kind of deconstructive force.

And we can also revisit the epigraph, in which Riggs's musings on silence, survival, and world-making return to us here as not just forms of resistance, but as other ways of understanding the folds and fissures in Being itself. Spatialized as *la frontera*, this is mixed space. Yet, as a mixed space inside and exterior to Being all at once, it is only mixed in the sense of modulation. *Other sounds are possible.* Those *other* sounds produce and reproduce worlds, marking not only silences that are heard in the otherwise by those who live otherwise, but also the internal differentiation of Black life in the sonic folds of the lower frequencies. A value of difference and dispersion rather that recurrences of unity, symmetry, and the hegemony that comes with such repetition. Inside *this* form of thinking, the closed future of pessimism and the abjection of blackness in the past and present is not so much surmounted as moved into thinking thought *otherwise*. In this *otherwise*, Zora Neale Hurston's taxonomy of Black expressive life in "Characteristics of Negro Expression" becomes something quite different than, well, a listing of characteristics of Black expressive life. It becomes, in the otherwise and in the modulated alteration of the lower frequencies, a semiotics of Black life as life measured by Black life itself, a discursive formation that makes possibility in the cracks, fissures, folds, and *la frontera* of this life, in this place, but also not in this place. *Difference and differentiation as first philosophy. Nonplace as a place for life.* This is less a question of Black being or being Black, as Warren's ontological transformation of Afropessimism would have it, and more a question of understanding the semiotic forms and discursive work of Black counterinhabitation (to rework Moten's phrasing). Supplementarity only disrupts if the otherwise is thought in relation to the closed system of antiblackness. In relation to itself, supplementarity enlivens conceptions of life and life possibility. Vibrancy. Vitality. Sound. Ecstasy. And another sense of time's flow. The future untied.

What did I do to be so black and blue? Armstrong's question. No answer.

Who am I when I am also black and blue? On the lower frequencies, this is also Armstrong's question. That question that has an answer. It is an answer in one word: tradition. Tradition, that is, in Baldwin's turn of phrase and characterization, as generated by "the relation Negroes bear to one another." This too is possible. And actual. And living.

Postscript Notes

> ... the motives hidden behind the mask are as numerous as the ambiguities the mask conceals.
> —RALPH ELLISON, "CHANGE THE JOKE AND SLIP THE YOKE"

As a final set of reflections, I want to write just a few concluding notes on ethics and excess and what it means for theorizing in a decolonial register. First, a note on ethics.

In the afterword to my book *So Unimaginable a Price: Baldwin and the Black Atlantic*, I paused in conclusion to think about the ethics of inheritance. That piece is short and suggestive, taking up James Baldwin's complicated and nuanced contemplation of the figures Aunt Jemima and Uncle Tom in many of the same terms as I did in the second chapter of the present book. Baldwin's argument is in some ways simple: As generations pass, we remember Jemima and Tom only as the *figures* they are, embodiments of abjection and concession to the work of white supremacy and white violence. That remembering is not wrong. They are, after all, figures from an abolitionist literary canon and then our common vernacular, which sought to gain at least some rhetorical distance from that canon and its compulsive turn to abjection. Figures make rhetoric and theory simple. We are secure in knowing that they are abject and can be wielded as scenes of atrocity's memory written onto the social body. The figures of Jemima and Tom also invite double readings, very much the figure of the slave woven throughout the chapters herein. Baldwin initiates just this reading when he reminds us that they had secrets, that they led lives in the kitchen after the white folks had gone away, and that those lives had conversations, words, touch, intimacy, and reflective life. What would it mean to witness that privacy? What would it mean to not just fabulate those conversations and reconceive, then reconsider, critical rhetorical elements of the past, but also to receive and handle their names with *care*? Care asks something of us in the name of the past. In figures and their figuration, memory is handed to us. How we handle that memory is a fraught and often despairing responsibility. Care asks us to see life in its complexity, and to see it under erasure, to see that secretion of the kitchen conversation after the white people leave. Baldwin asks a difficult question. It is a question I want to consider here as part of a concluding set of remarks.

There is no Aunt Jemima and Uncle Tom in these pages outside of Baldwin's occasional mention and invocation. Indeed, one of the most interesting parts of Baldwin, Wright, Fanon, and Afropessimism as considered here is how little they turn to inherited figures of abjection. Rather, and with good reason, they are concerned with the structural workings of white violence toward the construction and reproduction of closed systems of nihilism. That is the work of critical theory, and it helps us understand the conditions under which life, death, and social death are produced. Those systems produce Aunt Jemima and Uncle Tom, but the figures themselves are not central to the critical theoretical works discussed in the preceding chapters. It is true that the early Baldwin in "Everybody's Protest Novel" and in essays on Wright that follow will equivocate the character Bigger Thomas with Uncle Tom. This is something for which Wright probably never forgave Baldwin and who could blame him. That equivocation truncates Wright's work, reducing his fiction to only *Native Son* and perhaps bits and pieces of *Black Boy*. It also truncates our understanding of what Wright wanted to accomplish—and did, with great success—in terms of describing the broad and abiding affective life of white violence and its closed system. Yet Baldwin also understood this aspiration. In many ways my account of his nihilism is an account of Baldwin's Richard Wrightism. When Baldwin writes that every African American has a Bigger Thomas living inside his skull, he is at once giving Wright rare credit for a correct moral psychology and acknowledging the enduring significance and fundamental *accuracy* of the sociogeny at the foundation of Bigger's life. They share a conviction about the meaning and persistence of nihilism in an antiblack world. How to work with and from that is the other question. The other question splits midcentury African American literature in so many important ways.

In "Many Thousands Gone," an essay from 1951 that takes up Wright's work in important new ways following the publication of "Everybody's Protest Novel" just two years prior, Baldwin offers a nuanced revisit of Jemima and Tom, removing their demeaned and demeaning family titles while asking a question of

Wright that he may as well have been asking of himself: How ought we receive and handle the past? What are the ethics of inheriting struggle *and* survival? Struggle has its heroes. Perhaps survival has a story to tell, too. It is a question to be asked here. Again. And it is a story whose telling is about witnessing both what the past has said and what the past has never been able to say.

It is arguably the most important question in Black Atlantic theory.

The question is a very particular one for me as a white writer on Black texts. The texts I engage with, draw on, and reckon for our consideration of forms of Black knowing have been formed and forged in the terror of this nation, hemisphere, and oceanic space. Those texts are saturated with memory and history in very particular ways, much of which is offered by me to the reader for intratextual study and, with that intratextual study in place, readied for comparative, intertextual study. That has been my method here: offer readings of literary works, personal essays, philosophical psychology, and global Black critical theory that are then prepared for intertextual study. Intertextual study tells an important theoretical story, in this case about internal debates in the Black Americas about the dimensionality of being and the meaning of Black life under excessive conditions of antiblackness. We all read with interpretative frames, which for me here is the framing of deconstruction, social death, and bits and pieces from Hurston, Ellison, Anzaldúa, and others. My aim in this project and always is to be explicit about those framings. The hermeneutic event is its own thing and requires careful parsing if we want to be understood as critical readers. I am and will forever be a text worker. It is important work. I believe that. And it is work that, at its best moments, raises questions, offers some provisional answers in the declarative, and articulates some hopes for dispute and debate to follow. In other words, I have tried here to ethically enter into a tradition with respect, grace, and seriousness.

What is that ethical sensibility in this context?

For me, this sensibility concerns the ethics of reading inheritances and reading disputes inside the tradition around those inheritances. On the one hand, the decisive themes in this project are not my direct inheritances. I am and will forever be a text worker. What it means for, say, Baldwin to contest Wright on the question of African American folkways is a matter of the porch, the kitchen, and the grandparent's knee for both of them. It is not a secondary or tertiary communication. From those sites of knowledge production—profound sites of world making imaginaries—they made fiction, nonfiction, and critical theory that describes worlds described in acts of passing on inheritance. My work is a kind of tertiary witness in its best moments (of which I hope there are many), letting the text teach, then deploying my skills and sensitivities as a reader and writer in order to make that inheritance work between figures in a tradition I have spent much of my adult life reading, discussing, and thinking about. If a writer is successful and honest, then they bequeath to us readers real insight into their senses of inheritance, reckoning, and sometimes apostasy.

On the other hand, and I think this is crucially important, the question of nihilism is also no racially specific inheritance. If the nihilism of a Manichean, antiblack world is the atmosphere of interracial space, of a shared space and the *agon* constituting it, then inheritance is commonplace and a common place. This is something like what Baldwin describes as Americanness in his essay "The Discovery of What It Means to Be an American," in which he draws the lesson from exile that being American is about a common inheritance of rootlessness and the existential freedom that flows from it. In particular, I have in mind this opening remark: "And I found that my experience was shared by every American writer I knew in Paris. Like me, they had been divorced from their origins, and it turned out to make very little difference that the origins of white Americans were European and mine were African—they were no more at home in Europe than I was."[1]

The common place of home and the story of making that home—therein lies the question of inheritance in its most confounding yet utterly familiar sense. We surely inherit differently. We travel different paths and arrive at sites and citations of nihilism in specific and distinct ways. But we also arrive at one and the same deathworld that makes the Black abjection that makes the innocence of white life possible. This is why traditions, however separate, can also seem very familiar. Baldwin is right that the interracial world produces an inexorable presence of terror that make the world-ness of our world. Inhabiting it is the incarnation of inheritance. The history of inheritance is written on our bodies in so many registers: as an abstraction (a theory of race), existential meaning (innocence, guilt, resistance, refusal), and capacities and vulnerabilities in a deathworld (necropolitics, nihilism, hope, refusal again, resistance again, traitorous activity, revolution). Differences? Of course. Those differences give the world its violent energy and abject affect. Same world? In many ways, yes, of course. The meaning of our lives is negotiated in that world. Difference and sameness at the same time—this is Baldwin's perplexing insight. What it means to handle inheritance with care inside this shared and unshared world is a critical story about race in the Black Atlantic. It is also a story about what it means to write in response. Every response is a form of responsibility. Responsibility is responsiveness. We begin there when raising the question of ethics.

What strikes me as so interesting about our inheritance of the terms of nihilism in each of the figures treated here is how the question of ethics is raised, on each occasion, in the temporality of the intervention of the supplement.

Or *can* be raised in each thinker, each occasion, if we read the supplement's deconstructive work at the margins of the text of and about nihilism. Deconstruction is a form of responsibility, a responsiveness to a crisis of hegemony. If we think about the commonplace and common place of nihilism (and its companion concept pessimism), deconstructive opening of the system by way of the supplement *cares* for those forms of life folded in the interstices. That care is about care for inheritances. To see Jemima and Tom as folded and doubled temporalities. To call for a double reading of them as figures of the slave. And, through an engagement with that time and enacted in that reading, to move toward an understanding of their lower frequencies. "Aunt Jemima and Uncle Tom," Baldwin writes, "our creations, at the last evaded us; they had a life—their own, perhaps a better life than ours—and they would never tell us what it was."[2] It is precisely this moment of opacity, a moment in which the enigma refuses to appear and explain itself according to a measure and a meaning other than itself, that the decolonial work of reading under erasure becomes something like an ethics of inheritance. To inherit and read inheritance not as role model for struggle and a common or shared understanding, but rather as what Édouard Glissant called *the right to opacity*.[3] An ethics of inheritance cares for what does not tell its own story *to us*. Instead of telling for it or demanding its transparency or putting it under scrutiny and assumption of meaning, an ethics of inheritance *witnesses* its power to dismantle our own compulsion to comprehend, to disrupt our drive to seize it as our own insight, and therefore, in a gesture of humility and graciousness, to let it be what it always wanted to be: free on its own terms.

Deconstructive supplementarity against social death at the margins of nihilism. An ethics of inheritance—a readerly ethics of care and graciousness—maps our movement through the history of the interstices. Says yes to the ghost. Listens to the frequencies and opacities of traces. This is the demand of deconstruction as an ethics. It is also the demand of those who made worlds out of the impossible. A decolonial moment in acts of remembering.

Let me conclude where I began, between two films about the postcolonial.

If thinking after deconstruction and social death places the figure of the slave, saturated with refusal and new senses of relation in the interstices, remunerated by self to self rather than by the one who produced the figure, then what is the future of decolonial thought? That is a dense question. Put another way: What can be said about the space opened by deconstruction and how consideration of the supplement reopens the concept of life? It is interstitial. It is *la frontera*. It is where gesture, modulation, lower frequencies, disordered and chaotic thought, and all of those variations and modifications to systematicity find a space of play. That play is important. Play is the space of *poiesis*, the activity of bringing into being and the work of world-making. Play is possible when the imagination is given—or perhaps better, gives itself—a sense of distance from hegemonic force and the rendering of life in a one-dimensional, racialized, and exploitative frame. Any question of the decolonial *as such* is embedded in the literary history of a concept—the bookish moment of the tradition—and is also rooted in the particular exigencies of a community, a people, a state, a region, or a postcolonial formation. Thus, the specificities of this work are matters of place and moment. This is why the phrase *Black Americas* appears at key moments. At the same time, as I hope I have shown in interesting ways, the intersection of deconstruction and social death offer sites of reflection and contours of thinking *broadly*. That moment of breadth, if I have been successful as a theorist in the preceding pages, make it possible to conceive decolonial significance and signification in an expansive and voracious horizon. This expansive significance turns on the movement of the imagination *otherwise than* the terms of knowing and being structured by colonial logic. That *otherwise* is less intuitive and obvious than it might seem at first glance.

And so, in many ways, this brings me back to my opening reflection on Ousmane Sembène's 1968 film *Mandabi*. Sembène's aim in the film and across most of his early work is clear: document the place of the neocolonial in the postcolonial state, which is configured aesthetically, morally, and spatially in *Mandabi*. The aesthetics of the neocolonial in the postcolonial is screened as Ibrahima's *bou bou*, with the camera following him as he wanders through the city center in search of help cashing his money order, surrounded by bureaucrats—precursors, really, of the kleptocratic state that is to come in too many parts of postcolonial Africa—dressed in Western-style suits. The moral conflict and its distinction sits between the emerging kleptocratic ethic of the Western-suited bureaucrats and Ibrahima's embodiment of a Muslim ethic of generosity even (or perhaps especially) among the poor. This configuration gives weight to Ibrahima's declaration of outrage at the close of the film as he repeatedly bemoans and mourns the disappearance of decency in Senegal. The spatialization of these two configurations is plain, drawing a stark line between the city and the poor neighborhood at its edges, the neighborhood where Ibrahima and his two wives live among so many other struggling folk. What happens at that stark line, what happens when it is crossed, and the question of what it would mean to *not* cross it, to give up on the *mandabi*—the nephew's money order, sent from abroad, repeating colonial relations with a difference—and work instead inside the virtues of hospitality and communal life. This is where we catch sight of decolonial possibilities. The unthought yet thinkable in Sembène's film. Ibrahima's plea is a remembrance of the past, but also a promise of a possible future.

The strangers who appear at his door add to that temporality. They know of his generosity *now*, in the present. Everything is in the call to decency. But, also, nothing is in the call to decency. The neocolonial moment is obscene and cruel.

Perhaps one could witness this moment in *Mandabi* and see it as revolutionary, a decolonial moment that addresses the colonial hangover in the postcolonial state. Perhaps what is urgent in this moment is that Ibrahima and like-minded folk gather force behind a movement to jettison the bureaucrats and the emerging kleptocratic state and enact a second revolution to restore Senegal to *another kind of world*, one that eschews the West and what Western values have left in and for the postcolonial state. The hope of (re-)Africanization. I actually think this is what Sembène wants us to take away from the film. We can think of his own cameo in the film, which is not unlike his appearance in *La noire de . . .* as the organizer of the People's School who gazes contemptuously at Monsieur as the Frenchman returns to give some bit of remittance to Diouma's mother after the young woman's suicide. Sembène's cameo in *Mandabi* suggests a similar politics: He sits at a table in the post office, helping Ibrahima by reading a letter to him and giving friendly instructions on how to solve his problem, talking with him across a table draped in a cover with Che Guevara's face on it. The People's School, the pipe smoking revolutionary and resistance worker, the reference to El Che as a revolutionary icon, even Diouma's boyfriend hanging a portrait of Patrice Lumumba in his bedroom—in these moments, Sembène shows his ideological hand, so to speak. Decolonization means the embrace of something between the space of Ibrahima's poor neighborhood and that of the bustling wealth in the city's center. Or maybe something after and beyond those spaces. Decolonial thinking is as much a puzzle as it is a method. It is both time and space, set in the margins as an alternative time structure and space of struggle in the shadows of empire's cruel, obstinate sun.

But *Mandabi* also suggests a different kind of intervention, one that is less about insurgencies against the neocolonial state and more about what decency might mean outside the boundaries drawn between city and slum. City and slum manifest, geographically, the deconstructive play of life and death and also produce social death as the subjectivity of the slum and the slum dweller who ventures to the city. That is, the slum and the city bear a relation to one another. That relation is one of abjection—the slum is only a "slum" under the hegemonic gaze of the Western-suited city people—and also one of reactivity. Or some bit of reactivity. Ibrahima *sees* the decency of the Muslim ethic of hospitality in a flash, a flash generated by a contrast and violence that transforms the slum from the abject projection of the city into the virtue of everyday folks. We can see that seeing in two ways. First, we can see it as a moment of nostalgia for precolonial forms of life and their resistance to assimilation under colonial domination. Nostalgia in this sense is generated by contrast and the moral and political violence that flows from it: abjection speaking back against the terms of its marginalization and exclusion while also turning to what is revealed, in that abjection, about the possible virtues in the heart of the abject. This is Sembène's Négritude moment, creating a reversal of colonial terms as a strategy and praxis of resistance. And it is a potent claim on the African postcolonial imagination. Rightly so. Re-Africanization genuinely changes political culture.

Second, we might also see decency in terms of what Sembène's cameos in *La noire de . . .* and *Mandabi* both evoke and represent: the people. The people's school offers assistance to the people rooted in the lives of those left behind by neocolonial constructions of civic space. Committed to neither the precolonial forms of life nor whatever modernity has made of postcolonial Senegal, Sembène hints at another kind of thinking that is outside both the slum and the city center, but also inside them. That sense of intellectual space as a space of thinking *otherwise* than nostalgia or assimilation is the antechamber opened up in the decolonial moment. Not a decolonial *vision* but decoloniality as a modality of thinking what is, what was, and what will be in the open space of the exterior. Exterior to what? Exterior to the Manichean structure of colonialism, which infuses so much of how we imagine and know even in revolutionary critique and conceptions of what is to come. Not a decolonial *vision* but decoloniality as a modality of thinking and puzzling out what is, what was, and what will be in the open space of the interior. Interior to what? Interior to the Manichean structure of the colonialism that made social death, abjection, and moderated-mediated elements that structure the figure of the slave in order to close the system. Sembène appears in *La noire de . . .* inside the marginalized neighborhood. The authenticity of that placement, however, does not come from an idealized conception of the margin, but instead from the word *people* framed by the definite article. *The* people can also be located interior to the system. In *Mandabi*, Sembène appears inside the city and, in fact, inside the civic structure of its postcolonial life. But, with El Che as his table, his site of staging intervention, *the people* exceed the hegemony of neocolonial social and institutional space.

The people as a space of the ethical inheritance of decency. An ethics of inheritance is the excess inside the concept of the kleptocratic postcolonial state. And indeed of any state that produces abjection in order to be and to reproduce colonial forms of being.

That is the right word for this: *excess*. If we recall Jean-Marie Teno's *Clando*, we see another time of the postcolonial state, two generations removed from independence, and wholly and completely devoid of excess. In fact, so much of *Clando* is about scarcity: Scarcity of hope. Scarcity of affect outside of demoralized cynicism. Scarcity of desire. Scarcity of wealth. The clando of *Clando*—the unlicensed taxi as figure for postcolonial being and affect—is a story about what it would even mean to consider hope. To hope for hope. That hope for hope must take place outside but also inside. Sobgui is alienated and stagnated as an office worker. He is fired, jailed, and then escapes to Germany for time in exilic reflection. Germany is only more alienation. What does it mean to return? It certainly does not mean to return for revolution or assimilation, but instead some kind of in-between that is not a blend of both and instead something wholly other and different and searching. It means to understand that the neocolonial state is one massive prison for the political and existential imagination. So, the film concludes in the interrogative. Sobgui returns, but without a massive political vision. No wisdom is carried back to Cameroon. Only an emergent *sensibility*—an attunement to a different form of life, perhaps an unformed life. That is, he returns to the quotidian, to the busyness of the streets, but also to their slow paced, calm, and deliberative mode of being. What does that mean? Teno leaves us to imagine for ourselves what Sobgui (and Cameroon more broadly) might discover about his imagination as an intrusive and extrusive exile *inside* the essence of the neocolonial state. What is the excess? It is gone. Kleptocracy does that to a world. It steals everything. Another question, then. What can be *manufactured* as that excess? It is not waiting for him. It has to be crafted.

This moment of the imagination's encounter with the compulsion and necessity of *making* is the decolonial antechamber's moment of appearance. Or, perhaps better put, it is the antechamber's elevation to the status of structuring appearance. And nonappearance. And so of reading under erasure for how life persists in conditions of social death, not as the social life of social death that Jared Sexton puts under such scrutiny, but instead the life between social death and the social life of social death: the vernacular, the archipelagic, chaos, resistance, and refusal. Deconstruction helps us see the emergence of this moment with real clarity, which in the end is about making visible or articulable—to the extent that it is possible in an interracial political space—what is already there as part of the facticity of subaltern life. Speaking on its own terms. Refusing speaking in the terms of others. What, and how, and who is all this speaking? So many words. Here are a few. There are always more. *La frontera* is nothing if not proliferation.

Proliferation of the improper.

In the name of the virtue of the profane, proliferation is a profanity against a system that demands proper accounting, *apologia*, and shared public reckoning. Proliferation expands and embellishes an inheritance committed to the joys and pleasures of its own opacity. Inheritance is nomadic and wandering. It is movement on its own terms in the borderlands. Manifesting a first and sacred word, perhaps: freedom.

Acknowledgments

This book had strange origins.

Much of it was written in a flurry over fall 2023 and into winter 2024. I owe the motivation for that surge of writing to Andrew Benjamin, who invited me to contribute an essay on "the figure of the slave" to a journal issue he was editing, and from that essay, I caught sight of a longer project. That longer project had to do with the intersection, wholly in my own construction, of deconstruction and social death. When I posted a musing on this topic on my Facebook page, a number of friends expressed enthusiasm for the very idea. That enthusiasm, coupled with satisfaction upon completing the essay for Andrew, motivated me to come back to my writerly self.

I had to come back to that self because it had fled. Part of that fleeing had to do with the difficulties of relocation when I decided to leave my position at Amherst College for a new one at the University of Maryland. That was absolutely the right decision. I loved my time at Amherst College, but it was time to move to a more research-forward position. We so rarely have a chance at refresh in our profession. But relocations take a toll. New place, goodbye to old friends, missing old places, connecting with new friends, and finding a way to the DMV—so many pleasures, but also a taxing journey. Then, when I contracted COVID-19 in the summer of 2022, my difficulties with restarting as a writer intensified. The case wasn't bad at all. In fact, it was a mild flu at worst. But the aftermath was awful, mimicking Alzheimer's at random moments for weeks over that summer. I would wake up in the middle of drinking coffee and have no idea how I'd gotten there, how I'd made breakfast for my family, coffee for myself and my spouse, dressed myself, started the dishwasher. It took two and a half months to start coming back to my normal cognitive function. My fall semester of 2022 was a bit of a fog, then spring 2023 was more normal for me, but the experience of that summer stuck with me as a low-level constant panic. What if I am no longer a writer? What if I don't ever recover my capacity to read?

Luckily that has proven to be more worry than reality. This book is proof that I can still write—even if no one likes it, it is still a book with coherent chapters and an argument. For that reason, my first acknowledgment is to myself. I did not give up. I tried again and again until it worked, this writing thing. It was hard and I was scared, but I did it anyway. Patting myself on the back for all of that.

I have made some of my students listen to me talk about the process of writing and I'm thankful for that. Kanya Richards, Lisa Osei, and most of all Fatima Seck—I appreciate you all. To Marshal Washington, thank you for the daily conversation. To Ashley Newby, the same and especially for helping me parse some of the broader questions at the heart of this project. And when I pitched this project to Tom Lay at the Society for Phenomenology and Existential Philosophy in Toronto in the fall of 2023, he was enthusiastic, encouraging, and expressed an early belief in the argument that got me to a motivated place as a writer. Since then, more of the same. Thank you, Tom, for real.

Grant Farred, my friend. Phone calls about basketball, books and ideas, and the, um, shall we say, "vicissitudes of parenting"—those all meant a lot to me. You like these things short, so I will keep it so: Thank you for your intellectual friendship and all of the other forms of friendship. In our shared generation of scholars, there is no one better than you at this ideas game. Endless respect and affection.

As big as any thanks goes to Jami Weinstein, my daily writing check-in partner during the composition of this book. We've been friends for a good long while, Jami, and your sartorial excellence is very missed on this side of the Atlantic. Mostly, though, respect for your intellect and creativity, your politics and insistences, and I cannot tell you how much I appreciate your encouragement, your kind words, and your persistent presence as I wrote this.

Love and adoration to my two children, Miles Henry and Satchel Bee. You two are the best. And of course Marisa Parham, who is the best of the best. Thank you for enduring and maybe at times enjoying my terrible combination of attentiveness and disappearance. I hope the former makes the latter tolerable. That's all I got. The result is that this book got written. That ain't a bad thing, right?

Notes

Prologue: Sembène, Teno, and the Work of the Outside

1. Jacques Derrida, *Dissemination*, trans. Barbara Johnson (Chicago: University of Chicago Press, 1981), 25.

2. For an excellent account of both critical approaches to Anzaldúa and how critical rereading of that work is both possible and productive, see Andrea Pitts, *Nos/Otros: Gloria E. Anzaldúa, Multiplicitous Agency, and Resistance* (Albany: SUNY Press, 2022), especially the fifth chapter. My emphasis throughout this project will be on refusal rather than resistance, which is both fitted to Pitts's interpretation and veers from it in important ways.

3. Gloria Anzaldúa, *Borderlands/La Frontera: The New Mestiza* (San Francisco: Aunt Lute Books, 1987), 84.

4. Lindsey Stewart, *The Politics of Black Joy: Zora Neale Hurston and Neo-Abolitionism* (Evanston, IL: Northwestern University Press, 2021).

5. Zora Neale Hurston, "Characteristics of Negro Expression," in *Folklore, Memoirs, and Other Writings* (New York: Library of America, 1995), 833–34.

6. Ibid., 834.

7. Ibid., 835.

Introduction: Whithering the Decolonial

1. Zora Neale Hurston, "Characteristics of Negro Expression," in *Folklore, Memoirs, and Other Writings* (New York City: Penguin Books, 1995), 832.

2. See the special issue "The Figure of the Slave in the History of Philosophy," assembled by Andrew Benjamin and Justin Clemens, *Philosophy, Politics, and Critique* 1, no. 2 (2024).

3. It is important to note how the Black Atlantic tradition, in particular the region and traditions of the Black Americas, is *Western* in a deeply complicated and subversive sense rather than a "non-Western" tradition. On that topic, see my "Decolonizing the West," in *Decolonizing American Philosophy*, ed. Corey McCall and Philip McReynolds (Albany: SUNY Press, 2021), 63–81.

4. James Baldwin, "The Fire Next Time," in *The Price of the Ticket* (Boston: Beacon Press, 2021), 341.

5. See also Geo Maher, *Anticolonial Eruptions: Racial Hubris and the Cunning of Resistance* (Berkeley: University of California Press, 2022).

6. Frantz Fanon, *The Wretched of the Earth*, trans. Richard Philcox (New York: Grove Press, 2008), 10.

7. Aimé Césaire, *Discourse on Colonialism*, trans. Joan Pinkham (New York: Monthly Review Press, 2000), 73.

1. Social Death as a Kind of Deconstruction: The Figure of the Slave under Erasure

Part of this chapter originally appeared as "Deconstruction as a Kind of Social Death: The Figure of the Slave under Erasure," *Philosophy, Politics, Critique* 1, no. 2 (2024): 271–86.

1. As a matter of scholarship, I think it is important to note that Olufemi Taiwo's book *Against Decolonization* (London: Hurst, 2022) gets the questions of the colonial and decolonial precisely reverse. For Taiwo, decolonial prerogatives work with and from the Manichean structure of the world. But exactly the opposite is the case: Decolonization *contests and overturns* the idea of oppositional forces. This is not an interpretation peculiar to my own theorizing. It is in fact Frantz Fanon's position in the *ur-text* of decolonial thinking, *The Wretched of the Earth*.

2. Frantz Fanon, *The Wretched of the Earth*, trans. Richard Philcox (New York: Grove Press, 2004), 178.

3. Ibid.

4. Suzanne Césaire, "A Civilization's Discontent," trans. Michael Richardson and Krzysztof Fijalkowski, in *Refusal of the Shadow: Surrealism and the Caribbean* (New York: Verso Books, 1996), 100.

5. For economy of expression and in accordance with professional vernacular, I will refer to the white West as "the West" and "Western." The equivalence of whiteness/white people and "the West" or "the Western tradition" is something that needs to be troubled, as I have written elsewhere: see John E. Drabinski, "Decolonizing the West," in *Decolonizing American Philosophy*, eds. Corey McCall and Phillip McReynolds (Albany: SUNY Press, 2021), 63–80. This is because the black Atlantic world—the Caribbean, the United States and Canada, Black Europe and Britain—is produced in, by, and through what we call "the West," but that is not the focus of the present essay.

6. Orlando Patterson, *Slavery and Social Death* (Cambridge, MA: Harvard University Press, 1980).

7. Jacques Derrida, *Cinders*, trans. Ned Lukacher (Minneapolis: University of Minnesota Press, 2014).

8. For some detail on how each of these examples work from the unremunerated figure of the slave, see my "Social Death as a Kind of Deconstruction."

9. Jacques Derrida, *Dissemination*, trans. Barbara Johnson (Chicago: University of Chicago Press, 2021), 128.

10. Jacques Derrida, *Of Grammatology*, trans. Gayatri Spivak (Baltimore: Johns Hopkins University Press, 1997), 155.

11. Patterson, *Slavery and Social Death*, 44.

12. Ibid., 51.

13. I have in mind here Emmanuel Levinas's work on the psyche as subjectivity that draws breath from its other, making (ethical) life from that other and its world. See, Emmanuel Levinas, *Otherwise than Being, or Beyond Essence*, trans. Alphonso Lingis (Pittsburgh: Duquesne University Press, 2011), 68–74.

14. Lisa Guenther, *Solitary Confinement* (Minneapolis: University of Minnesota Press, 2006).

15. Aimé Césaire, "Notebook of a Return to the Native Land," trans. Clayton Eshleman and Annette J. Smith, in *Aimé Césaire: The Collected Poetry* (Berkeley: University of California Press, 1983), 37.

16. Frantz Fanon, *Black Skin, White Masks*, trans. Richard Philcox (New York: Grove Press, 2008), 119. Fanon also discusses colonial amputation in terms of the mutation of subjectivity in cross-Atlantic travel, where the Black subject's Caribbeanness is amputated by time in a France to which he cannot belong (7), as well as in a general comment that "I hailed the world, and the world amputated my enthusiasm" (94).

17. Ibid., 119.

18. On the deep and complicated ambivalence of Derrida and Algeria, see the fantastic work in Grant Farred's essay "Nostalgeria: Derrida, Before and After Fanon," *South Atlantic Quarterly* 112, no. 1 (2013): 145–62.

19. Fanon, *Black Skin, White Masks*, 1–2.

20. Ibid., 21.

21. Fanon, *The Wretched of the Earth*, 19.

22. On the question of passage and limit, I am drawing on Len Lawlor's long meditation (across many essays and books) on the phrase from Derrida's *Introduction to The Origin of Geometry* "passage to the limit," in particular the fifth chapter of Lawlor's excellent *Derrida and Husserl: The Basic Problem of Phenomenology* (Bloomington: Indiana University Press, 2002).

23. Jacques Derrida, *Who's Afraid of Philosophy: Right to Philosophy 1*, trans. Jan Plug (Stanford, CA: Stanford University Press, 2002), 105.

24. Jacques Derrida, *Monolingualism of the Other; or, the Prosthesis of Origin*, trans. Patrick Mensah (Palo Alto, CA: Stanford University Press, 1998), 39–40.

25. Patrick Chamoiseau, *School Days*, trans. Linda Coverdale (Lincoln: University of Nebraska Press, 1997), 21.

2. Racial Formation and the Remainder in Baldwin's Nonfiction

1. For a very different but also very interesting account of Baldwin and rage, see Myisha Cherry, "On James Baldwin and Black Rage," *Critical Philosophy of Race* 10, no. 1 (2022): 1–21. Cherry frames Baldwin in terms of philosophical psychology and the constellation of concepts from that field of inquiry, whereas, as we shall see, my concern is with how rage is a formal indicator of the structure of being. I will spare the reader a long excursus on the difference between philosophical psychology and ontology, but it is an important difference that has real consequences for thinking through the ultimate meaning of Baldwin's work.

2. Raoul Peck, *James Baldwin: I Am Not Your Negro* (New York: Vintage International, 2017), 3.

3. James Baldwin, "The Fire Next Time," in *The Price of the Ticket* (Boston: Beacon Press, 2021), 340.

4. On this notion of founding wounds, see my "Reconciliation and Founding Wounds," *Humanity* 4, no. 1 (2013): 117–32. Baldwin does not consider with any sustained attention the companion founding wound: conquest, mass displacement, and genocide of indigenous people. This is no small issue when talking about his theorization of the historical and foundational structure of the nation and deserves sustained attention that I cannot give here. I think the best place for starting on this sort of reflection is his discussion of Hollywood cinema and the idea of the hero, one of which is the cowboy—a white conqueror and defender of expansive imperialism. In those brief remarks, Baldwin expresses anxiety and rage about the white hero while also proclaiming an intuitive connection to the "Indian" as a fellow displaced person, a fellow nonwhite person sharing the same white racist interracial space. That act of identification requires real scrutiny, for sure, but it is where Baldwin opens up space for our consideration.

In any case, it is true that Baldwin's origin stories repeatedly fail to take on the historical-memorial burden of anti-indigenous violence. That leaves an abyss at the center of what also enables his discourse. This is another sense of supplement to be explored. I do not take it on here—it requires a scholarly precision I do not yet have—but it should be acknowledged as a critical component to theorizing the long vision of Baldwin as a thinker.

5. Michael Omi and Howard Winant, *Racial Formation in the United States*, 3rd ed. (New York: Routledge, 2015), 129.

6. Ibid., 127.

7. James Baldwin, "Notes of a Native Son," in *The Price of the Ticket*, 155.

8. Ibid.

9. On this peculiar relation, see my "The Poetics of Beautiful Blackness: On Baldwin and Négritude," in *James Baldwin in Context*, ed. Quentin Miller (Cambridge: Cambridge University Press, 2019), 233–43.
10. James Baldwin, "Encounter on the Seine: Black Meets Brown," in *The Price of the Ticket*, 50.
11. Ibid.
12. James Baldwin, "The Discovery of What It Means to Be an American," in ibid., 179.
13. James Baldwin, "Princes and Powers," in ibid., 55.
14. Edith Wyschogrod, *Spirit in Ashes* (New Haven, CT: Yale University Press, 1985), 17–18.
15. Aimé Césaire, *Discourse on Colonialism*, trans. Joan Pinkham (New York: Monthly Review Press, 2001), 36.
16. Wyschogrod, *Spirit in Ashes*, 16.
17. Achille Mbembe, *Necropolitics* (Durham, NC: Duke University Press, 2020), 66.
18. Wyschogrod, *Spirit in Ashes*, 18.
19. James Baldwin, "Everybody's Protest Novel," in *The Price of the Ticket*, 44–45.
20. James Baldwin, "Many Thousands Gone," in ibid., 77.
21. Ibid.
22. Ibid.
23. Ibid., 78.
24. Cheryl Dunye, dir., *The Watermelon Woman* (New York: First Run Features, 1996), DVD.
25. Ibid.
26. Ibid., emphasis mine.
27. Jacques Derrida and Maurizio Ferraris, *The Taste for the Secret*, trans. Giacomo Donis (Malden, MA: Polity Press, 2001), 32.
28. Ibid., 7.
29. Ibid., 57.

3. Nihilism and the Refusal of Refusal in Wright and Fanon

1. Geo Maher, *Anticolonial Eruptions: Racial Hubris and the Cunning of Resistance* (Berkeley: University of California Press, 2022).
2. Richard Wright, *The Man Who Lived Underground* (New York: Library of America, 2021).
3. Richard Wright, *The Outsider* (New York: Harper Perennial, 2012), 503.
4. Richard Wright, "The Man Who Lived Underground," in *Eight Men* (New York: Harper Perennial, 2008), 84.
5. Richard Wright, "The Man Who Was Almost a Man," in ibid., 7.
6. Richard Wright, *Native Son* (New York: Harper Perennial, 2005), 7, 8.

7. Achille Mbembe, "Necropolitics," trans. Libby Meintjes, *Public Culture* 15, no. 1 (2003): 7.
8. Wright, "The Man Who Was Almost a Man," 10.
9. Ibid., 18.
10. Wright, "The Man Who Lived Underground," 24.
11. Ibid., 58.
12. Ibid., 83–84.
13. Ibid.
14. Frantz Fanon, *Black Skin, White Masks*, trans. Richard Philcox (New York: Grove Press, 2008), 45. The lecherous character of this and other passages is not incidental or occasional, but instead part of the text itself in which women, for Fanon, are visible as sexual objects/proto-subjects for men. See, for example, Gwen Bergner, "Who Is That Masked Woman? Or, the Role of Gender in Fanon's *Black Skin, White Masks*," *PMLA* 110, no. 1 (1995): 75–88.
15. Ibid.
16. Fanon, *Black Skin, White Masks*, 41.
17. Ibid., xvi.
18. Ibid., 92.
19. W. E. B. Du Bois, *Souls of Black Folk* (Oxford: Oxford University Press, 2007), 3.
20. Wright, "The Man Who Was Almost a Man," 18. Emphasis mine.
21. Ibid., 8.
22. Ibid., 9.
23. Fanon, *Black Skin, White Masks*, 94, 119.
24. Ibid., 96.
25. Du Bois, *Souls of Black Folk*, 3.
26. Fanon, *Black Skin, White Masks*, 118.
27. Frantz Fanon, "Racism and Culture," trans. Haakon Chevalier, in *Toward the African Revolution* (New York: Grove Books, 1994), 37.
28. Ibid.
29. Ibid.
30. Richard Wright, "The Literature of the Negro in the United States," in *Black Power: Three Books from Exile* (New York: Harper Perennial, 2023), 773.
31. See Paul Jay's excellent work on Gloria Anzaldúa and how *la frontera* is a space of hybridization/creolization in the mode of the improvisational, *Global Matters: The Transnational Turn in Literary Studies* (Ithaca, NY: Cornell University Press, 2014), 77, 205.
32. On this, see my "Wright and the Violence of Tradition," in *Atlantic Theory: On the Vicissitudes of Relation* (Edinburgh: Edinburgh University Press, 2025).
33. Richard Wright, "Tradition and Industrialization," in *Black Power*, 723.
34. Frantz Fanon, "Richard Wright's White Man, Listen!," trans. Steven Corcoran, in *Alienation and Freedom* (London: Bloomsbury Publishing, 2018), 640.

Fanon would have encountered these ideas from Wright at the 1956 Paris Congress, where Wright presented the essay "Tradition and Industrialization."

35. Fanon, *Black Skin, White Masks*, 118.
36. Ralph Ellison, "Richard Wright's Blues," in *Shadow and Act* (New York: Vintage, 1995), 79.
37. Ellison, "The World and the Jug," in ibid., 107–43.
38. James Baldwin, "Many Thousands Gone," in *The Price of the Ticket* (Boston: Beacon Press, 2021), 82.
39. Ralph Ellison, *Invisible Man* (New York: Vintage Books, 1995), 8.

4. The Lower Frequencies after Afropessimism

1. Marlon Riggs, dir., *Tongues Untied* (San Francisco: California Newsreel, 1989), DVD.
2. Richard Wright, "The Man Who Lived Underground," in *Eight Men* (New York: Harper Perennial, 2008), 83–84.
3. Frantz Fanon, *The Wretched of the Earth*, trans. Richard Philcox (New York: Grove Press, 2004), 50.
4. Ibid.
5. Richard Wright, "Tradition and Industrialization," in *Black Power: Three Books from Exile* (New York: Harper Perennial, 2008), 727–28.
6. Frantz Fanon, "West Indians and Africans," trans. Haakon Chevalier (New York: Grove Press, 1988), 27.
7. Martin Heidegger, *Being and Time*, trans. John Macquarrie and Edward Robinson (New York: Harper & Row, 1962), 38.
8. Ibid., 41.
9. Frantz Fanon, *Black Skin, White Masks*, trans. Richard Philcox (New York: Grove Press, 2008), xii.
10. Zakiyyah Iman Jackson, *Becoming Human: Matter and Meaning in an Antiblack World* (New York: New York University Press, 2020), 77.
11. Calvin Warren, *Ontological Terror: Blackness, Nihilism, and Emancipation* (Durham, NC: Duke University Press, 2018), 9.
12. Ibid.
13. Ibid., 124.
14. Jared Sexton, *Black Masculinity and the Cinema of Policing* (New York: Palgrave, 2017), viii.
15. See Anthony Paul Farley, "Perfecting Slavery," *Loyola University Chicago Law Journal* 36, no. 1 (2004): 244.
16. Sexton, "The Social Life of Social Death," *Intensions* 5 (Fall/Winter 2011): 31.
17. Fred Moten, "Black Op," *PMLA* 123, no. 5 (2008): 1745.
18. Sexton refers to Frank Wilderson in deploying this phrase *longue durée* in the context of Afropessimist thinking, a phrase that, for me, is important as a way of marking the depth of the sedimentation of antiblackness in the white lifeworld,

Black deathworld (borrowing from the reflections on James Baldwin in chapter 2). Sedimentation is important because it helps explain the viral, contagious, and pathogenic character of antiblackness itself and its intensity across all social forms. See Jared Sexton, "Ante-Anti-Blackness: Afterthoughts," *Lateral: Journal of the Cultural Studies Association* 1, no. 1 (2012), https://csalateral.org/issue/1/ante-anti-blackness-afterthoughts-sexton.

19. Sexton, "The Social Life of Social Death," 28.

20. See the treatment of this idea in chapter 3 and the primary source text, Frantz Fanon, "Racism and Culture," trans. Haakon Chevalier, in *Toward the African Revolution* (New York: Grove Press, 2022), 37.

21. One exception to this is the "Historicity and Guilt" chapter of David Marriott's *Whither Fanon? Studies in the Blackness of Being* (Palo Alto, CA: Stanford University Press, 2018), 73–122. Marriott's work, however, conceives both language and being in Fanon's terms—which makes sense, of course, given that the book is explicitly a pessimistic interrogation of Fanon and Fanonian thinking. But as I hope to have shown, the limit to Fanon's work lies primarily in his undertheorization of Being as such, and therefore also his truncated conception of language.

22. Martin Heidegger, "Letter on Humanism," trans. Frank A. Capuzzi and J. Glenn Gray, in *Basic Writings* (New York: HarperCollins, 1993), 234.

23. Heidegger, "Letter on Humanism," 217.

24. Fanon, *Black Skin, White Masks*, 1–2.

25. Ibid., 21.

26. Ralph Ellison, *Invisible Man* (New York: Vintage Books, 1990), 581.

27. Ibid., 7. Emphasis mine.

28. Ibid., 8.

29. Ellison, "Blues People," 256.

Postscript Notes

1. James Baldwin, "The Discovery of What It Means to Be an American," in *The Price of the Ticket* (Boston: Beacon Press, 2021), 179.

2. James Baldwin, "Many Thousands Gone," in ibid., 78.

3. Édouard Glissant, *Poetics of Relation*, trans. Betsy Wing (Ann Arbor: University of Michigan Press, 2000), 189–90.

Index

abjection, 5, 14–18, 29, 31, 33–36, 43–48, 55, 59, 60, 66, 67, 71, 72, 80–86, 89–98, 101, 104, 105, 109, 110, 118, 120, 122, 126, 128, 144, 149–52, 156, 166, 168, 169, 171, 174, 175
adornment, 16, 17, 20, 36
Adorno, Theodor, 23
affect, 1, 5, 11, 16, 23, 26, 27, 33, 40, 44, 63, 73–77, 79, 81, 86, 91, 95, 102–4, 113, 116–25, 130, 135–37, 140, 149, 153, 154, 157, 158, 169, 171, 176, 180
Africa, 8, 9, 27, 34, 36, 41, 44, 48, 83, 123, 135, 141, 171, 173, 174, 175
Algeria, 24, 127, 183
alienation, 11, 12, 36, 63, 83–85, 103, 108, 114–17, 127, 135, 159, 161, 162, 176
angularity, 16, 17, 20, 36
antestructure, 26
antiblackness, 5, 6, 29, 32, 33, 41, 75, 85, 90–95, 103, 105, 106, 116, 117, 122, 124, 127, 128, 135, 138–40, 143, 144, 149, 150, 152, 155, 157, 158–66, 170, 187, 188
anticolonial, 64, 67, 105, 119, 127, 131, 140
Anzaldúa, Gloria, 4–6, 19, 29, 64, 165, 170, 181
apocalyptic, 33, 67, 105, 118, 124, 125, 127, 137
Armstrong, Louis, 128, 133, 164, 165, 167
asymmetry, 16, 17, 20, 21, 28, 40
atrocity, 7, 9, 11, 25, 28, 49, 71, 79–81, 103, 104, 143, 168
Aunt Jemima, 92–101, 168, 169, 172

Baldwin, James, 6, 28, 31–33, 36, 48, 70–102, 103, 105, 107, 127, 132, 140, 167–72
being, 2, 3, 5, 7, 10, 16–25, 32–43, 46–48, 54, 58, 59, 62–64, 67, 68, 72–77, 81, 83, 84, 87–93, 95, 98–108, 111, 113, 114, 117–24, 127, 130, 132, 133, 135–39, 142, 144–66, 170, 171, 173, 175, 176
Black Atlantic, 6, 7, 23, 25, 29, 33, 50, 102, 135, 136, 144, 147, 150, 168, 170, 171, 182
blues, 32, 60, 123–30, 133, 137, 156, 157, 163, 165
borders, 9, 61, 104, 130
Brathwaite, Kamau, 36, 44

caste, 54, 55, 85
Césaire, Aimé, 7, 34, 35, 58–60, 87, 123, 125, 150
Césaire, Suzanne, 42, 43
Chamoiseau, Patrick, 44, 68
closure, 4, 6, 9, 21, 32, 33, 37–39, 42, 44–48, 51, 53, 54, 56, 63, 66, 67, 104, 107, 124, 136, 138, 139, 147, 149, 153, 156, 157, 159, 160
colonialism, 1–2, 6–14, 21, 25, 28, 35, 36, 40–47, 50, 59–68, 87, 102, 115–18, 124, 130, 135, 136, 140, 144, 159, 162, 163, 175
creole, 32, 36, 44, 66–68, 123, 124
cultural production, 1, 21, 29, 34, 59, 104, 126, 137, 147, 153–55

deathworld, 8, 73, 78, 79, 86–91, 95, 98, 99, 103, 124, 126, 129, 139, 140, 143, 171, 188

189

decolonial, 1–4, 6, 10, 18, 19, 26, 29, 34–40, 44–49, 59–67, 74, 101, 129, 130, 132, 133, 168, 172–76, 182n1
decolonization, 7, 28, 35, 37, 40, 44, 47, 58–62, 66, 130, 174
deferral, 39, 52, 53, 63, 111
delay, 39, 52, 53
desire, 8, 10–13, 16, 29, 34, 36, 43, 57, 58, 86, 89, 93, 96, 103, 108, 110, 111, 115–17, 120, 122, 125, 127, 130, 131, 140, 141, 146, 148, 149, 157, 161, 176
diachrony, 4, 57, 99, 100, 133
dialectic, 4, 26, 31–33, 54–58, 72–74, 77, 82–89, 92, 95, 98–100, 106, 130–32
diction, 32, 51, 68, 115, 129, 161–63
différance, 4, 31, 38, 51–53
dimensionality, 16, 17, 33, 104, 112, 170
dislocation, 5, 99
displacement, 7, 184n4
double reading, 15, 17, 31, 51, 52, 55, 105, 168, 172
double session, 53, 58, 63, 77, 93, 98, 129, 130–33, 141
doubled discourse, 17, 60, 132, 133
Du Bois, W. E. B., 81, 118, 119, 121, 122, 135, 148
Dunye, Cheryl, 95–98, 100

elliptical, 21, 26, 95, 97, 100, 111
Ellison, Ralph, 29, 30, 33, 60, 129, 131–33, 137, 163–70
embodiment, 15, 20, 34, 57, 58, 117, 122, 135, 136, 168, 173
empire, 1–5, 24, 27, 38, 39, 42, 48, 49, 53, 105, 136, 142, 157
enslavement, 1, 5, 6, 24, 26, 39, 42, 46, 57, 102, 110, 153, 166
epistemology, 3, 49, 50, 75, 76, 95, 96, 137, 149
erasure, 20, 28–30, 37, 38, 46, 50, 51, 58–60, 68, 69, 93, 95, 97–100, 104, 105, 108, 112, 115, 132–34, 152, 164, 169, 172, 176
estrangement, 10, 85, 108, 160, 161
event, 1, 5, 7–9, 13, 18, 26, 27, 33, 38, 39, 41, 42, 44, 46, 48, 68, 87, 125, 130, 144, 149, 159, 160, 165, 170
excess, 3–7, 14, 65, 113, 140, 168, 170, 175, 176
exemplarity, 26–28
exile, 8, 30, 54, 55, 57, 70, 75, 83–85, 151, 152, 155, 156, 171, 176

exploitation, 6, 7, 13, 27, 34, 36, 38, 47, 61, 113, 150
exteriority, vi, 19, 53, 55, 59, 73, 83, 89, 95, 99, 106, 131, 132

facticity, 106, 144, 145, 147, 176
Fanon, Frantz, 7, 28, 31–44, 48, 58, 60–68, 74, 90, 102–108, 114–43, 146–52, 156–58, 161–65, 169
Farley, Anthony, 153
fecundity, 29, 37, 45, 100, 147, 148
frontera, 4–7, 14, 19, 29, 30, 32, 36–40, 60, 63–65, 90, 99, 105, 106, 129, 130, 132, 133, 165, 166, 172, 176

generosity, 11–14, 124, 127, 173, 174
geography, 5, 11, 12, 35, 61, 70, 112, 141
ghettoization, 3, 71, 77
Gilroy, Paul, 59
Glissant, Édouard, 21, 36, 71, 172
global north, 1
global south, 1, 8, 38, 39

Hegel, G. W. F., 27, 48, 50, 56, 58, 131
hegemony, 2, 10, 12, 28, 51, 64, 65, 77, 103, 106, 115, 132, 137, 141, 142, 144, 158, 163, 166, 172, 175
Heidegger, Martin, 20, 37, 63, 64, 68, 135–39, 144–62, 165
home, 5, 17, 36, 62, 75, 84, 85, 92, 110, 121, 156, 160–62, 171
hospitality, 9, 13, 173, 174
humanism, 32, 35, 59, 60, 67, 68, 74, 90, 101, 117, 125, 142, 143, 147, 151
Hurston, Zora Neale, 15–17, 20, 21, 30, 133, 166, 170
hybrid, 83, 84, 126

identity, 4, 6, 7, 11, 37, 46, 47, 68, 70–72, 77–90, 98, 99, 106, 120, 127, 134, 165
ideological, 28, 31, 45, 55, 56, 80, 86, 96, 103, 109, 117–19, 122, 124, 129, 140, 161, 174
imagination, 1–3, 5, 7, 9, 10, 12, 13, 26, 27, 29, 31, 36, 44, 49, 61, 82, 88, 92, 93, 96–99, 103, 105, 106, 111, 112, 136, 140, 142–46, 152, 153, 158, 162, 173, 175, 176
inheritance, 1, 15, 27, 36, 43, 49, 74, 78, 84, 85, 135, 136, 140, 146–48, 168, 170–72, 175, 177

INDEX

191

interracial, 16, 17, 25, 32, 55, 62, 72, 78, 82, 84, 94, 98, 101, 106–8, 115–19, 122, 127, 129, 131, 132, 135–37, 140, 143, 144, 148, 153, 163, 165, 171, 176, 184n4
interstitial, 14, 20, 28–34, 42, 55, 66, 67, 99, 130, 132, 133, 165, 172
intraracial, 35, 107

JanMohamed, Abdul, 107
jazz, 7, 60, 89, 125

Kant, Immanuel, 27, 48, 50
kleptocracy, 7–9, 14, 173–76

Lacan, Jacques, 157
Levinas, Emmanuel, 25, 40, 49, 99, 183n13
liberation, 36, 39, 41, 51, 61, 67, 74, 108, 110, 111, 128, 134, 142, 143, 148, 158
libidinal, 146
Locke, John, 27, 48, 50, 63
logocentrism, vi, 19
Lumumba, Patrice, 12, 174

Manichean, 1, 2, 5, 7, 9, 14, 28, 34, 35, 39, 41, 61, 64, 66, 126, 131, 132, 142, 144, 171, 175, 182n1
Mbembe, Achille, 33, 86–88, 111, 152
melancholy, 11, 81, 84, 102
metropole, 1, 2, 9, 10, 18, 34, 36, 41, 61, 62, 158
Middle Passage, 1, 6, 7, 36
monolingualism, 63–66, 68, 69
Moten, Fred, 154–56, 163, 166
multilingualism, 65, 68
music, 17, 18, 123–30, 137, 156, 158, 164, 165

natal, 73, 77, 78, 85, 107, 108, 111, 114, 115, 123, 135
nationalism, 82
necropolitics, 38, 86, 88, 109, 110, 112, 119–21, 140, 143, 171
neocolonial, 7–14, 18, 35, 37, 42, 68, 102, 173–76
nonbeing, 42, 43, 59, 63, 67, 93, 98, 102, 108, 117, 119, 123, 135, 138, 146–50, 160

ontology, 3, 20, 21, 28, 29, 32, 33, 49, 75, 76, 83, 85, 95, 102, 106, 112, 117, 118, 135–39, 144, 145, 147–66
opacity, 23, 29, 34, 98, 99, 172, 177
optimism, 137, 142, 143, 154, 155, 156, 166

otherwise, 2–8, 12, 16, 18, 20, 21, 29, 30, 33, 34, 37, 40, 42, 58–67, 71, 88, 90, 95, 98, 101, 104, 118, 124, 126, 158, 164–66, 173, 175

parasitic, 23, 51, 52, 53, 63, 165
parricide, 121
pathogen, 11, 12, 29, 153, 154, 187n18
Peck, Raoul, 31, 73–76, 82
phallus, 112, 158
pharmakon, 4, 51, 53, 104, 137
pidgin, 66, 67, 123
plantation, 25, 27, 68, 78, 95, 96, 111, 120, 162
poiesis, 2, 71, 82, 129, 172
postcolonial, 6–12, 18, 34–47, 50, 61, 66, 67, 68, 101, 125, 130, 172, 173, 175, 176
race, 2, 20, 25, 27, 36, 42, 49, 50, 58, 78–83, 89, 96, 117, 144, 150, 152, 171
racial formation, 70, 72, 77, 78–83, 85, 86, 88, 89, 92, 100, 101
reconciliation, 4, 85
rage, 11, 67, 74, 75, 77, 82, 90, 92, 102, 119, 138
recognition, 3, 73, 74, 101, 108, 116, 131, 132, 149
refusal, 4, 6, 12, 14–17, 20–22, 27, 29, 31, 32, 34, 37, 55, 58–62, 66–68, 82, 89, 90, 96, 98–100, 108, 118, 125, 126, 128–33, 138, 141, 171, 176, 181n2
remainder, 32, 33, 43, 61, 67, 68, 73, 85, 89, 90, 93, 98
repressive, 3, 8, 45, 65, 72, 140
resistance, 4, 6, 12, 14, 21, 31, 32, 34, 42, 55, 58, 59, 66, 72, 77, 90, 91, 94, 98, 99, 103, 105, 108, 119, 121, 124, 125, 131, 132, 138, 154, 157, 158, 166, 171, 174–76
revolutionary, 1, 2, 12, 15, 22, 23, 41, 42, 57, 59, 67, 89, 90, 103–5, 116, 118, 119, 128, 131, 132, 140–43, 158, 174, 175
Riggs, Marlon, 134, 137, 166

secret, 90, 93, 96–98, 100, 101, 105–7, 127, 132, 133, 137, 168, 169
sedimentation, 22, 72, 103, 187n18
Sembène, Ousmane, 7, 9, 10, 12–14, 35, 174, 175, 181
Senghor, Léopold, 12
Sexton, Jared, 32, 146, 153–56, 176
sexuality, 74, 96, 115, 118, 136

signification, 3, 20, 25, 28, 52, 72, 90, 120, 132, 139, 173
silence, 20, 29, 30, 49, 97, 134, 136, 137, 166
slavery, 7, 23, 14–26, 30, 33, 38, 45, 46, 53–55, 58, 78, 87, 109, 113, 151, 153, 158–60
sociogeny, 7, 29, 42, 95, 102, 103, 116, 118, 126, 148, 149, 154, 169
sociological, 46, 53, 57, 129, 140
spatiality, 3, 4, 30, 36, 39, 47, 65, 99, 112, 117
Spivak, Gayatri, 19, 21, 29, 30, 55, 60, 150
subaltern, 6, 19, 20, 26, 27, 30, 50, 55–60, 65, 67, 68, 94, 126, 144, 150, 154, 159, 161, 176
sublation, 4, 99
supplement, 4, 12, 15, 25, 26, 28, 30–33, 43–60, 64–69, 73, 81, 83, 89, 90, 92, 93, 99, 104, 106, 118, 126, 129–33, 137, 139, 157, 163–66, 171, 172, 184n4
surrealism, 43, 129
syntax, 63, 162

Teno, Jean-Marie, 7, 8, 12–15, 35, 176
terror, 3, 7, 9, 21, 25, 39, 41, 71, 74, 80, 82, 88, 112, 128, 146 147, 154, 170, 171
trace, 4, 24, 37, 42, 50, 51, 61, 96, 97, 98, 104, 106, 114, 129, 133, 134, 135, 172

tradition, 6, 7, 9, 15, 20, 22, 23, 25, 27, 29, 36, 45, 46, 48, 50, 58, 61, 82, 102, 105, 106, 125, 127, 132, 135–37, 141–44, 151, 159, 167, 170, 171, 173, 182n3

Uncle Tom, 90–94, 100, 168, 169, 172
undigestible, 65, 165

vernacular, 7, 10, 12, 16, 30, 33, 36, 40, 60, 68, 71, 84, 89, 100, 104, 105, 123, 124, 126–30, 133, 134, 161, 163, 168, 176, 118, 131, 182

Warren, Calvin, 32, 33, 146, 149–53, 156, 157, 159, 165, 166
white gaze, 20, 21, 66, 70–72, 85, 89–94, 108, 121, 122, 131, 132, 135, 140, 163
whiteness, 80, 81, 85, 89, 115, 116, 118, 131, 182n5
Wilderson, Frank, 11, 32, 38, 157, 187n18
witness, 2, 7, 21, 63, 73, 80, 83, 93, 102, 103, 107, 108, 113, 118, 132, 140, 151, 166, 169, 170, 172, 174
world-making, 6, 12, 15, 21, 29, 39, 43, 57, 62, 66, 67, 86, 99, 126, 129, 131, 132, 153, 166, 173
Wright, Richard, 7, 28, 31–33, 48, 90–92, 102, 104–35, 139–43, 152, 154, 155, 158, 169, 170, 186n34
Wyschogrod, Edith, 86–88

zombification, 63, 64, 117

JOHN E. DRABINSKI is Professor of African American and Africana Studies and English at the University of Maryland. He is author of *So Unimaginable a Price: Baldwin and the Black Atlantic* (2025), *Atlantic Theory: On the Vicissitudes of Relation* (2025), *Glissant and the Middle Passage: Philosophy, Beginning, Abyss* (2019), *Theorizing Glissant: Sites and Citations* (2015), *Levinas and the Postcolonial: Race, Nation, Other* (2011), *Godard Between Identity and Difference* (2008), and *Sensibility and Singularity: The Problem of Phenomenology in Levinas* (2001).

www.ingramcontent.com/pod-product-compliance
Lightning Source LLC
Chambersburg PA
CBHW020411080526
44584CB00014B/1281